Brer Rabbit, Uncle Remus,
and the 'Cornfield Journalist'

HARRIS HURST

Joel Chandler Harris

1848-1908

Brer Rabbit, Uncle Remus, and the 'Cornfield Journalist'

The Tale of

Joel Chandler Harris

by Walter M. Brasch

Mercer University Press

2000

© 2000 Walter M. Brasch
Mercer University Press
6316 Peake Road
Macon, Georgia 31210-3960

First Edition.

Book Design by Mary Frances Burt
Jacket Design by Jim Burt

∞ The paper used in this publication meets the minimum requirements of American
National Standard for Information Sciences—Permanence of Paper for Printed Library
Materials, ANSI Z39.48-1984.

Library of Congress Cataloging-in-Publication Data

Brasch, Walter M., 1945-
    Brer Rabbit, Uncle Remus, and the "cornfield journalist": the
    tale of Joel Chandler Harris /
    by Walter M. Brasch.--1st ed.
        p. cm.
    Includes bibliographical references and index.
    ISBN 0-86554-696-7 (alk. paper)
        1. Harris, Joel Chandler, 1848-1908. 2. Authors, American--
    19th century--Biography. 3. Journalists--Georgia--Biography.
    4. Remus, Uncle (Fictitious character) 5. Brer Rabbit
    (Fictitious character) 6. Afro-Americans in literature. 7.
    Folklore in literature. 8. Georgia--In literature.

PS1813B73 2000

00-032878

Critical Praise

"Exhaustively researched, cogently organized, and briskly written, *Brer Rabbit, Uncle Remus, and The 'Cornfield Journalist'* is a model of the transdisciplinary study. Incorporating history, literary criticism, journalism, and other fields, it adds much to our knowledge of a complex man and the complex environment in which he lived."

—Wayne Mixon, professor of history, Augusta (Ga.) State University; author, "The Ultimate Irrelevance of Race: Joel Chandler Harris and Uncle Remus in Their Time" and *Southern Writers and the New Southern Movement, 1865-1913*.

"Walter Brasch's energetic and engaging biography reconstructs the active professional life and rich sociological and historical legacy of Joel Chandler Harris as a journalist and dialect writer. Brasch does a masterful job of integrating Harris's writings, events in his life, correspondence with family, colleagues, and publishers, critics' and reviewers' responses, book sales figures, and extensive examples of his popular culture impact to demonstrate how Harris's career was an important sociological gloss on the Reconstruction, post-Reconstruction, and turn-of-the-century South.

"Brasch portrays Harris as a complex and thoughtful journalist and writer, a liberal conservative for his day, whose extremely popular portraits of Black character and Black speech and folklore in his times have stirred up controversies but have also had a larger influence than we realize on later writers and on the media, generally.

"Incorporating an extensive array of hitherto unpublished or overlooked material on Harris's life and legacy, Brasch brings Harris back—as a major late nineteenth century journalist who promoted racial understanding and helped an international readership appreciate the sociological, linguistic, and folkloristic legacy of the Old South become New.

"Among the book's strongest points are Brasch's analysis of Harris's use of Black speech and the critics' and linguists' evolving responses to his dialect and to Harris as a dialect writer; his commentary on Harris's presentations of North-South and racial reconciliation themes over several years; his analysis of the racial controversies surrounding the Uncle Remus tales; and his inventories of the literary and popular culture influences of Brer Rabbit and the Uncle Remus tales—from Mark Twain to Toni Morrison, from Ralph Ellison to Van Dyke Parks and Julius Lester, from community theatre productions to picture books, records, cassettes, and videos; from Coca-Cola ads to Disney's 'Song of the South' and Splash Mountain.

"Further, the book's impressive gallery of seventy photographs is the most extensive gathering of Harris-related images ever published."

—R. Bruce Bickley, Jr., professor of English, Florida State University; author of *Joel Chandler Harris* (1978, rev. 1987) and *Critical Essays on Joel Chandler Harris* (1981); and senior compiler, *Joel Chandler Harris: A Reference Guide* (1978) and *Joel Chandler Harris, An Annotated Bibliography of Criticism, 1977-1996: With Supplement, 1892-1976* (1997).

Books by Walter M. Brasch

A Comprehensive Annotated Bibliography of American Black English
(with Ila Wales Brasch)

Black English and the Mass Media

Cartoon Monickers: An Insight Into the Animation Industry

Columbia County Place Names

The Press and the State: Sociohistorical and Contemporary Interpretations
(with Dana R. Ulloth)

A ZIM Self-Portrait

Forerunners of Revolution: Muckrakers and the American Social Conscience

With Just Cause: Unionization of the American Journalist

Enquiring Minds and Space Aliens:
Wandering Through the Mass Media and Popular Culture

Sex and the Single Beer Can: Probing the Media and American Culture

forthcoming:
Before the First Snow (novel)

Betrayed: Death of an American Newspaper

Dedication

For Kashatten Klug Cheltaverta—a wise, heroic friend who was also the best research assistant anyone could ever have.

And, as always, to my parents Milton and Helen Haskin Brasch; and to my wife, Rosemary R. Brasch, each of whom has helped make me a better person and a better journalist.

Joel Chandler Harris

Advice to Writers
for the Daily Press

When you've got a thing to say,
Say it! Don't take half a day.
When your tale's got little in it,
Crowd the whole thing in a minute.
Life is short—a fleeting vapor,
Don't you fill the whole blamed paper
With a tale which, at a pinch,
Could be cornered in an inch.
Boil her down until she simmers,
Polish her until she glimmers.
When you've got a thing to say,
Say it! Don't take half a day!

—*Joel Chandler Harris*

Preface
xix

Acknowledgements
xxix

Chronology
xxxiii

"An Editor Must Have a Purpose"
xxxvii

Chapter 1
'A Spice of the Devil'
1

Chapter 2
'Pink Top from Old Put'
23

Chapter 3
'I Will See What I Can Do'
41

Chapter 4
'A Deep and Wide Influence'
61

Chapter 5
'Very Close to the Untutored Spirit of Humanity'
89

Chapter 6
'Mow Down the Old Prejudices That Rattle in the Wind'
113

Chapter 7
'His Habits are Simple…His Wants are Few'
129

Chapter 8
'Distorted Words and Illiterate Grammar'
147

Chapter 9
'The Other Fellow'
181

Chapter 10
'The Good Old Times We Used to Have'
213

Chapter 11
'Neighbor Knowledge'
239

Chapter 12
'An Excellent Thing to Die By'
255

Chapter 13
'A National Heritage'
269

Chapter 14
'A Bad Odor Among the Younger Generation'
289

Addendum
327

Appendix 1
"A Mother's Wisdom: Essie Harris and Respect"
339

Appendix 2
The Uncle Remus Museum
341

Appendix 3
The Wren's Nest
343

Appendix 4
The Wonderful Tar-Baby Story
350

Appendix 5
A Brief Overview of American Black English
359

Bibliography
369

Index
383

About the Author
393

Illustrations

Atlanta Constitution: 211, 277

Brasch, Walter M.: TK

Brer Bear: 282

Brer Fox: 164, 172, 282

Brer Rabbit: 159, 164, 172, 179, 288, 316, 319

Copyrights: 64, 95

Eatonton Male Academy: 3

Eatonton, Georgia: 288, 293

Estill, J.H.: 30

Free Joe: 101

Funeral Scene: 259-260

Grady, Henry W.: 30, 185

Harris, Charles Collier: 225, 229

Harris, Esther LaRose: 32, 229, 230, 338, 344

Harris, Evelyn: 192, 329, 338

Harris, Joel Chandler: ii, x, xxxvi, 22, 27, 30, 35, 40, 88, 110, 128, 132, 140, 146, 154, 180, 185, 222, 225, 226, 230, 237, 238, 251, 263, 268, 273

Harris Jr., Joel Chandler: 192, 226, 338

Harris, Julia Collier: 241, 330

Harris, Julian: 330, 338

Harris, Lillian: 192, 338,

Harris, Lucien: 338

Harris, Mary: 125

Harris, Mildred: 192, 237, 338

Howell Jr., Clark: 185

Illustrations from books: 60, 69, 159, 164, 171, 172, 179, 219, 282, 288, 316, 319

Imhotep, Akbar: 348

Letters: 12, 216

Ohl, J. K.: 185

Reed, Wallace P.: 185

Riley, James Whitcomb: 140

Roberts, Frank Sloval: 30

Savannah Morning News: 39

Stanton, Frank L.: 185

Terrell, George: 47

The Countryman: 15

The Little Boy: 171

Turnwold: 9, 21

U.S. Census Record: xxxviii

Uncle Remus Museum: 342

Uncle Remus: 60, 69, 171, 282

Uncle Remus's Magazine: 244, 254

Westview Cemetery: 263

Wren's Nest: 131, 132, 135, 145, 320, 344, 347, 348

Credits

From the Collections of:

Atlanta Historical Center: 211

Century Magazine: 101

Emory University: xxxvii, 3, 9, 12, 21, 22, 32, 40, 64, 95, 131, 146, 154, 164, 172, 179, 180, 185, 212, 216, 219, 222, 238 (originally: World's Work), 244, 263, 268, 329, 336

Savannah Morning News: 39

Uncle Remus Museum: 15

U.S. Census Bureau: xxxviii

U.S. Post Office (Eatonton, Ga.): 316

Winsell, Keith, 273, 282

Wren's Nest: 27, 29, 35, 47, 60, 69, 88, 112, 126, 128, 132, 140 (original photo by Moore & Stephenson), 193 159, 171, 225, 226, 229, 230, 237, 241, 254, 260-61, 277, 330, 342 (original photo by Francis E. Price)

Original Photography:

Renn, Rick: 135, 145, 288, 293, 320, 340, 345

Stanyard, Ray (Florida State University Research in Review): 346

Brer Rabbit, Uncle Remus, and the 'Cornfield Journalist'

xvi

Letter to Julian Harris; 6 July 1908

"[Joel Chandler Harris] was a genius; and furthermore he was a man who in his private life, in its modesty, its simplicity, its kindliness and refinement, illustrated the very quality which we must all of us like to see typical of the homes of the nation;…[H]e never wrote anything which did not make a man or woman reading it feel a little better, feel that his or her impulses for good had been strengthened, feel a more resolute purpose to do with cheerfulness and courage and with good sense and charity, whatever duty was next to be done. No writer was ever less didactic; but, quite unconsciously, every reader of his writings, learned to set a new and higher value upon courage, upon honesty, upon truth, upon generosity, upon all of those qualities that make a man a good man in his family, a good neighbor, a good citizen in peace or war."

—Theodore Roosevelt

Letter to Julia Collier Harris; 28 June 1917

"From the moment when I first saw his writings, I was an ardent admirer…[His] writings gave to me, as they gave to so many thousands of others, something that we got nowhere else.…I certainly do not care for books…unless one feels moved by something high and fine, so that one feels braver and gentler, with a keener indignation against wrong, and more sensitive sympathy for suffering, because of having read them.

"Joel Chandler Harris gave all of this to me, and to my family—for his books were among those to which the children listened most eagerly when their mother read aloud. Aside from the immortal B'Rabbit stories, and the children's stories, many of his sketches were among the most striking and powerful permanent contributions to literature that have been produced on this side of the ocean."

—Theodore Roosevelt

Preface

"Who?"

The student who asked the question was one of thirty-two in an upper-division journalism course that fused history, philosophy, and social issues. In passing, I had mentioned Uncle Remus to help illustrate a point. About half of the class wrote down the name, not knowing who he was; the other half just let it slip past their note-taking. All except one student who dared to ask "Who was this Uncle Remus?"

No one knew. I had thought that the tales, which have been translated into almost forty languages, were known by every schoolchild in America. Thomas Wentworth Higginson, Thomas Nelson Page, Mark Twain, George Washington Cable, James Whitcomb Riley, and dozens of other major nineteenth century writers praised him and acknowledged they were influenced by his narrative style. Page himself praised Harris for being "the creator of the most delightful world that American Childhood has known, and of the charming population that inhabit it to the great pleasure and edification of those grown up."[1]

Beatrix Potter's *The Tale of Peter Rabbit* (1902) is a direct descendant of the Brer Rabbit tales, complete with names and characterization, although Potter never publicly acknowledged her literary debt to Harris. Certainly, my students should at least have heard about Uncle Remus, Brer Rabbit, and the Tar-Baby. But they hadn't. I hastily tried to explain Uncle Remus and Joel Chandler Harris.

In the next class, I spoke more about Harris and Remus, and their roles in American journalism and society. I first gave a brief background about similar tales that are part of the folklore of numerous civilizations and cultures. I then explained how most twentieth century folklorists praised Harris, and how linguists pointed out that his vivid depiction of spoken Black dialect has helped generations of readers to better understand not only a creolized language, but also to appreciate the culture of the people who spoke it.

Because I knew my student audience, I also discussed the sexual connotations of the Remus tales. Soon, we were discussing human nature, the use of dialect in stories, the role of folklore in the American social conscience, and the vaporous nature of fame. It became one of my better discussions—and it became obvious that although Harris was known by almost every literate American at one time, recent generations of Americans do not know him or his writings.

It is impossible to fully describe a person's life. All that a journalist or historian can do is try to condense a part of that life into a meaningful book or movie, which covers with accuracy, honesty, and fairness those facts and issues that will help others better understand not only the subject, but themselves and society as well.

The task is even more difficult when the subject is a web of contradictions. Joel Chandler Harris is such a subject, and the contradictions begin with the date of his birth. In his mid-teens, his age "suddenly" changed, to make him younger than he was; as a young journalist, he "resumed" his actual age, but hid it again as he approached middle-age until his family, friends, and the public accepted a birth date that was two—or three—years later than it was.

His mother never married; his father ran off soon after his son's birth. He internalized society's malicious attacks upon those with red hair, and the Irish, America's most recent wave of immigrants.[2] He experienced the discrimination society inflicts upon those not of the majority, but at the same time he refused to believe anyone was truly unkind to him. He admitted to being a bad student and a prankster, but was excited by knowledge, and enjoyed reading newspapers, magazines, and books, especially the classics.

He wrote extensively about the values he learned in his youth and how he missed everything about that rural isolation that introduced him to numerous kind and nurturing friends; but as he matured, he preferred to live in metropolitan cities to advance his career. He was a leader of the "New South," but clung to the philosophy that had established the "Old South."

He believed in peaceful resolution to conflict, and wanted people to love him, but wrote forcefully on controversial issues. He was a segregationist, but fought for racial equality, justice—and integration. He was unyielding in his opposition to mob violence and vigilante justice, but believed not only in states' rights, but that the South would solve its own problems if the federal government did not interfere.

During the Civil War, he despised Lincoln. After the war, not only did he praise the assassinated president as one of the greatest men in history—Harris's other two heroes were Robert E. Lee and "Stonewall" Jackson—but condemned Jefferson Davis for his "restless petulance and his ridiculous rhetoric," and as a man who "no longer has the authority to represent anybody or anything save his own splenetic passions."

Like most journalists, Harris harbored a love/hate relationship with his job, complained about this "grinding business," and wished to be out of it. But, even after he made his reputation and financial security as a literary writer, he refused to give up daily newspaper journalism.

Working two related jobs left him mentally and physically exhausted; to survive, he created and was finally consumed by two distinct personalities. The "other fellow," as he called his literary self, even despised and scorned the journalist self.

As Joel Chandler Harris, the writer of short stories, novels, and Uncle Remus tales, he was shy, reclusive, secretive, afraid to be in the public, afraid to let others know anything about his life. Even when offered huge fees, as much as ten times the annual salary of most Americans, to go on a two- or three-week speaking tour, he refused, perhaps because of his fear of the public, perhaps because of his fear he would embarrass himself by his stutter.

As a journalist and in his private life, he was Joe Harris, still shy, self-deprecating, and modest, but relatively eloquent, especially when among friends. He enjoyed chatting with fellow journalists and the public, often took the reigns of a horsecart-streetcar so the driver could have lunch, helped create the first professional baseball league in the South, and was a city councilman. He was unafraid of controversy, or of asserting his beliefs with the masses and with publishers. He refused to believe he was a folklorist, but his studies into folklore, and his writing of the tales told to him by American Blacks, thinly-disguised allegories of life, made him one of the nation's leading folklorists.

Like most journalists, with the help of his family, he kept scrapbooks not only of most of his newspaper paragraphs, editorials, articles and essays, but also what others wrote about him. The journalist introduced the tales; the literary writer told them. Underlying both personalities was a humble and unpretentious man who lived simply, provided for the comfort of a large family, friends, and even strangers, and wanted nothing more than to be loved—and to write.

Harris was born into controversy, and become one of the nation's most popular and beloved writers during his life. After his death, the controversy continued as numerous critics, especially during the Civil Rights Cycle—many of whom neither read nor understood the Uncle Remus tales—attacked him as racist. Among their arguments were that he perpetuated the stereotype of the "happy-go-lucky darky," that his use of American Black English in the tales is little more than a White man's racist interpretation, and that by not capitalizing the word "negro," Harris proved he was racist. However, Harris's definitive character portrayal of Blacks shows a wide range of emotion and beliefs; the animal tales, themselves, are reflective of the oral tradition of numerous cultures that is often interpreted as revolutionary. Linguists have proven that the American Black English of the stories is relatively accurate interpretations, reflective of a West African language base. It doesn't take an historian or literature critic to know that it would be wrong to ascribe racism to Harris on the basis of not capitalizing "negro," especially since he didn't capitalize most common nouns, including those of the "democrat" and "republican" political parties and even his own beloved "south." Nevertheless, many critics mistakenly believe that by disregarding one of the nation's most important storytellers they are burying what they believe are racist depictions of Southern plantation life.

Of his stories, Harris once claimed, "There is nothing here but an old negro man, a little boy, and a dull reporter."[3] He called himself an "accidental author" and a "cornfield journalist," but he was wrong. The public, if not always the critics, loved his stories, making him one of the most popular and respected writers of the late nineteenth century. Politicians, business executives, and the working class all praised him. President Theodore Roosevelt called him a genius, and said that his works are "the most

striking and powerful permanent contributions to literature that have been produced on this side of the ocean." Andrew Carnegie said that in addition to "giving a helping hand to all the world," Harris "has won the hearts of all the children, and that's glory enough for one man." A small Brer Rabbit mascot sat near the edge of the desk of Samuel Gompers, founding president of the American Federation of Labor, and always went with him whenever he traveled. An hour the former cigar-maker spent with Harris in Atlanta was "an hour of the most unalloyed joy I have ever experienced."[4]

Mark Twain and others attested to Harris's literary impact. Twain himself declared, "Uncle Remus is most deftly drawn and is a lovable and delightful creature; he and the little boy and their relations with each other are bright, fine literature, and worthy to live." James C. Derby, one of the nation's most distinguished book editors during the latter half of the nineteenth century, characterized Harris as "the very best delineator of Southern negro character which the country developed. [His] dialectic stories, in which the shrewd wit and sententious sayings of 'Uncle Remus' are given, have never been equaled."[5] In 1897, William Baskervill, professor of English at Vanderbilt and the nation's foremost critic of Southern literature of the nineteenth century, pointed out in *Southern Writers* that Uncle Remus was "one of the very few original creations of American writers worthy of a place in the gallery of immortals," that the stories were "the most valuable and permanent contribution to American letters in the last quarter of this century," and that Harris was "the most sympathetic, the most original, the truest delineator of this larger life [and its] manners, amusements, dialect, folklore, humor, pathos, and character."[6] That same year, the *Library of the World's Best Literature*, edited by nationally-known author/journalist Charles Dudley Warner, devoted fourteen pages to Harris's life and stories. Walter

Hines Page, one of the nation's most influential editors and publishers during the late nineteenth and early twentieth centuries, boldly stated that Harris's first compilation of Uncle Remus tales was "so great a piece of literature that if all the histories and records of slave-life in the South were blotted out, a diligent antiquarian thousands of years hence could reconstruct it in its essential features from the three human figures that Mr. Harris has used—Uncle Remus, the little boy, and Miss Sally."[7]

R. Bruce Bickley, Jr. and Hugh P. Keenan, two of the leading experts on the life of Joel Chandler Harris, state in their 1997 bibliography, "With Uncle Remus's help, Harris led his black and poor white characters out of their shanties, past the Big House of the old plantation era, and openly down the Big Road into the twentieth century."[8]

J. Mason Brewer, one of the nation's most-respected folklorists, called the Uncle Remus tales "The first, and still the most significant and authentic, volume of Negro animal tales..."[9] Harold W. Thompson, president of the American Folklore Society, pointed out: "There is no doubt that the Uncle Remus stories head the list of our country's folktales, and there should be no doubt that their author must be included in the roster of the dozen American writers who have contributed most to the world's literature."[10]

Author-folklorist Julius Lester, in the foreword of *The Tales of Uncle Remus* (1987), the first of four reworkings of the Uncle Remus tales, noted: "Although Harris never studied folklore, and was embarrassed when others acclaimed him a folklorist, his integrity regarding the tales was exemplary and remarkable."[11]

However, Harris wrote far more than the Uncle Remus/Brer Rabbit tales. Of his short stories, the *New York Times* of 7 May 1904, declared, that Harris "easily stands among the very best of the story tellers and is at the same time in full possession of the old-fashioned

disposition to exercise his story-telling abilities in making his readers acquainted with one company after another of the delightful characters of which his imagination seems to hold an unlimited supply." Journalist-author Bret Harte, who would later become recognized as one of the nation's outstanding short story writers, in 1899 placed Harris among five writers he considered to be America's top short story writers.

Underlying the story of Joel Chandler Harris and his influence upon literature and folklore is his transcription of American Black English speech. Stella Brewer Brookes, one of the nation's outstanding folklorists and a principal authority on the life of Harris, concluded: "[He] stands among the greatest writers of dialect in the world. He developed to the utmost the gift of recording the speech of the plantation Negro. So accurately and fully has he reproduced the dialect that persons in Georgia who have heard the speech of some of the ante-bellum Negroes can almost hear them speaking, through Uncle Remus."[12]

According to Louis D. Rubin, professor of literature at the University of North Carolina, and author of several books about regional literature: "…Harris worked importantly to undercut the plantation literary tradition. He not only shifted the center of attention from the lordly master and lovely lady to the black slave, but he made the plain folk of the village the focus of the non-Negro stories, thereby opening the way for much realistic southern fiction of a latter day."[13]

During the early part of the twentieth century, C. Alphonso Smith, distinguished literary scholar and specialist in American literature, underscored Harris's contribution to folklore, language, literature, and American society:

> [T]he language of Uncle Remus is more interesting than his philosophy. In the picturesqueness of his phrases, in the unexpectedness of his comparisons, in

the variety of his figures of speech, in the perfect harmony between the thing said and the way of saying it, the reader finds not only a keen aesthetic delight but even an intellectual satisfaction.... He leaves the impression not of weakness but of strength, not of contractedness but of freedom. What he says he has not only been through but seen through and felt through....

In the character of Uncle Remus the author has done more than add a new figure to literature; he has typified a race and thus perpetuated a civilization [and] laid the foundation for scientific study of negro folk-lore. His work has, therefore, a purely historical and ethnological value not possessed by any other volume of short stories in American literature.... In the knowledge of negro life and the sympathy with negro character shown in the Uncle Remus stories there is suggested a better method for the solution of the negro problem in America than can be found in all the political platforms or merely legal enactments that American statesmanship has yet devised.[14]

The public heaped more praise upon Harris's dialect stories than upon those of his contemporaries; only Mark Twain exceeded Harris's popularity and critical acclaim, and even then it was for works that may have included American Black English but were not identified as dialect tales. Several journalists and critics from that era suggested that the reason Harris's tales may have been more popular than those written in Gullah and other languages may have been because Gullah and the New Orleans creole, even in transcription, were harder to understand than that of the Middle Georgia dialect of the Uncle Remus stories. However, it is equally probable that the circulation of the *Atlanta Constitution*, one of the largest in the country, gave Harris the base for popular interest in the tales.

Threading its way through almost all of Harris's animal fables is the trickster, the character many of us secretly wish were a part of our own lives, the apparently weaker character who uses cunning and mental agility to overcome stupidity and undaunted strength positioned against him, even if it might become self-destructive eventually. The trickster tales have origins throughout the world in almost all time frames. The coyote and raven are the tricksters of the North American Indians; the jackal is India's trickster; the bear is the trickster for several eastern European countries; in Brazil, it is the tortoise; Reynard the Fox is France's trickster; Anansi, the spider, is the trickster of the Caribbean Blacks. Brer Rabbit himself is everything a trickster should be, as well as cruel, malicious, and deceitful. Later American tricksters have been more benign.

For contemporary Americans, the ultimate trickster is Bugs Bunny, who uses his wits to forever escape the hunter Elmer Fudd, the Wild West bandit Yosemite Sam, the whirling and snapping Tasmanian Devil, or even super-alien Marvin the Martian. Others we admire are the Roadrunner, who continually outruns the Coyote; Rocky and Bullwinkle, who foil Cold War spies Boris and Natasha; Roger Rabbit, Disney's unacknowledged tribute to Tex Avery, who had originally molded Warner Brothers' Bugs; the Animaniacs, who elude the Warner Brothers security force; and innumerable other cartoon combinations. In film, *The Sting* is the ultimate trickster movie; in television, it could be Bret and Bart Maverick.

In only seventy-five minutes, I didn't have the time to tell my students all there was to know about Joel Chandler Harris, the contradictions in his life, and the innumerable social issues he brought forth. Nor could I explain much about folklore and linguistics and how Harris wove them through his tales so America could better understand itself. Perhaps this book will help do that.

"We are mysteriously bound, indeed, not only to the living but to the dead, and to all who ever lived."

—Joel Chandler Harris

Acknowledgements

The intellectual challenge of research is a fitting companion to the drudgery and loneliness of writing, and it was no different with this book. Joel Chandler Harris's articles, essays, editorials, short stories, tales, and novels opened a new intellectual challenge. But, between the lines of about forty-five years of published writing were personal essays and journals, notes, manuscript drafts, hundreds of letters to and from Harris, reviews and critiques of his work, contracts, royalty statements, and the ephemera that many of us discard daily, yet Harris kept, and now served to help illuminate the other published work. It was an "immersion" within the primary documents that gave me a better insight into his life, and provided that intellectual stimulation of locating sources, verifying accuracy, and synthesizing seemingly non-related information into an organic whole.

The challenge continued as I explored the social issues of Harris's life, and looked into the criticisms others from a different era placed upon the creator of Uncle Remus, the compiler of Black folktales, the writer of stories about the common people, and the incisive wit who wrote some of the best editorials in American newspaper and magazine journalism.

But, if all a researcher can do is to categorize and analyze what has been previously written, then whatever the researcher has to say is not only flat but incomplete as well. Writers need to talk with people, to ask questions, to challenge others' minds and, in so doing, also be challenged. Fortunately, to help me tell this tale, I have been most appreciative of the assistance, and discussions, of many persons.

Rick Renn of Columbus, Georgia, helped track down critical information and original documents in Eatonton and Atlanta. His willing assistance, intellectual curiosity, and enthusiastic love of learning were invaluable, and shall always be remembered and appreciated. Also assisting were Denise and Tabitha Mathews, and Mark Coile, also of Columbus, Georgia.

Providing additional useful information were several dozen people, from residents of Eatonton and Atlanta to corporate executives whose firms used Uncle Remus memorabilia and images. I am especially indebted to Michael Rose and Yen Tang at the Atlanta History Center; Beverly B. Allen, Steve Ennis, Linda Matthews, and Kathy Shoemaker of the special collections department at Emory University's Woodruff Library, which has done an outstanding job of accessing, classifying, cataloguing, and making available the bulk of the Joel Chandler Harris papers;[15] Carole Mumford, former executive director of the Joel Chandler Harris Association and museum in Atlanta; Norma Watterson, curator of the Uncle Remus Museum in Eatonton who came to the museum in 1984 and "meant to stay only two weeks"; Michele Smith, publisher of the *Eatonton Messenger*; Lynda Ramage, owner of the Rosewood Bed and Breakfast in Eatonton and chair of Putnam County's tourism council; Kenneth H. Thomas, Jr., of Atlanta; Dr. Keith Winsell of Greensboro; and William Eugene Page of Nicanopy, Florida.

Jo Crossley at the Bloomsburg University library, assisted by Alex Shiner, was also most helpful—and most patient—while buried under an avalanche of interlibrary loan requests. Other assistance was provided by Phil Menzies and Tim Colton, both of Durham, North Carolina; and Prof. Bill Knight of Western Illinois

University. James Bender, Catherine Kelly, Jennifer Neumer, and David Powers assisted with clerical details at various times during the past five years.

I was pleased that five experts in the life and lore of Joel Chandler Harris served not only as "fact checkers," but also made several useful suggestions. Providing insightful comments were Dr. R. Bruce Bickley, Jr., professor of English at Florida State University; Dr. Hugh T. Keenan, professor emeritus of English at Georgia State University; Dr. Wayne Mixon, professor of history and department chair at Augusta (Ga.) State University; Carole Mumford; and Brian P. O'Shea, content manager for Cox Interactive Media. As always, Rosemary R. Brasch also read the manuscript, made many valuable suggestions, and endured me during the creative process.

Several dozen persons have written about the Uncle Remus tales and the life of their author, but I am especially indebted to the outstanding biographies written by R. Bruce Bickley Jr., Paul H. Cousins, Thomas H. English, Alvin F. Harlow, Julia Collier Harris, and Robert L. Wiggins which provided a basis for understanding more about Harris than my own earlier explorations into the forms of American Black English and folklore and their West African origins. The bibliography by William Bradley Strickland of Harris's magazine and book writings provided a means to understand the volume and breadth of Harris's writings. I am also indebted to Dr. Bickley's outstanding comprehensive bibliographies of Harris's writings, and articles about Harris in both academic and popular media.

At Mercer University Press, Dr. Marc A. Jolley ably, and with my appreciation, directed publication, assisted by senior editor Edmon L. Rowell, Jr., marketing director Margaret Shannon, and editorial assistant Kevin Manus.

Brer Rabbit, Uncle Remus, and the 'Cornfield Journalist' is not intended to be a literary critique of the Uncle

Remus stories and Harris's other writings, an analysis of the Brer Rabbit folklore, a full and critical biography of Harris's life, or a probing "pop psych" insight into his mind. It *is* intended to be the tale of a journalist and his legacy, a tale that, hopefully, will stimulate others not only to better understand this one journalist's life and writings, but to reflect upon their own lives, and spur them into their own intellectually-satisfying investigations of life and society.

—Walter M. Brasch, Ph.D.

---

[1] Thomas Nelson Page, "Introduction" to fortieth year anniversary edition of Joel Chandler Harris's, *Uncle Remus: His Songs and Sayings*, v.

[2] Interestingly, in his first book, Harris included an ethnic joke ridiculing the Irish.

[3] Joel Chandler Harris, *Uncle Remus and His Friends*, x.

[4] Letter from Samuel Gompers to R. Lee Guard, 19 May 1907.

[5] J. C. Derby, *Fifty Years Among Authors, Books and Publishers*, 433.

[6] William Baskervill, *Southern Writers*, 67, 43, 46.

[7] Quoted in Burton J. Hendrick, *The Training of an American: The Early Life and Letters of Walter H. Page*, 332.

[8] R. Bruce Bickley, Jr. and Hugh Keenan, *Joel Chandler Harris, An Annotated Bibliography of Criticism, 1977-1996: With Supplement, 1892-1976*, xxi.

[9] J. Mason Brewer, *American Negro Folklore*, 3.

[10] Quoted in Stella Brewer Brookes, *Joel Chandler Harris, Folklorist*, xiii.

[11] Julius Lester, *The Tales of Uncle Remus*, xiii.

[12] Stella Brewer Brookes, *Joel Chandler Harris, Folklorist*, 111.

[13] Louis D. Rubin, "Uncle Remus and the Ubiquitous Rabbit," 784-804 passim.

[14] C. Alphonso Smith, "Joel Chandler Harris," 143-44, 128-29.

[15] Most of the original letters, memos, and contracts cited in footnotes are from Special Collections of Emory University's Woodruff Library. Materials from other collections are cited in the footnotes.

Chronology

1846	Probable year that Joel Chandler Harris was born to Mary Harris in Eatonton, Putnam County, Georgia.
9 Dec 1848	Birth date that Harris and subsequent generations of the public and scholars have accepted.
1856	Begins formal schooling in Eatonton
1862	Works as printer's devil for *The Countryman* on Joseph Addison Turner's plantation, Turnwold; hears African-American folktales from slaves and publishes a few essays, reviews, and poems.
1866	Typesetter for the *Macon Telegraph*; private secretary to William Evelyn of *New Orleans Crescent Monthly*.
1867	Printer and editor for *Monroe Advertiser* of Forsyth, Georgia.
1870	Associate editor of *Savannah Morning News*.
1873	Marries Mary Esther LaRose of Upton, Quebec, Canada
1874	Julian LaRose Harris is born.
1875	Lucien Harris is born.
1876	Evan Howell Harris is born
1876	Moves to Atlanta to flee yellow fever plague. Becomes associate editor of *Atlanta Constitution*. Writes first Uncle Remus sketch.
1877	Mary Harris moves into the home of her son, daughter-in-law, and their three children.
1878	*The Romance of Rockville*, his first novel, is serialized in the *Constitution*. Evelyn Harris is born; Harris's third child, Evan Howell Harris, dies of measles at age of nineteen months.
1879	*Constitution* publishes his first Uncle Remus tale; Mary Esther "Rosebud" Harris is born.
1880	*Uncle Remus, His Songs and Sayings* is published.

1881   Moves into the Wren's Nest in West End, Atlanta

1882   Meets novelists Mark Twain and George Washington Cable,
            and publisher James R. Osgood in New Orleans, but declines to
            take part in a lecture tour. Lillian Harris is born; Mary Esther
            dies of diphtheria at age of three.

1883   *Nights With Uncle Remus* published. Linton Harris is born.

1884   "Free Joe," his most famous short story, is published in *Century
            Illustrated Monthly Magazine; Mingo and Other Sketches in Black
            and White* is published.

1885   Mildred Harris is born.

1888   Joel Chandler Harris, Jr. is born.

1890   Linton Harris dies from diphtheria.

1891   Mary Harris, his mother, dies.

1892   *On the Plantation*, the first of three fictionalized auto-
            biographies, is published.

1895   New edition of *Uncle Remus, His Songs and His Sayings* is
            published, with illustrations by A. B. Frost.

1900   Retires from the *Atlanta Constitution*.

1902   Receives honorary doctorate of literature from Emory
            University.

1905   Elected a member of the Academy of Arts and Letters.
            Honored by President Theodore Roosevelt in Atlanta.

1906   With his son, Julian, founds *Uncle Remus's Magazine*; first issue
            is June 1907.

3 July 1908   Dies in Atlanta.

[Chronology is edited and abridged from *Joel Chandler Harris* (1987),
by R. Bruce Bickley.]

Joel Chandler Harris at his desk in the *Constitution*

An editor must have a purpose

An editor must have a purpose. He must have some object in view beyond the mere expression of an opinion or the publication of a newspaper. The purpose may be either moral, social or political, but it must be well designed and pursued constantly.

I shudder when I think of the opportunities the editors in Georgia are allowing to slip by. It grieves me to see them harping steadily upon the same old prejudices and moving in worn ruts of a period that was soul-destroying in its narrowness. There never has been a time when an editor with a purpose could accomplish more for his state and his country than at present.

What a legacy for one's conscience to know that one has been instrumental in mowing down the old prejudices that rattle in the wind like dry weeds! How comforting to know that one has given a new impulse to timid convictions! But an editor with a purpose can do more than this: he can sweep away all false conditions in society and politics and bring his fellows back to the sweet simplicity of the ancient days. Provided he be earnest. That is everything.

What if it requires a generation of time to reform a generation of men? The flight of the swallow is swift, but it conveys no idea of permanency. A good writer need not be an editor, but an editor needs to be a writer, and a vigorous one; no gifts of intellect will compensate for a lack of purpose. Let him play the politician if he will, but always as an editor.

In the South, John Forsyth made an impression that will be permanent, in the North Samuel Bowles. These men were editors with a purpose, and whatever part they took in politics was subservient to that purpose. In the South to-day we sadly need the resurrecting hand of editors with a purpose; who will supply that need?

Joel Chandler Harris

(*Sunday Gazette*; 5 October 1878)

Dwelling-houses numbered in the order of visitation.	Families numbered in the order of visitation.	The Name of every Person whose usual place of abode on the first day of June, 1850, was in this family.	Age.	Sex.	Color, white, black, or mulatto.	
1	2	3	4	5	6	
4	4	Matilda Cuthbert	25	F	M	
4	"	Thomas "	18	M	M	
4	"	Daniel "	2	M	M	
4	4	Mary "	10	F	M	
4	5	Eugenia "	2/12	F	M	
557	557	Ann Harris	50	F		
4	"	Ann Finman	70	F		
4	4	Mary Harris	30	F		
"	4	Joel	3	M		
558	558	Elizabeth Reed	78	F		
4	4	Robert Jones	29	M		
559	559	Josh Spurmmon	49	M		
4	4	A. S. Penmman	43	F		
"	"					

U.S. Census Record, 1850

Chapter 1

'A Spice of the Devil'

In the chambers of the United States Senate, 27 January 1837, Senator John C. Calhoun of South Carolina, one of the nation's most brilliant politicians and orators, spoke out in defense of slavery. Reflecting the views of much of America, both North and South, Calhoun argued that a "divine providence" had brought together the two races—the White, European race, to be the masters; the Black, African race, to be the slaves. The Blacks, said Calhoun, were genetically and morally inferior, and slavery was not an evil but the will of God. The best life for slaves was only on a plantation, he said to the cheers of his fellow senators, and it would be the plantation that would give Blacks character and meaning.

It was into this way of life that Joel Chandler Harris was born in 1846[1] in Eatonton, Putnam County, Georgia[2], which he later remembered as a "primitive little village in the cotton country, where the planters came to buy and sell."[3] His mother was Mary Harris, an educated woman with a quick wit who was of Scottish descent from a respected middle-Georgian family. In her mid-20s, she had run off with what may have been an alcoholic itinerant day laborer, possibly an Irish immigrant[4] who knew "of the bitter opposition of Miss Mary's family, and that he would never be received or recognized by them [and was] not strong enough to stand up under such conditions," according to Julia Collier Harris, Joel Chandler Harris's daughter-in-law.[5] Mary Harris, about twenty-eight years old when she gave birth, never married and reportedly did not mention the father's name after he deserted her; the name Joel was from Dr. Joel Branham, attending physician at the birth; Chandler was that of Mary's uncle.

Mary Harris, who rejected several marriage proposals to devote her life to her only son, supported herself and her son by her work as a seamstress, and from the assistance of several of the county's more prominent citizens. Dr. Joel Branham's brother, Dr. Henry Branham, who had married Mary Harris's aunt, provided financial assistance; Andrew Reid, a prosperous neighbor, had provided a cottage for Mary, her mother and son, and later paid for the boy's school tuition.

Mary Harris, an avid reader, instilled in her son the love of language and literature. When Harris was six, maybe eight, years old, his mother first read him Oliver Goldsmith's episodic novel, *The Vicar of Wakefield* (1766), the story of an affluent city-bred preacher who is forced to move to a rural area; an underlying theme was that of a seduced woman who was forced to live as a social outcast, perhaps not so unlike Mary Harris's story. Harris later recalled:

> My desire to write—to give expression to my thoughts—grew out of hearing my mother read "The Vicar of Wakefield." I was too young to appreciate the story, but there was something in the style or something in the humor of that remarkable little book that struck my fancy, and I straight away fell to composing little tales, in which the principal character, whether hero or heroine, silenced the other characters by crying "Fudge!" at every possible opportunity. None of these little tales have been preserved, but I am convinced that since their keynote was "Fudge!" they must have been very close to human nature.[6]

However, except for reading and writing, in which he excelled, Harris wasn't one of the better students at the Eatonton Male Academy.[7] What he *was* was one of the school's better pranksters, although several of his pranks caused more than mere laughter. "He once knocked a wasps' nest into a boy's face, stinging him seriously [and] later burned the same friend on the neck with a pancake flipper," wrote biographer and literary critic R. Bruce Bickley, Jr. He tricked another boyhood friend into "jumping into a muddy pen swarming with fiercely biting hog fleas."[8]

"Like Brer Rabbit, he made up for his lack of size by his agility and shrewdness, and there was a spice of the devil in him as well," wrote Julia Collier Harris.[9] That "spice" was probably a "cover" for his innate shyness. The blue-eyed, ruddy-complexioned young boy was sensitive about being short and having red hair and freckles; he stammered when he was in a crowd or unfamiliar places,

Eatonton Male Academy

appeared sickly, and most of all was shy in front of any group he did not know well. This sensitivity, wrote Bruce Bickley, "made him acutely aware of the subtle gestures, glances, and innuendoes that often convey enormous meanings." It was a sensitivity that ironically helped Harris become an excellent observer of life.

As he matured, Harris saw some of the discrimination his mother had experienced for being an unwed mother, and thought of himself as among the disadvantaged, although the people of Eatonton, unlike much of America, had more to do than complain about an unwed mother and her red-haired son. Harris believed he was ugly and unloved, a cast-off not only because of his "bastard" status but because he was the son of an Irish immigrant. During the mid-nineteenth century, the Irish were treated poorly by Americans of all regions, some of it because most were Catholic in a religiously-intolerant America, some because they were of the lower classes. Harris also considered his red hair, more identified with Irish than American Southerners, as a mark of shame; others compounded his alienation by calling him a "red-headed bastard." As an adult, he was still shy, still sensitive about his red hair—his mother's hair had been red when she was young, but it had turned brown—and usually wore a felt hat in public, even indoors. Even when his hair and mustache turned from red to a sandy blond, he still believed they were "fiery red." Whatever the reasons for his shyness and insecurity, Harris may have developed an understanding of a small part of what American Blacks suffered. In one of the many contradictions in his own life, Harris internalized society's attacks upon red-haired Irish bastards but believed the people of Eatonton were kind to him:

It is a great blessing for a young fellow in the clutches of poverty to be raised among such people as those who lived in Eatonton when I was a boy, and whose descendants still live there. I have not the slightest difficulty in the world in referring all that I have ever done or hope to do to the kindly interest which the people of Eatonton took in my welfare when I was too young to know of the troubles which inhabit the world by right of discovery and possession.[10]

In a diary-letter written in 1870, Harris revealed his insecurity:

I am morbidly sensitive. With some people the quality of sensitiveness adds to their refinement and is quite a charm. With me it is an affliction—a disease— that has cost me more mortification and grief than anything in the world—or everything put together. The least hint—a word—a gesture—is enough to put me in a frenzy.... The least coolness on the part of a friend—the slightest rebuff tortures me beyond expression, and I wished a thousand times that I was dead and buried and out of sight.... You cannot con- ceive to what an extent this feeling goes with me. It is *worse* than *death* itself. It is horrible. My dearest friends have no idea how often they have crucified me.

By the time he was fifteen years old, and determined to be a writer, Joe Harris—as he was then known and would be known by friends and colleagues in journal- ism—was restless with life at the academy. His education came not from classes, but from going to the Eatonton post office and country store almost every day to sit upon a battered couch and read newspapers and magazines

which the postmaster surreptitiously provided to him before delivering them to their subscribers. In March 1862, while scanning papers at the Eatonton post office, Harris responded to a classified ad in the first issue of *The Countryman*:

WANTED:

An active, intelligent white boy, 14 or 15 years of age, is wanted at this office, to learn the printing business.

March 4, 1862.[11]

The publisher was Joseph Addison Turner, son of Billy Turner, a well-known author and Georgia politician; his mother, Lucy, was from an aristocratic Virginia family. At the time he had placed the ad for a printer's devil, Turner himself was not only a journalist, but a lawyer, former state senator, and owner of Turnwold, a 950-acre plantation about nine miles from Eatonton.[12] While practicing law, Turner had created several publications, including the literary journal *Turner's Monthly*, followed by *The Independent Press* in 1854, which survived almost two years, and *The Plantation*, a quarterly literary journal that survived only four issues in 1860, but which included Black dialect verses almost two decades before the nation would begin to see a proliferation of dialect material in its mass media.

Turner had met the young Harris boy several times when he had brought sewing to Mary Harris's home. He was sufficiently impressed with Harris's intellectual curiosity and desire to be a writer, and hired him as a printer's devil (apprentice) for *The Countryman*, a three-column 9-inch by 12 inch four page newspaper, published Tuesdays. *The Countryman*—"independent in everything—neutral in nothing"—was modeled primarily upon England's literary and often anti-establishment "Little Papers," especially *The Tattler* (1709-1711), edited by Richard Steele; and *The Spectator* (1711-1712, 1714), edited by Steele and Joseph Addison, for whom Turner was named. In a "Prospectus" to readers, Turner explained *The Countryman*'s role:

> It is our aim to fill our Little Paper with Essays, Poems, Sketches, Agricultural Articles, and choice miscellany.—We do not intend to publish anything that is dull, didactic, or prosy. We wish to make a neatly printed, select Little Paper—a pleasant companion for the leisure hour, and to relieve the minds of our people somewhat from the engrossing topic of war news.[13]

The newspaper, which would be Turner's passion for almost four years, would be the nation's only plantation newspaper, eventually reaching subscribers throughout the South and achieving a circulation of about 2,000, making it one of the larger circulation newspapers in the South.

Turner was a benevolent slave-owner—or as benevolent as any slave-owner could have been—to the twenty or so slaves he had owned. He treated his slaves fairly, and even gave them patches of land to grow their own crops to earn their own incomes. "The sons of the richest men were put into the fields to work side by side with the negroes," Harris later wrote about the plantation life of Middle Georgia, "and were thus taught to understand the importance of individual effort that leads to personal independence.... [T]here was a cordial and even affectionate understanding between the slaves and their owners, that perhaps had no parallel elsewhere."[14] Turner, however, was one of many exceptions to the

nature of the slave-owner. Secure in his own belief that kindness produces mutual tolerance and respect, Turner never worried about his slaves running away or revolting. Other owners, however, constantly feared what might happen if the Blacks—in Putnam County alone, almost three-fourths of all residents were slaves—would rise up against not only the owners but the plantation system as well. Nevertheless, as benevolent as he was, there was never a question as to Turner's beliefs of White superiority and the value and necessity to maintain the slavery system. On the back cover of the first issue of *The Plantation*, Turner outlined the magazine's purpose:

> The special feature of this Journal will be a defence of Negro slavery—real, unqualified, unreserved—in a moral, social and political point of view. In whatever aspect the question presents itself, "The Plantation" will be found the champion of this "peculiar institution" of the South, and will counsel that section to maintain its just rights under the Constitution, and as sovereign States, in the teeth of all opposition, at all hazard, and to the last extremity.[15]

Even after abolition and the end of the Civil War, Turner would oppose voting rights for freed Blacks, stating he didn't believe "negroes have intelligence or principle enough to be allowed to vote."[16] Turner's compassion—and fierce defense of segregation—influenced the impressionable young printer's devil until later in his own life when he modified his own thinking to argue for Negro rights.

As a child, Harris had been an actor in a mock-minstrel comic ensemble known as the Gully Minstrels, named for the red-clay Big Gully which divided the town, and where Harris and his friends played after school.

Printing Office at Turnwold

Charles A. Leonard, one of Harris's friends, recalled: "Hut [Adams] was the manager, I was the treasurer, and Joe the clown, with a fiddle he couldn't play. But he would make a noise that would bring down the house. The price of admission was ten pins [which was used as a currency barter during the War], and it was not long before the treasurer was stuck on pins, and no exchange."[17]

Harris would soon understand that the racial stereotypes created by burnt-cork Whites were little more than fanciful imaginations of the Whites' racism.[18] "The exhibitions of minstrelsy…are, like many other things in this life, an illusion," Harris would write two decades after the Civil War, letting his readers know that the minstrel shows "represent nothing on the earth, except the abnormal development of a most extraordinary burlesque.[19]

At Turnwold, Harris hunted rabbits and small game with the slaves, visited their one-room cabins, talked with them, and listened and learned from their stories of animals and of people. More importantly, he developed an understanding of how their tales were a part of their culture. Not only did he remember their stories, he absorbed how the slaves told them, with the language and the special inflections. It was here that he became friends with "Uncle" George Terrell and "Aunt" Betsy Evans[20]—both of them well-known as ginger cake makers—whom Harris years later refashioned into the essence of Uncle Remus and Aunt Minervy Ann, although he acknowledged that the personalities and experiences of several slaves also become a part of his two main fictional characters. The Little Boy, to whom Uncle Remus told his tales, may have been based partially upon Harris himself. But, Harris had another explanation. "Did it never occur to you that *you* might be the *little boy* in 'Uncle Remus'?" Harris wrote to Joe Syd Turner, son of Turnwold's owner, and his boyhood companion who would eventually become a judge. "I suppose you have forgotten the comical tricks that you played on old George Terrell, and the way you wheedled him out of a part of his gingercakes and cider. Lord! those were the wonderfullest days we shall ever see."[21]

As for the young Harris, he worked as hard as any slave boy; his wages, common for an apprentice, were clothing, room, and board. Unlike most apprentices, he received an education he could never have received in a one-room school. He had his own room in a house in which the print shop foreman also lived and who, with dramatic flourishes, often read to him stories from the classics. Turner, architect of a significant improvement in the state's public education system, taught him how to set type and design a newspaper page, and also gave the young boy free access to over 2,000 books, including the classics from his and his brother's libraries; the young Harris, who also set lines of the classics into type to be used as "fillers" when other stories ran short, often stayed up late, reading the books by firelight. Turner drilled the boy constantly in the essentials of writing, and taught him that writers must be inquisitive, curious, and observant. Turner, said Harris, "was a good writer with a fine taste in literature"[22] who "took an abiding interest in my welfare, directed my reading, gave me good advice, and the benefit of his wisdom and experience at every turn."[23] In interviews with other journalists, Harris would state categorically that Turner was "a miscellaneous genius."[24]

Although Harris would eventually become one of the most-loved writers in America, his first attempt to become a published journalist was rejected. In an insightful and prophetic letter to Harris, Turner advised the young would-be journalist to "study simplicity, and artlessness of style," while avoiding the flowery Victorian phrasing popular in literature; he believed the young boy had "a talent for writing," advised him "to cultivate it,"

"Countryman" Office,
Turnwold, (near Eatonton) Ga.)),
Eds. Commonwealth—   June 2, 1863.

Sirs:—I send you an article for the
Commonwealth, which, if you see fit, publish, otherwise, burn it up. On no account, let my name be
known. Hoping that you may soon receive a thousand
reams of nice paper, (which is the best wish that any
newspaper can receive now-adays), I remain your
                    friend, JCHarris
P.S.— I have an original tale for the Commonwealth
Entitled, "A Night Hunt." Must I send it?
                                JCHarris.

Query letter from Joel Chandler Harris, 1863

and predicted, "There is a glorious field just ahead of you for Southern writers."[25]

Upset by rejection but inspired to keep writing, Harris began his journalistic career by sneaking into *The Countryman* short articles—most of them humor paragraphs, many twisted around puns—and signing them "The Countryman's Devil." The youthful prankster also managed to get at least one hoax into the newspaper, writing about an ape-man from Australia, crediting the "discovery" to "Otway's Travels in Australia." However, the story had "legs," and was reprinted as fact hundreds of times by newspapers and magazines during the next four decades, long after the original source was no longer remembered.[26]

Bedeviling Turner, Harris says he "[set] my articles from the [type] 'case' instead of committing them to paper, and thus leaving no evidence of authorship. I supposed that this was a huge joke; but, as Mr. Turner read the proof of every line that went into his paper, it is probable that he understood the situation and abetted it."[27] With other Georgia newspapers reprinting many of these capsulized bits of humor, Turner encouraged the young boy to continue writing, this time with poems, which Harris loved, and longer articles. Many of Harris's stories during his four years on *The Countryman* were inspired by the events of the Civil War and its impact upon the people, and may have been clumsy and thinly-disguised rallying cries for the South. Before the war, Turner had begged Georgia not to secede, but after war was declared he unselfishly provided clothes and food to the Confederate army. Harris, however, did not serve in the Confederate Army, although by the end of the war, with the Confederacy taking teenage boys, he was of an age that he would have been drafted. Turner—himself exempt from the draft because of a chronic deterioration of the thigh bone which first attacked him during childhood—provides one of the reasons Harris wasn't drafted. In a list of employees provided to the Confederate government at the end of 1864, Turner noted: "Compositor—Joel C. Harris—19 years old.[28] Weighs only about 100 pounds. Frail and feeble. Not fit for military service. Exempt under state and confederate law, as a compositor."[29]

A month after Turner reported Harris's status to the Confederate government, the left wing of General William T. Sherman's 62,000-man army, the 20th Army Corps of Pennsylvania Germans under command of General Henry Slocum, slashed through Middle Georgia and destroyed about fifty plantations, taking horses, mules, and supplies, and raiding Turner's printing plant, hat factory, tannery, and distillery. To save his pet pony, Butterfly, Harris rode into a swamp, then "rode through the bushes like the wind, a stray bullet occasionally whizzing past him,"[30] according to his friend Forrest Adair. Slocum's troops did not find Butterfly, but they did find Harris and planned to imprison him when Slocum himself, "pleased with his boldness and ready wit... ordered him to be left alone."[31] Harris, however, would report little of the confusion and terror of the raid in a subsequent romanticized autobiographical novel, *On the Plantation* (1892); and as part of a children's novel, *The Story of Aaron* (1896).

Just as Harris readily learned Black language and culture from the Turnwold slaves, he also learned of another culture from the Yankees. "Their broken English [Pennsylvania Dutch] amused me greatly [and I] followed them into [Turner's hat] factory just to hear them talk," Harris wrote.

About half of Turnwold's slaves, mostly the field slaves, moved on with the army; the others remained loyal to Turner even after Federal troops ordered them emancipated.

After the Union soldiers had left, and while he was walking back to Turnwold, Harris saw an old man and a woman. Against a fence, the old Black woman was shivering; at her feet was an old Black man. Harris asked the woman what was wrong. She replied, "He dead, suh! But bless God, he died free." The story was first published in *The Countryman*; Harris would repeat the story innumerable times during the next four decades, and included it in *On the Plantation*.

For at least two years, while paper was scarce in the Confederacy, Turner continued to publish *The Countryman*, begging his readers to sell to him rags for five to ten cents a pound so he could then make his own paper. But, it would be politics not economics that would close the newspaper. In the 9 May 1865 issue, Turner told his readers:

THE·COUNTRYMAN.

By J. A. TURNER. ——"INDEPENDENT IN EVERYTHING—NEUTRAL IN NOTHING"—— $3 A Year.

VOL. XX. TURNWOLD (NEAR EATONTON) GA., TUESDAY, MAY 23, 1865. NO. 21.

The Five Points.

The yankees have whipped us, and they have it in their power to do with us as they please. They say they want a great republic on the American continent, and they desire the south as an integral part of that republic. Now would it not be better for them to *reconcile* us, if possible? We would be worth a great deal more to them, if they *would* reconcile us. Is there not a document, much venerated by the yankees, called the Declaration of Independence, in which something is said about all government having as its only true basis, the "consent of the governed?"

It strikes us that there is something of this kind on record; but really, it has been so long since we had any communication with the outside world, owing to "the blockade," that we cannot be certain Yet this is our recollection.

With this recollection on our mind, we also remember that there was once a very celebrated English clergyman by the name of Colton, who finally got too much sense in his head for this world, and so committed suicide, in order that he might go to another. He wrote a book of aphorisms entitled Lacon, and in this book occurs the following paragraph:

"They that are in power, should be extremely cautious to commit the execution of their plans, not only to those who are *able*, but to those who are *willing*; as servants, and instruments, it is their duty to do their best, but their employers are never so sure of them, as when their duty is also their *pleasure*. To commit the execution of a purpose to one who disapproves of the plan of it, is to employ but one *third* of the man; his heart, and his head are against you—you have commanded only his hands."

The yankees desire a great North American republic, and in order to obtain it, they must, under the present circumstances, partially "commit the execution of their purpose to those who disapprove of the plan of it"—to wit, the southern people. Gentlemen yankees, in the course you are pursuing towards the southern people, "you employ but one *third* of the man—his heart and his head are against you—you have commanded only his hands."

Now, Messrs. yankees, in the formation of your great republic, do you not want the heart and the head of the southern man, as well as his hands? If so, you must grant us the following five points, as

a matter of grace—not of right—for you have whipped us, and have a right to do as you please :

1.—A new flag.—Our people have so long fought against the United States flag, and it has waved over the bloody graves of so many of them, and over so many of their ruined homes, and burned towns, and villages, that you cannot expect to command their hearts and heads, though you do their hands, in its support.

2.—A new constitution should be agreed upon, because the old one is not sufficiently explicit as to our rights.

3.—A full and complete acknowledgement of our state rights, and state sovereignty should be accorded us—together with complete recognition of our institution of slavery.

4.—An abnegation of the idea that our people became rebels, or were guilty of treason when they seceded, and waged war against the north—they owing allegiance to their respective states alone.

5.—A consolidation of the war debt of the two sections.

Now, if the yankees will accede to the foregoing five points, then we can have the great republic they desire, on the American continent. Then they can command our hearts and heads, as well as our hands.

We submit it to the northern people, is not this programme worthy of your serious contemplation? We do not expect you to adopt it, but you ought to do so. You are the victors—you have everything in your hands, and you can afford to be generous. Will you be so? Mr. Webster once told you of your triumphs—your triumphs in art—your triumphs in science—your triumphs over your sterile soil. Now you have had a triumph greater than all—the triumph in arms over the southern people. As Mr. Webster counseled you to obtain a yet greater triumph over your prejudices, so do we counsel you the same. If you want a great American republic, conquer your prejudices, and give us good terms.

The Democratic Party.

The destruction of the democratic party was the "Iliad of all our woes." The union of that party, upon some common ground, is the only hope we have left of popular government upon the American continent. Let that party again reunite upon the ancient land-marks, and all will yet be well.

The Death of Lincoln.

The most unfortunate thing that has occurred, for the people of the south, is the death of Pr. Lincoln. In the first place, it deprives us of a ruler, who, we believe, had no wormwood and gall—no spleen—no malignity—no revenge in his constitution. A "fellow of infinite jest," the milk of human kindness had not soured in his bosom, and we believe he knew how to regard the feelings of an honorable fallen foe. We have no idea that we have profited by the change made in the rulers of the United States.

And again : We see that some of the northern presses are disposed to hold our people responsible for the assassination of their president. This is all wrong. Had the proposal for Lincoln's assassination been put to our people, we opine it would have obtained very few, if any votes. We think our people knew their interest better. But so it is, the northern people are disposed to hold the southern people responsible for the death of Lincoln. They are wrong, in this, as we have said : but it matters not with us whether they are right, or wrong. They have the power, and revenge for Lincoln's death will be one of the elements that will enter into the excuse for inflicting summary punishment upon us. Therefore it is unfortunate for us, in this regard, that Lincoln was killed.

And we will merely allude to the precedent set in this matter of assassination. Having been once introduced upon this continent, there is no knowing where it is to end. We may well pause, and ask ourselves if the bowl and the dagger are to rule on this side the Atlantic, as they have done on the other side.

The Negroes.

We suppose the yankees design setting the negroes "free." Poor negroes! Once they had guardians, and protectors. Now they have none. They will live to curse the day when they were set "free." By setting the negroes "free," the yankees will destroy the best resources of the American government to pay its debt, and make the condition of the blacks a thousand fold worse than ever it was. But the experiment must be made. Let it be done. We warn the American people of the evils of emancipation. Yet it will come. We wash our hands of all the evils that will flow from it.

As an editor, I was once bold as a lion. That was when I had a country. Now, it seems, I have none. That, I fear, has gone. Our people, it seems to me, are ready to bow their necks to take the yoke, Gen. Lee's army has been captured, and the balance of our armies, through their generals, are negotiating an abolition of our flag, and our country. If I cannot edit a paper as a freeman, I will edit none at all. Until I know the weight of the chains I have to wear, I shall publish a quarter sheet, but shall have nothing to say on political affairs. I will write upon no subject upon which I cannot freely speak my mind. All business matters between my subscribers and myself, will be adjusted, unless I am robbed of everything.

He dated the commentary 3 May. In a "P.S." to his readers, dated two days later, Turner added: "Since writing the above, I learn that Gen. Johnston has surrendered to Sherman. Of course, therefore, we are an overpowered, and, *for the present*, a conquered people. Before resuming the publication of a full sheet, I shall have to wait and see what regulations my masters make concerning the press."[32] The military arrested Turner on 26 June 1865, charged him with printing articles "disloyal" to the federal government, harassed and imprisoned him in Macon. Because of restrictions placed by the federal government upon Southern newspapers and in violation of First Amendment rights, Turner suspended publication of *The Countryman* between 27 June 1865 and 30 January 1866. Finally, on 8 May 1866, with Turnwold no longer producing the crops it once did, and the military occupation placing even stronger restrictions upon freedom of the press, Turner closed *The Countryman*. In the final issue, Turner told his readers that although he still lived at Turnwold, "I have a home and country no longer. Living in the same spot where I always did, I am, nevertheless, an exile and wanderer."[33] His readers understood.

The war destroyed families and businesses. Without slaves, the South's agriculture base was doomed. The plantation era was over. "The old plantation…has passed away, but the hand of time, inexorable, yet tender, has woven about it the sweet suggestions of poetry and romance, memorials that neither death nor decay can destroy," Harris would later write in the *Atlanta Constitution* of 9 December 1877.

The Plantation Era was replaced by the era of tenant farmer who was essentially still a slave of the land and the owner, but who now had to care for himself and his family.

Darwin Turner, almost a century after the Civil War ended, claimed that Harris "clung philosophically and emotionally to the dream of a utopian plantation society," and "shaped reality to conform to his dream."[34] Turner also claimed to have understood why Harris set most of his fiction on a plantation:

> Abandoned by a father whom he had never known, Harris projected a utopia in which each deserving Anglo-Saxon American is satiated with love from childhood to death. As a child he is entertained, comforted, and advised by a devoted black nurse or a slave playmate who was more faithful than a pet hound. As an adult, he is attended by servants who, like dutiful genies, live only for his pleasure while he, like an indulgent father, protects them and supervises their growth. Such a utopia had existed, or had been possible, Harris imagined, on plantations before the Civil War.[35]

Of course, Harris had only White boys for playmates and never had a Black nurse-mammy, but he did have older Black males as role models. Nevertheless, the plantation life, so embedded within the young boy's mind,

and the destruction of the South's economy would be the base of his most remembered writing.

---

[1] James Wood Davidson, in *Living Writers of the South*, published in 1869, stated that Harris was born 8 December 1846. In *Oddities in Southern Life and Character*, published in 1883, Henry Watterson, editor of the *Louisville Courier Journal*, stated that Harris was born 6 December 1846. However, most persons who knew Harris believed he was born in 1848. In 1886, Harris wrote he was born 9 December 1848, and subsequent generations have accepted that to be his official birth date. However, W. J. Rorabaugh and Kenneth H. Thomas, Jr. have independently found several documents, including census records, that indicate Harris was probably born in 1845 or 1846. In a family Bible, Harris's birth was recorded as 9 December 1845. In the 1850 U.S. census, Harris is identified as being three years old, the 1860 census has him being fourteen years old, indicating an 1846 birth date. Rorabaugh and Thomas believe that Harris—or more probably his mother—at the beginning of the Civil War may have added two years to his actual birth date so he would be too young for the draft. The 1870 Census suggests an 1846 birth, the 1880 Census suggests an 1845 birth. By 1890, Harris was claiming an 1848 birth date. In 1881, with publication of his first book, Harris who had stated he was born in 1845, began stating he was born in 1848.

[2] Putnam County, incorporated in 1807, was named for General Israel Putnam of Massachusetts, a Revolutionary War hero. Eatonton, incorporated in 1809, was named for General William Eaton of Connecticut, who led American troops against pirates four years earlier.

[3] James B. Morrow, "Joel Chandler Harris Talks of Himself and Uncle Remus," 5-6.

[4] There are numerous speculations who Harris's father was, including the possibility he was William Roby, a red-haired, alcoholic groundskeeper. The 1850 census lists a twenty-five-year old William Roby as being a resident of Putnam County. The outstanding genealogy study of the Harris family is being done by Kenneth H. Thomas of Atlanta. Thomas says that even the common belief that the father was an itinerant day-laborer and an alcoholic may not be accurate since it was common to use that description against anyone of "ill-repute."

[5] Julia Collier Harris, *The Life and Letters of Joel Chandler Harris*, 7.

6 Joel Chandler Harris, "An Accidental Author," 418-19.

7 The school was also known as the Eatonton Academy for Boys.

8 R. Bruce Bickley, Jr., "Joel Chandler Harris," 191.

9 Julia Collier Harris, *The Life and Letters of Joel Chandler Harris*, 12.

10 Joel Chandler Harris, "Joel Chandler Harris Talks of Himself," *Atlanta Daily News*, 10 October 1900, 1.

11 There is still one more reason why Harris may have stated he was born in 1848 instead of two or three years earlier. If he was born in 1845 or 1846, he might have been too old to meet Turner's requirement to be a printer's devil. Claiming an 1848 birth date would have made him the ideal age for a printing apprenticeship.

12 Turnwold—Turner's wold—was the name William Turner, Joseph's brother, had given the family homestead, as well as Joseph's plantation.

13 [Joseph Addison Turner], "Prospectus," *The Countryman*, 15 April 1862, [4].

14 Joel Chandler Harris, *Stories of Georgia*, 241. Ironically, one of the nation's most vigorous opponents of slavery was William H. Seward, Abraham Lincoln's secretary of state. In 1819, at the age of eighteen, having briefly dropped out of Union College, Seward spent six months as a teacher on the Turnwold plantation. Although Seward saw the relative humanity of Joseph Addison Turner's father, he also saw the brutality of the other slave owners. Many historians believe that Seward's unyielding abolitionist views were a primary reason the Republican party denied him the presidential nomination in 1860, preferring the more moderate Abraham Lincoln.

15 [Joseph Addison Turner], prospectus, *The Plantation*, back cover, March 1860.

16 [Joseph Addison Turner], "What Is to Become of the Negro?" *The Countryman*, 13 February 1866, 17.

17 Quoted in *"Uncle Remus": Joel Chandler Harris as Seen and Remembered by a Few of His Friends*, ed. Ivy L. Lee, 18.

18 Minstrels used burnt-cork to blacken their white faces and hands, then applied white creams to their lips to create an exaggerated stage appearance.

19 Joel Chandler Harris, "Negro Customs," *The Youth's Companion*, 11 June 1885, 238.

20 It was common for Blacks to call an older Black male "Uncle," and an older Black female "Aunt" or "Aunty," even if they were not related. When they were related, it was usually from the mother's side of the family, the result of children of slaves usually being kept with the mother while the father was often sold to another plantation.

21 Quoted in Julia Collier Harris, *The Life and Letters of Joel Chandler Harris*, 159-60.

22 Quoted in Julia Collier Harris, *Joel Chandler Harris: Editor and Essayist*, 248.

23 Quoted in Myrta Lockett Avary, *Joel Chandler Harris and His Home*, 6.

24 Quoted in James B. Morrow, "Joel Chandler Harris Talks of Himself and Uncle Remus," 6.

25 [Joseph Addison Turner], "To a Young Correspondent," *The Countryman*, 27 October 1862, 40.

26 The original article, "The Doo-Dang," was printed in *The Countryman*, 21 April 1863, 12.

27 Joel Chandler Harris, "An Accidental Author," 419.

28 If Harris's birth date was at the end of 1848, he would have been almost sixteen years old. However, if he was born in late 1845 or 1846, as certain documents indicate, he would have been nineteen, the age Turner believed was accurate.

29 Turner's personal correspondence to the Confederate States of America of 29 October 1864. The Confederate States of America, well aware of the value of the mass media, especially newspapers, exempted all printers.

30 Forrest Adair, "Joel Chandler Harris—Master Builder," 49.

31 Ibid.

32 J. A. Turner, "To My Patrons," *The Countryman*, 9 May 1865, [1].

33 [Joseph Addison Turner], "Adieu," *The Countryman*, 8 May 1866, 118.

34 Darwin T. Turner, "Daddy Joel Harris," 24, 22.

35 Ibid., 21-22

Main House at Turnwold

Joel Chandler Harris, May 17, 1868

Chapter 2

'Pink Top from Old Put'

Following the war, Joe Harris, like many in the South, was impoverished and unemployed. The meager savings he had accumulated selling rabbit skins for twenty cents each was all in the now-useless Confederate money. With little to sustain him, Harris left the plantation to become a typesetter for six months on the *Macon Telegraph*, owned by William A. Reid, a former resident of Eatonton. Joseph Addison Turner, who had been trying to create another newspaper, may have laid the groundwork that led Reid to hire Harris.[1] Reflecting upon the quality of journalism after the Civil War, Harris noted:

> There was not much that was original or interesting in Georgia journalism in that day and time. The State was in the hands of the carpet-baggers, and the newspapers reflected in very large degree the gloom and the hopelessness of that direful period. The editors abused the Republicans in their editorial columns day after day, and made no effort to enlarge their news service, or to increase the scope of their duties or their influence. Journalism in Georgia, in short, was in a rut, and there it was content to jog.[2]

Like most newspapers at the time, the *Telegraph* was staffed by itinerant tramp printers and reporters, all of whom worked, played, and drank equally hard, something Harris had not previously encountered. A practical joker while a youth, Harris now found himself the butt of innumerable office pranks, among them his first experience with becoming drunk—then having it exposed to the public through the news columns.[3] It would not be the last time.

In an era of personal journalism—a precursor of the "yellow journalism" of the 1890s, "jazz journalism" of the 1920s, and tabloid journalism of the 1980s and 1990s, in which reporters invaded private lives and characterized their subjects by appearance and manners—Harris found even more excuse to turn inward as the staff referred to him, in conversation and print, as "Pink Top from Old Put." References to his red hair would continue in many of the state's newspapers for more than a decade.

At the *Telegraph*, in addition to his regular job as a typesetter, Harris wrote shorts, "puffs" for local businesses, and reviews of books and magazines. Reviewing the *Crescent Monthly* of New Orleans, Harris praised the literary magazine, stating that it was likely "to develop and foster Southern talent to an extent that will show to the world that the Southern mind has more genius that it has ever had credit for."[4] Five months later, still hoping to become a full-time writer, Harris left the *Telegraph*, with few regrets, to move to New Orleans and become secretary to William Evelyn, a former Confederate officer who had founded the *Crescent Monthly*.

In New Orleans, Harris wrote several verses for the local newspapers, and met journalist-novelist Lafcadio Hearn, who impressed him as "a specialist in almost every branch of information"; unlike Hearn, Harris never used the city as a background for any of his writings.[5]

Six months after coming to New Orleans, lonely, homesick, and seeking to do more writing, Harris returned to Georgia to become an editor for the weekly *Monroe Advertiser*, published in Forsyth by James P. Harrison, a friend and former employee at Turnwold who had recently bought the newspaper. In his career of less than five years, Harris had been on the staff of a weekly plantation newspaper, a daily newspaper, a monthly literary magazine, and now a weekly general circulation newspaper.

Harris later recalled that for the *Advertiser* he "set all the type, pulled the press, kept the books, swept the floor, and wrapped the papers for mailing; my mechanical, accounting, and menial duties being concealed from the vulgar hilarity and comment of the world outside of Forsyth by the honorable and impressive title of *Editor*."[6] For all of that, he was paid fifteen dollars a month. After a year writing junk copy, Harris was finally moving his hoped-for career foreword, writing numerous sketches and vignettes about rural life, investigative stories about political corruption and bureaucratic inefficiency, and humor paragraphs[7]—"bright thoughts, witty 'personal notes,' and sarcastic 'news items,' each expressed in a few succinct lines full of fun."[8] However, as with the paragraphs written by most Southern White journalists, and a few Northern ones, many were racist by today's standards. Yet, Harris tore into Blacks—occasionally referring to them as "negroes," "colored," and "darkeys," other times as "niggers"—no more so than he punctured politicians, businesses, and social institutions.[9]

Other Georgia newspapers reprinted many of his humorous paragraphs and political barbs, giving him a regional audience. "Of our young writers,—writers of energy, hope and ability, who promise to become men of mark in letters,—there are few, if any, who rank higher than Chandler Harris,"[10] prophesized author/critic James Wood Davidson in *Living Writers of the South*, a comprehensive overview published in 1869. Underlying that "energy, hope and ability" was a sensitive young man, desperate to be loved and encased by fears and doubts.

On 29 February 1868, Joseph Addison Turner died at the age of 41, impoverished and broken by the Civil War. To Joel Chandler Harris, it was as if the father he always

wanted had left him. Only his mother, the profession of journalism, and now a newly-found friend carried him through what could have been a continuing depression.

Harris and Georgia Harrison Starke, sister of the *Monroe Advertiser* publisher, developed what would become a lifetime platonic friendship. Julia Collier Harris described Starke as "a young matron, a woman of geniality and common sense [who] was fond of books and had a cultivated and discerning mind. Her manners were unaffected and sincere and she was in full sympathy with youth."[11] It was a friendship that would help pull Harris out of depression several times. "I never knew what a real friend was until I went to Forsyth," Harris recalled.[12]

In the fall of 1870, Harris reluctantly left the Forsyth paper to become associate editor of the *Savannah Morning News*, the largest circulation newspaper in Georgia, and one of the South's most respected newspapers. His salary was forty dollars a week, considerably higher than most journalists were then earning. "Forty dollars was enough to keep me for a year, in a way in which I had been accustomed to live. I was the biggest man in the world, I thought," Harris told a reporter almost three decades later.[13]

The editor of the *Savannah Morning News* was William Tappan Thompson, a humorist and one of the South's more popular writers of regional fiction; the publisher was J. H. Estill, its owner as of 1868. Together, they had made the *Morning News* one of the state's better newspapers, a force opposing the political extremes which were dividing the state.

Not long after moving to Savannah, and perhaps once again depressed about being away from friends during the Christmas season, Harris wrote Georgia Starke a long letter explaining his torment at leaving Forsyth and his close friends:

Joel Chandler Harris, 1869

My history is a peculiarly sad and unfortunate one—
and those three years in Forsyth are the brightest of
my life. They are a precious memorial of what would
otherwise be as bleak and as desolate as winter....
[James P. Harrison] treated me throughout with a
kindness and consideration which I am not sure I
deserved. Indeed, the whole family seemed to vie with
each other in their kindness and in the expression of
their goodwill.... If I had consulted my desires—my
personal feelings, I mean—I would have remained on
the 'Advertiser'; but in this miserable world, personal
predilections are often sacrificed for gain.... [It was] a
matter of business simply, and had nothing to do with
my friendship or personal feelings.[14]

Harris was in Savannah to improve his career, not to
make friends, as he explained to Starke:

I don't expect to make any friends here—for the
simple reason that I shall not try. I haven't room in my
heart for them. My love, my friendship, and my
esteem are exhausted on the few friends I already
have. You see, I am conservative in my disposition and
suspicious of new faces. I wouldn't give even the
memory of my friends for the balance of the world. I
have an absolute horror of strangers, and as for making friends of them now, it is not to be thought of. I am
determined to put myself to the test at once—so that
I may know exactly what is in me. In order to do this,
I will have to trust entirely to merit for success,
instead of depending upon the biased judgment of
friends. By this means my capabilities—if I have
any—will show themselves.[15]

At the *Morning News*, as at the *Monroe Advertiser*,
Harris did almost every job on the newspaper. He set
type; he wrote features; and when William Thompson
took extended summer vacations, he was in charge of the

Four of Georgia's better journalists visited Lookout Mountain in July 1871.
With Joel Chandler Harris (wearing a light hat) were Frank Sloval Roberts to
his right; J. H. Estill, sitting on lower ledge; and Henry W. Grady, standing.

editorial page. His biting editorials, often laced with sarcasm, tore into injustices of all kinds, as he threw the newspaper's support behind the working class and, against the popular will, the newly-freed Blacks of the South. But while at the *Morning News*, he was best remembered for writing "Affairs of Georgia," a daily column of paragraphs about the people and politics of Georgia which brought him recognition as the state's leading humor columnist during the six years he wrote the column. Harris could disguise many of his own political thoughts in the language of the freed Blacks. Although he believed in the plantation system, and like almost all of the South and many in the North believed in segregation, Harris also believed in human rights. In blistering editorials, in one of the nation's largest newspapers, he called for tolerance and respect for all people, and condemned violence, no matter who it was directed against. He never doubted that the government was correct to remove the Cherokees from Georgia in the late 1830s. Perhaps, he argued, the Indians needed to be segregated from the White population, and placed onto their own lands to preserve and protect their own culure. But, unlike most Americans, he attacked the federal government for the brutality the Army used to force the Indians from their homelands and onto government-imposed reservations, both during and after the Civil War. He saw this as a pillage of a people by a dominant culture that was not only afraid of another people, but who greedily wanted the land and resources. It was the dichotomy in his earlier life that drove Harris to demand equality for all people, and gave many segregationists a reason to spit out their invective that he was a liberal, while decades later those who thought they were liberals branded him racist. He "abhorred bigotry [and] looked upon all men as his brothers," Julia Collier Harris wrote a decade after his death.[16]

During 1872, while staying at Savannah's Florida House, Harris met Mary Esther (Essie) LaRose, a vivacious and intelligent seventeen-year-old fourth-generation French-Canadian from Quebec who was also boarding at the house with her parents; her father, Pierre LaRose, captain of the steamer Lizzie Baker, had temporarily moved to the port city, northern terminus of his runs to Palatka, Florida. Essie "was small, dainty, and coquettish; her dark eyes sparkled with innocent mischief, and she wore her brown hair in ringlets. Her mother dressed her with French taste, and the piquant combination of modish figure and simple convent manners made a deep impression."[17]

After almost a year of courtship, Harris married Essie on 21 April 1873; she was eighteen, he was twenty-six, admitting twenty-four. Throughout Harris's life, Essie would shield and protect him, providing him the love and support he so long needed. Evelyn Harris, looking back upon his parents' relationship, four decades after his father died and a decade after his mother's death, remembered:

> Mother was one of the strongest, certainly the most constant and effective influence in his mature life. She possessed those qualities of good humor, determination, and rare mental poise which made her an ideal mate for a shy, retiring, home-loving man....
>
> [She had] an alert mind, a dauntless spirit and a keen sense of humor [although she didn't appreciate the practical jokes her husband enjoying playing on friends and colleagues.] She had inherited from her father a practical outlook on life and habits of economy which enabled her to overcome the difficult and unfamiliar problems and responsibilities which constantly confronted her. From her mother, came her strong sense of justice, her uncompromising attitude

Esther LaRose Harris, 1873

in matters of principle, her extreme modesty and devotion.

Marrying a man of high ideals, a dreamer who held in light regard the material problems of life, but whose love of home and deep sense of family responsibilities were unusually and strikingly developed, she brought to the union those attributes which made their life together one of harmony and happiness....

It was her thrift and indomitable energy that aided the growing family to carry on happily through the early difficult years. It was she who protected him from interruptions and annoyances that he might be undisturbed in his creative work. She encouraged and inspired him, dispelled his fears and doubts and cherished the warm praise an acclaim from which he never ceased to shrink.[18]

Three years and two children after marriage, six years after Harris first came to Savannah, the young Harris family, like thousands of others, fled a yellow fever epidemic sweeping up the coastal area, which eventually claimed almost a thousand lives. Atlanta was sufficiently inland to be relatively safe. For a little more than a month, Harris and his family survived on savings and occasional work for James P. Harrison, Harris's former editor at the *Monroe Advertiser* and currently editor of the *Christian Index and Cultivator*, published in Decatur.

In a chance meeting in Atlanta in October, Harris renewed his friendship with Henry W. Grady, about to become managing editor of a reorganized *Constitution*.[19] The *Atlanta Constitution* had been founded in 1868 as a voice to unify the people of the South in their reluctance to accept the martial law of Reconstruction. As long as Whites continued to believe that the "darky" was a "happy-go-lucky" banjo-strumming, foot-shuffling soul with a strong back and limited mental powers, all was well. But now, during the chaos of Reconstruction, a frightened White population thought freed Blacks would steal money, property, and "White women's virtue." They also believed the Blacks who were put into political office by the Northern armies of occupation would destroy the economy and political structure that had been developed over two centuries. The *Constitution* was named to reaffirm that although the South had tried to secede and caused a four-year civil war, the Northern armies of occupation had no right to violate the Constitution in order to reunify the country. Its first editor was Carey W. Styles, a militant former Confederate officer; a year later, a more moderate J. R. Barwick became editor.

The *Constitution* struggled a few years until 1872 when it faced competition from the newly-created *Herald* which declared it would be an active champion of the people's rights, expose fraud and corruption, and serve as the voice of a people who were still being ruled by a punitive North. Within a few months, twenty-two-year-old Henry Grady bought a one-third interest in the *Herald* and helped give it the strength to compete with the *Constitution*. However, the competition financially drained each newspaper, and the *Herald* went bankrupt within three years. During the next few months, Grady unsuccessfully tried to create another Atlanta newspaper, spent some months in New York City, then was lured to the *Constitution* when Evan P. Howell—loyal Southerner, former Confederate artillery officer, and a liberal in most social issues—became editor-in-chief and half owner.

The *Constitution*'s increasing strength would benefit not only from its editorial excellence but also from the advantages that came with the federal government making Atlanta the state capital in 1868 at the expense of Milledgeville, and a subsequent population shift to the new capital. The U.S. census of 1870 reported Atlanta with a population of 21,000; Savannah, the state's largest

Joel Chandler Harris, 1873

city, had 28,000. A decade later, Atlanta had 37,000, while Savannah had increased to only 30,000.

Harris and Grady had first met when Grady was a dynamic young editor in Rome, Georgia, and Harris was associate editor in Forsyth. They had formed a journalistic and personal bond, both being young, intelligent, single journalists in rural Georgia. Grady had abruptly resigned as editor of the *Rome Courier* when the publisher believed that one of Grady's investigations would upset the power-brokers of the city. Within a day, Grady bought out the *Rome Commercial* and the *Rome Daily*, merged them, and put the investigative story about city corruption into the new newspaper.

The 23 April 1873, issue of the *Constitution* had run a biographical sketch about Harris, who at that time was on the Savannah paper, citing him as one of the region's best humor writers. Now that Harris was in Atlanta in the early fall of 1876, Henry Grady—who was recently named managing editor of the *Constitution* after being editor of the *Atlanta Herald*, followed by four months as a freelance correspondent for several major newspapers— quickly recognized the advantages of having the state's leading humor columnist on the *Constitution*. He offered Harris a part-time temporary job as paragrapher and editorial writer at twenty-five dollars a week, considerably less than he had been paid by the *Morning News*, but more than enough to help sustain him during his family's self-imposed exile from Savannah. Within a month, the *Constitution* offered him a full-time job, with an additional five dollars a week as night telegraph editor. William Tappan Thompson was eager for Harris to return to Savannah but because of a recession that followed the epidemic was forced to cut Harris's salary. Nevertheless, Harris worried less about taking a temporary salary cut than being disloyal to the *Morning News*, about leaving the people who had been a part of his life the past six years and whether he could succeed in the new state capital. Only after Thompson encouraged Harris to take the new job did he resign from the *Morning News*. His first official day as "fixture on the editorial staff" of the *Constitution*, as the newspaper reported, was 21 November 1876. During the next two weeks, the *Constitution* would reprint several comments by other newspapers praising Harris and the *Constitution* for hiring him. "The wittiest man of the Georgia press," declared the *Cartersville Express*; "the brightest wit on the Georgia press," proclaimed the *Warrenton Clipper*; a paragrapher with a "sagacious, racy and able pen [who is] a genial, clever gentleman [with] few, if any, equals his age, in Georgia journalism," trumpeted the *Bainbridge Democrat*.[20]

It was at the *Constitution*, where Harris spent twenty-fours years as chief editorial writer and associate editor, that he earned his greatest fame in both newspaper journalism and literary folklore.

----

[1] Paul M. Cousins, *Joel Chandler Harris*, 68.

[2] Joel Chandler Harris, *Life and Works of Henry W. Grady*, 23.

[3] See "The Question Partially Solved," *Macon Daily Telegraph*, 5 August 1866, 3.

[4] [Joel Chandler Harris], review, *Macon Telegraph*, 26 May 1866.

[5] Paul M. Cousins, *Joel Chandler Harris*, 76.

[6] Quoted in James B. Morrow, "Joel Chandler Harris Talks of Himself and Uncle Remus," 6, then in a slightly different form in Julia Collier Harris, *The Life and Letters of Joel Chandler Harris*, 63.

[7] Today's "paragraphers" are stand-up comedians who use not newspapers, but comedy clubs and television.

[8] Robert Lemuel Wiggins, *The Life of Joel Chandler Harris*, 76.

[9] After using the word "nigger" in his paragraphs during the 1870s, Harris almost always used the word "negro" in his articles and in his fiction narratives. Because "nigger" was in common usage, in both North and South, Harris occasionally used it in dialogue, reflecting what was, not would should be. Critics say that his failure, or refusal, to capitalize the name "Negro" in his writings proves he was a racist, even in his times. However, Harris also lower-cased most descriptive names, including the political parties "democrat" and "republican," and his much-loved "south."

[10] James Wood Davidson, *Living Writers of the South*, 256-57.

[11] Julia Collier Harris, *The Life and Letters of Joel Chandler Harris*, 69.

[12] Letter from Joel Chandler Harris to Georgia Harrison Starke, 9 December 1870.

[13] James B. Morrow, "Joel Chandler Harris Talks of Himself and Uncle Remus," 5.

[14] Letter from Joel Chandler Harris to Georgia Starke, 9 December 1870.

[15] Ibid.

[16] Julia Collier Harris, "Joel Chandler Harris—Fearless Editor," 10.

[17] Julia Collier Harris, *The Life and Letters of Joel Chandler Harris*, 111.

[18] Evelyn Harris, *A Little Story*, 2, 8-9, 3.

[19] The newspaper had two separate editions—the *Atlanta Daily Constitution* and the *Atlanta Weekly Constitution*. In all references, *Constitution* refers to the newspaper itself, whether the daily or Sunday edition.

[20] See John Henry Lowery, *Joel Chandler Harris: His Journalistic Rise to Literary Fame*, 29

The Morning News has the largest city and mail circulation of any paper published in Savannah.

Affairs in Georgia.

Atlanta will soon have a new bank with a capital of two hundred thousand dollars. Mr. Cofer, late of Americus, will be President.

It is said that the object of the recent visit of Governor Smith to Macon was to confer with prominent men as to the best means of negotiating the new loan authorized by the Legislature.

Three negroes were drowned in Heard county recently.

Mr. Joseph May, who was shot recently in Heard county, is dead. Thomaston, the murderer, has disappeared, but his father has been held in bail as accessory.

A "deeply-veiled female" is worrying the Atlanta reporters.

The family of Col. R. A. Alston, of Atlanta, has entirely recovered from the recent serious illness that visited every member thereof.

A negro girl was burned to death in Troup county recently.

A negro boy was burned to death in Twiggs county last week.

Three negro women and a negro man were drowned in the Chattahoochee recently.

The serenity of Forsyth is somewhat disturbed by a case of infanticide, the parties to the transaction being negroes.

A man named Bone killed a man named Burton in Forsyth county last Saturday.

Capt. John A. Davis has taken the agency of the Southwestern Railroad and Central Railroad Bank in Albany.

Talbotton will never be comforted with anything less than a telegraph office.

Columbus is fixing up her ice works.

Four negro children have been burned to death in Talbot county recently.

A negro woman was burned to death in Elbert county last week.

Camilla wants a base ball club and a debating society.

From all accounts, the average Columbus girl is not averse to taking unto herself a mate. A young man from the country visited Columbus recently, was introduced to a girl after supper and the twain were made one before bed-time.

Meningitis has visited Elberton.

Dawson has a few cases of small-pox.

Mr. William James, of Dawson, was shot and seriously wounded by a negro recently.

The Elberton Gazette is talking about building a seventy-five thousand dollar railroad from that town to the Air-Line road.

The Columbus Sun has this in regard to Rev. Lovick Pierce: This venerable and wonderful man is very near ninety years of age. In a short talk that he made in St. Luke's Church, last Sunday, he stated he had been preaching sixty-eight years, and if he lived until the 15th of August next, he will have been a member of the church sev-

the New York Sun, is still recreating in Florida.

The debaters of Live Oak are discussing whether capital punishment shall be abolished.

The Key West Dispatch says: "From a careful examination among our cigar manufactories, we are enabled to state that the weekly supply of cigars made in this city amounts to the modest number of 472,000, worth at the factories $35,400."

The body of Edward Homan, steward of the bark Cleone, was found near the railroad wharf in Pensacola last week. Deceased during a fit of insanity, caused by fever, jumped overboard and was drowned.

The Tallahassee Sentinel says : Madison Guilliam was stabbed in the throat on last Saturday night at Centreville, by Charles Gardner, and died two hours after. We have not learned the cause of the stabbing. Both parties were colored. Gardner made his escape, and so far has avoided pursuit, though active steps were taken to arrest him. He is supposed to be lying about the Georgia line, where he has relatives living. Gardner is about 5 feet, 6 or 7 inches in height, with a small face, somewhat pockmarked; weighs 135 to 140 pounds, and is between 30 and 35 years of age.

The editor of the Tampa Peninsular has been visiting an orange grove, and while intoxicated—with the beauties of the scene—wrote as follows: " The orange trees are putting forth, and in a very few days the trees will put on a white and beautiful as well as fragrant robe. The large yellow oranges that still remain on them will personate the golden breast-pins of the blushing bride of spring, and we can feast our eyes on a lovely as well as a sight that, could enjoy a more extended view of, would cause us to be proud of our country, and we could then boast of it as one of the most attractive States of the Union."

A most cold-blooded and heartless murder was committed in Manatee county on the 16th ult., in the vicinity of Fort Ogden. The victim was an Irishman, known as "Fred," employed as a boat hand, the perpetrator being one Marion Allen. Fred was shot while asleep, in the presence of eye-witnesses. The murderer at once fled, but the citizens of the county were at once aroused, and he was taken a few days after, and sent on his way to the jail at Key West. Our informant states that the sheriff, and particularly the citizens, are entitled to great credit for their untiring efforts, day and night, to effect his arrest. He was found secreted in a dense swamp, in which he was tracked for over a mile.

The Tallahassee Sentinel has this: The first case under the Civil Rights bill, passed at the late regular session of the Legislature, was brought before Mr. West, Justice of the Peace, in this city, on Thursday last. Mr. Charles is the owner of the skating rink here, and claims the right of admitting who he pleases to his institution. Bradley Robinson, a colored man, wanted to try his skill on skates, but was refused the privilege, and ejected from the hall. On his making complaint to Mr. West, Mr. Charles was summoned before him, but owing to an inform-

protect them, in some places, have bee killed, and tender plants and Englis peas in bloom are killed. We will hav but little fruit, and vegetables will b later than usual this season. Last yea I had corn up as early as the middle o January, and it passed safely through th light frosts we had and came to maturit

The fine steam saw mill of Messrs. L. Burns & Co., at this city, which h been undergoing repairs for some tim will start again in a few days, which w add something to the life of our litt city.

The proposed convention of mill me to meet in your city, is an importa move that will be followed by good r sults to the mill men and the owners timber land. The lumber business the pine-belt country of the South getting to be immense. Georgia als ships about one hundred and seventy-t millions of feet, most of which goes foreign markets and yields a fair pric bringing nearly two millions of dolla into the State. This business must i crease because Canada and Maine h been comparatively exhausted.

The project of a line of road fro Chicago to Savannah is certainly a gra scheme and seems to bid fair to succee Savannah has no need to dread her co mercial future. With her present capit trade and business energy it will be utter impossible to retard her progress.

I believe in the course of the next qu ter of a century, and perhaps earlier, th all of the seaport cities of Georgia w be in a high state of prosperity. Geor is the natural outlet for the West, and t day will come when her importing a exporting will be done through our por Besides, we will eventually supply t West with manufactured cotton goods.

The South and the West are so situat as to be finally inseparably united as co mercial allies which, when establishe will result in their becoming politi allies. Bind a people together with chord of gold and they will stand sho der to shoulder in peace or war to keep from being broken. The South will ve gradually but surely absorb the cott manufactures of New England. It is n unfrequently the case that we round expressions of alarm on this subject in h journals.

The emancipation proclamation was decree that brought poverty and lament tion upon the South, but she will ari and grow in wealth and power again, a to some extent at the expense of N England capital.

As soon as her cotton manufactur find that the South can put up goo cheaper than she can, they will commen to leave her soil for the South, like r leave a sinking ship. They are sharp men generally get to be, and in ten yea a large part of manufacturing New En land will change their latitude for a mo salubrious climate.

I hope that your cotton factory in S vannah may prove as great a success the Eagle and Phoenix Manufacturi Company of Columbus has done. If does, it may lead to the establishment others on our coast.

Observer.

A Colored Conference Invades T White House.—I saw this morning a da cloud in white chokers moving on th White House, and made one of a curio

Typical "Shorts" colulmn, written by Joel Chandler Harris
(*Savannah Morning News*; March 11, 1873)

Joel Chandler Harris, about 1877

Chapter 3

'I Will See What I Can Do'

J ust as American society relegated Blacks, whether slave or
free, to a secondary role, American writers ignored the Black
as a character. But, there were a few exceptions. During the
Colonial-Revolutionary Cycle of American Black English, ending
shortly before the nineteenth century,[1] a number of travelers'
commentaries had quoted the language of slaves, and a dozen or
so plays were written with characters speaking forms of American
Black English, although the accuracy was questionable and the
stereotypes prevalent.

The stereotypes continued through the subsequent
Antebellum Cycle with the popularity of the minstrel show, with
Whites in burnt-cork blackface telling jokes and stories, and playing musical numbers to the amusement of most of the nation,
both North and South. William Gilmore Simms, one of the
South's better Antebellum writers, accurately portrayed the field
language of the slave, but he was an apologist for slavery, depicting the slave in ways that were acceptable to White prejudices.
Although the widely-distributed slave narratives often told the
truth about slavery, while exaggerating the facts, most were written by abolitionist Whites, few of whom understood Black
language or culture.

Several White writers did try to portray Blacks accurately.
James Fenimore Cooper, the first significant American novelist,
saw Blacks as contributing to the growth of the new nation.
Cooper's portrayal of Blacks in *The Spy* (1821), *Satanstoe* (1845),

and *Redskins* (1846) shows a basic understanding of slaves and their lives, although his recording of Black language was inconsistent. In Edgar Allan Poe's "The Gold Bug," a seriocomical tale about White greed, the freed slave Jupiter speaks a variety of American Black English, and has a few stereotypical traits common to the era. However, he is treated not as incidental to the plot, as was common with most other writers, but as a major character. The tale was first published as a two-part serial in the June 21 and June 28, 1843, issues of the *Philadelphia Dollar Newspaper* then reprinted in other newspapers, becoming one of Poe's more popular stories. *Uncle Tom's Cabin* (1852), Harriet Beecher Stowe's powerful indictment of slavery—which Joel Chandler Harris praised as having "made a more vivid impression upon my mind than anything I have ever read since"[2]— humanized the racial conflict in America and emphasized that even if writers made Blacks the literary equal to Whites in characterization, they were still no more than chattel to the White nation.

After the Civil War, Blacks continued gaining stronger and more accurate roles in Ameican literature. Sidney and Clifford Lanier's dialect poem, "The Power of Prayer," first published in the 26 May 1875 issue of the *Macon Telegraph*, and its subsequent publication in *Scribner's Monthly*, had been one of the first dialect poems to awaken White America to the beauty and power of American Black English. Three years later, *Scribner's Monthly*, which had actively sought out Southern writers, published twenty-five-year-old Irwin Russell's poetic operetta, "Christmas-Night in the Quarters," a poem Joel Chandler Harris had read and admired. In the forward to a collection of Russell's poems, Harris noted:

Irwin Russell was among the first...of Southern
writers to appreciate the literary possibilities of the
negro character, and of the unique relations existing
between the two races before the war, and was among
the first to develop them.... [I]t seems to me that
some of Irwin Russell's negro-character studies rise to
the level of what, in a large way we term literature....
"Christmas-Night in the Quarters" is inimitable. It
combines the features of a character study with a
series of bold and striking plantation pictures that
have never been surpassed. In this remarkable
group...the old life before the war is reproduced with
a fidelity that is marvelous.

But the most wonderful thing about the dialect
poetry of Irwin Russell is his accurate conception of
the negro character. The dialect is not always the
best,—it is often carelessly written,—but the negro is
there, the old-fashioned unadulterated negro, who is
still dear to the Southern heart. There is no straining
after effect—indeed, the poems produce their result
by indirection; but I do not know where could be
found to-day a happier or more perfect representation
of negro character.[3]

Joseph Addison Turner, for an essay in *The
Countryman*, a few months after its first issue, argued: "I
do emphatically wish us to have a Southern literature.
And prominent in our books I wish the negro placed. The
literature of any country should be a true reflex, in letters,
of the manners, customs, institutions, and local scenery
of that country...Let them write about things at home,
and round them."[4] It was Joel Chandler Harris, Turner's
apprentice, more than any other American author of the
post-war era, who would make the American Black a primary figure in literature, and in so doing helped change
the nation's perception of American Blacks, their languages, and cultures.

For several years, Sam W. Small, an excellent observer of people and their customs but a poor recorder of Black language, had been writing a popular column of anecdotes and sketches of Black life. As a literary device, he had created an elderly Black, Uncle Si. When the *Constitution* was sold in 1876, and the new publisher, Evan P. Howell, reorganized the staff, Small resigned and bought a part of a newly-formed newspaper combination, the *Atlanta Evening Telegram* and the *Sunday Herald*. Howell's solution to the probable loss of subscribers to the competing newspaper was to ask Harris, who had written several dialect poems, to take over the column in addition to his other responsibilities. "I don't know what I can do," Harris responded, "for I have never done anything along that line, but I do know the old-time Middle Georgia Negro pretty well and I will see what I can do."[5]

The first two dialect tales, written while Harris was still a temporary employee, appeared 26 October 1876. "Markham's Ball," a 150-word sketch that poked fun at a Republican politician, and "Jeems Roberson's Last Illness," a 200-word sketch about a man who thought he could tame a mule, were street sketches, two men discussing something or someone else. During the remainder of the year, Harris wrote seven other sketches for the *Constitution*, some with the "Cracker" dialect, some with variations of American Black English. In "Uncle Remus and the Savannah Darkey" published 18 November 1876, Harris showed he was aware of dialect differentiation by recording separate dialects for the plantation slaves from Middle Georgia and those from coastal Savannah. "Revival Hymn," published 18 January 1877, is believed to be the first dialect poem Harris wrote for the *Constitution*. The poem was quickly reprinted by several Southern newspapers and in the November 1877 issue of *Harper's*.

Many of Harris's stories included a character named Remus, an urban Black who visited the newspaper office to chat with the editors, primarily about social issues and problems of both Whites and freed slaves during Reconstruction. The character was possibly named for the town gardener in Forsyth. Uncle Remus, himself, was a foil, a character who projected Harris's philosophies and ideas, including his views of race relations and the South.[6]

In "The Night Before Christmas," Harris described Uncle Remus:

> The figure of the old man, as he stood smiling upon the crowd of negroes, was picturesque in the extreme. He seemed to be taller than all the rest; and, notwithstanding his venerable appearance, he moved and spoke with all the vigor of youth. He had always exercized authority over his fellow-servants. He had been the captain of the cornpile, the stoutest at the log-rolling, the swiftest with the hoe, the neatest with the plough, and the plantation hands still looked upon him as their leader....
>
> "His voice was strong, and powerful, and its range was as astonishing as its volume. More than this, the melody...was charged with a mysterious and pathetic tenderness.[7]

With the failure of the *Evening Telegram* and *Sunday Herald*, Sam W. Small returned to the *Constitution* and resumed writing the Uncle Si columns. Harris, who returned to writing about scenes of rural Georgia, later said he was pleased to give up the dialect sketches. Writing the Uncle Remus stories "came hard to Harris at first," Small wrote several years later, "since he had culti- vated no ambitions for literary adventure, and Mrs. Harris used to say that 'Joe would rather take a licking than grind out one of those stories.' In fact, only

affections for and loyalty to the wishes of Captain Howell kept up the production of the 'Uncle Remus' stories..."[8]

In October 1877, after a nine-month lapse, the *Constitution* published another Uncle Remus sketch, "Uncle Remus as a Rebel." Harris explained the break as being the time that the former slave became a farmer, failed, and returned to Atlanta to again chat with the editors at the *Constitution* to tell them he was more comfortable living on the plantation with Mars Jeems. The lure of the comfort of the plantation life, as opposed to the uncertainties and problems in Reconstruction, would be a theme that threaded its way through many of Harris's tales.

Harris had no intention to continue the tales. A political appointment changed all that. In March 1878, Rutherford B. Hayes appointed Small commissioner to the Paris Exposition, and Harris again resumed writing dialect tales. Julia Collier Harris later recalled that Small's resignation "became the means of releasing this rich store of myths and legends which had slumbered for years in an obscure compartment of [my father-in-law's] memory."[9]

During the next ten months, Harris wrote thirteen urban Uncle Remus tales, and created a written folk history. Uncle Remus, said Harris, was comprised of

...three or four darkies whom I had known [including Uncle George Terrell of Turnwold]. I just walloped them together into one person and called him Uncle Remus. You must remember that the negro is sometimes a genius and original philosopher....[10]

[He] plays many parts. But in my mind—as he appears to the inner eye—he is more surely an individual than the majority of people I meet. All my other characters are delineations—types—suggestions—experiments—but Uncle Remus alone is a development.[11]

"Uncle" George Terrell, early 1880s

The character, in various stories spread over Antebellum and Reconstruction eras, ranges from tragic to comic to "minstrel darky," reflecting both Harris's and society's interpretations. Literary scholar C. Alphonso Smith pointed out in 1911:

> It is only after repeated readings that one realizes how completely the character of Uncle Remus is revealed, or rather how completely he is made to reveal himself. There are not many subjects within his range, or beyond it, on which he has not somewhere registered an interesting opinion.... Never in American literature has an author succeeded better in harmonizing a typical character with an individual character."[12]

For a biographical sketch, Sam W. Small praised Harris for having "placed negro dialect poetry as a distinctive feature in the literature of the country," and noted that no one ever wrote better dialect tales than Harris:

> Versatile and always brilliant, [Harris] furnishes some of the most readable editorials of the day, and his humorous and striking political paragraphs are the delight of every right-thinking pair of journalistic shears in the land. He is laborious and careful in the preparation of his matter, and has caused less profanity among compositors than almost any other high moral editor in the United States....
>
> For the poetical deliverances of [Uncle Remus] there are neither peers nor imitators....
>
> It was from observation and actual contact with [plantation life] that the matter and inspiration of "Uncle Remus" were drawn; and the popularity won by faithful renditions is proof of their realistic merits.[13]

Harris realized he needed to put Remus onto a plantation and have him tell stories from his cabin to a little White boy, thus intertwining the lives and folklore of slaves with the White culture. However, the tales Uncle Remus told the Little Boy had none of the obscenities and sexual suggestion common in most of the stories that Blacks told primarily among adults at night and not meant to be heard by children. Harris was probably aware of the connotations, but he was also aware that tales told to children needed to be cleansed. However, Harris may not have understood all of the sexual connotations and the spirit of rebellion within the tales—no matter how close Harris was to Blacks and their folklore, they were not going to tell their Southern friend everything.

In April 1878, Joel Chandler Harris contracted the measles; within two weeks, he had written an Uncle Remus sketch in which the old plantation philosopher had also contracted the illness.[14] But the spread of disease did not end with Harris's fiction: three of Harris's nine children would die of childhood illnesses. Evan Howell Harris, named for the *Constitution*'s publisher, died the following month at the age of nineteen months from complications from the measles. Harris always carried the burden that because he had contracted the illness, he may have brought about young Evan's death. Two other children would also die during their childhoods—Mary Esther in 1882 at the age of three, and Linton in 1890 at the age of seven, both from diphtheria. Within a couple of months of Evan's death, Essie took Julian and Lucien to her parents' home in Upton, Quebec, to avoid the humidity and potential health problems of an Atlanta summer. It was just one of several extended summer vacations Essie would take in Canada. Harris, who so wanted love and acceptance as a child, would try to be the perfect husband and father to his children, spending significant time with them when

they were at home, writing them lengthy letters when they were visiting their grandparents' home in Canada.

During the days, Harris had the work and friendship at the *Constitution*; at night, he suffered from the isolation from his family and continual memories of the death of his youngest son. During the summer that Evan died, Harris finished his first novel, staying just ahead of publication dates in the *Constitution*. Between April and September 1878, the *Weekly Constitution* published Harris' serialized 50,000-word novel, *The Romance of Rockville*, a first attempt that Harris himself admitted was not very good. The book had probably been a catharsis for his grief and subsequent loneliness; a major plot line included the death of the son of an unmarried woman, and its impact upon a family. Harris's fourth son, Evelyn, would be born that September in Canada, the last month that the novel ran in the *Constitution*.

Evan's death may have led Harris to drink even more. However, it was Mary Harris who at least temporarily broke her son of a decade-long alcohol dependency. Julia Collier Harris says: "[Mary Harris called her son] into her room one night and told him that the quality of his work was suffering, and that he now had three boys for whom he was responsible, and that she wanted him to leave off drinking altogether. He listened respectfully, took what she said in good part, and followed her advice."[15] After a temporary break, Harris probably continued drinking heavily, although he sternly wrote to his children to avoid becoming alcoholics.[16] For his entire life, Harris would be an active and caring parent who spent as much time with his children as possible; later, as they grew up, he frequently wrote to them, almost always enclosing money.[17]

Loved at home, praised at work, Joel Chandler Harris could have lived his entire life as an obscure Southern journalist had he not changed the direction of the Uncle

Remus stories. In the January 1877 issue of *The Arena*, W. S. Scarborough had brought to public attention the importance of Black folklore and language within folk tales. In the December issue of *Lippincott's Magazine*, William Owens discussed the folklore of the Southern Black, but much of it was inaccurate. For a *Constitution* review, Harris pointed out that the article was "remarkable for what it omits rather than for what it contains," and criticized Owens's research:

> The author is even at a loss to account for the prefix 'Buh'...which the negroes give to the animals that figure into their stories, as 'Buh Rabbit,' 'Buh Wolf,' etc. We judge from the tone of Mr. Owen's [sic] article that he is familiar only with the lore of the non-descript beings who live on the coast, otherwise he would have no difficulty in determining the derivation of the word 'buh.' The real southern darkey pronounces the word as though it were written 'brer,' and he confines it to the animals themselves—for instance: "Den bimeby, Mr. Fox, he see Mr. Rabbit comin' 'long, an' he say, 'howdy Brer Rabbit—how you gittin' 'long dese days?"[18]

The articles by Scarborough and Owens—along with the writings of William Orrie Toggle, a Georgian who collected tales of the Creek Indians—stirred Harris's interest in folklore and language.[19] In an article for *Lippincott's* almost a decade later, Harris acknowledged that although he "had absorbed the stories, songs, and myths" that he had first heard on Turnwold, until he read Owens's article he "had no idea of their literary value." The Uncle Remus tales would have their structure in the form that Chaucer used for *The Canterbury Tales* and Boccaccio used for the *Decameron*; however, Harris would use only one major narrator for his tales.

The first of a series of almost three dozen Uncle Remus plantation fables, each published weekly, none of them with a byline, was "The Story of Mr. Rabbit and Mr. Fox as Told by Uncle Remus," published 20 July 1879. That first tale briefly introduced the characters who would be more fully developed through other tales. His leading character would be Uncle Remus, the beloved elderly former plantation slave who lived through the Antebellum, Civil War, and Reconstruction eras, a polite man of great wisdom who distrusted most of what Whites said but was bound by loyalty to his masters. Supporting characters were the Little Boy, six-year-old son of the plantation owners, who visited Uncle Remus in his cabin at night; and Miss Sally and Master John, the Little Boy's parents, who were often coincidental to the narrative. Remus was the teacher; the Little Boy, the student; and their discussions set the tone for both a literary and philosophical series of stories. Literary critic Dennis F. Brestensky explains:

> Remus can be admired for his teaching abilities—he can listen as well as lecture, he can balance freedom and discipline, and he is confident enough to let his student constantly question his authority....
>
> [M]ost of his philosophical beliefs are imparted to the boy as part of the initiation-into-life motif. Remus's basic philosophical position is one of resigned acceptance of life [but he] can also be skeptical....
>
> He is more than a superficial observer and thinker; he is imaginative and can see connections between disparate objects—all of which give him stature as a character and a person.[20]

The featured animals of the folktales that Uncle Remus would tell his young friend were the Rabbit, whose mission in life seemed to be to use his wits to take a little more than his fair share from animals much stronger than he; and the Fox, the wily, conniving antagonist who would develop plans to trap the rabbit, only to be foiled.

Brer Rabbit originally was not a rabbit; Brer Fox was not a fox. Both the rabbit and the fox were American adaptations of animals native to the West Coast of Africa. The characteristics of the American fox are normally swiftness and a lovable sly or crafty intelligence, somewhat the same characteristics attributed to Brer Rabbit.

The fox of the Uncle Remus tales is more greedy, more plotting, and less intelligent. In the West African tales, the animal was probably a jackal or hyena, both of which share many of the same characteristics that distinguish Brer Fox. Because there were no jackals and hyenas in America, the slaves had to adapt an animal that appeared to be similar to the ones they knew in their ancestral homelands of Sierra Leone, Ghana, and Nigeria.

The slaves also adapted one of their own animals that was the classic African trickster into the closest appearing American animal. The American rabbit is not known for the characteristics that the slaves gave to Brer Rabbit. However, the cunnie rabbit is. This species is not a rabbit at all, but a rabbit-sized animal with round small ears, large eyes, and a build similar to the American hare. It is better known in modern West Africa as the chevrotain, a mouse deer. This particular cud-chewing animal is a forest-dweller known to be extremely clever, ingenious, and elusive. In African folklore, it is often endowed with magical knowledge.

The etymological history of the cunnie rabbit and its adaptation to the American slave tales is even more interesting. Both *cunnie* and *rabbit* are English names. *Cunnard*, meaning *knowing*, is the Middle English name

for the Western European rabbit. From *cunnard* came *cunning*, and then *cony*, the name most Americans in the eighteenth and nineteenth centuries called the hare. A *cunningaire* ("cunning hare"), the nearly-obsolete term, or *cony hare*, the more acceptable nineteenth century name, was a rabbit warren.

During the late eighteenth and nineteenth centuries, the American slaves merged some zoological knowledge—the chevrotain of their ancestral homelands that looked like the American hare—with some nebulous linguistic adaptation from two continents to determine that the cony was the chevrotain, and that cunning was one of the main characteristics of the trickster animal they called Brer Rabbit.

Two published stories about a rabbit and a tar-baby, combined with what Harris had heard on the Turnwold plantation, set the base for Harris's most famous tale, which probably had its origins within several African and Caribbean cultures, although folklorists and anthropologists have also traced the stories and possible origins to almost all cultures, including those of Canada, Brazil, India, Spain, and Portugal.[21] Most tar-baby stories involve animals, one of which tricks an adversary into trying to say "howdy" to a mound of tar made to look like a child. The animal adversary becomes mad when the tar-baby says nothing, eventually striking the tar-baby. With each blow, the animal adversary becomes further and further trapped by the tar, and the animal which had put out the tar-baby then captures the easy prey, only to be tricked into letting the tarred animal free.

In the July 1870 issue of *Lippincott's*, Thaddeus Norris discussed Black folklore and hoodoo, and presented one version of the tar-baby tale. In Norris's tale, a farmer creates a tar-baby to trap a rabbit which was stealing peas; however, when the farmer frees the rabbit to prepare him for dinner, the rabbit escapes by punching a tar-covered paw into the farmer's eyes. William Owens's article from *Lippincott's* seven years later presented another story that included the trickster rabbit. A Gullah version collected by A. M. H. Christensen from South Carolina was published in the *Springfield* (Massachusetts) *Republican*.

In its 16 November 1879, issue, less than two years after Harris first read Owens's article, the *Constitution* published "Brer Rabbit, Brer Fox and the Tar-Baby." Once again, there was Uncle Remus, the Little Boy's teacher who, unlike earlier stories, told the tale from his own cabin, not "The Big House." All future tales would be told from the cabin. In Harris's tar-baby story, Uncle Remus tells the Little Boy the story about a fox who uses a tar-baby to trap a rabbit for dinner. Upon greeting the tar baby, the rabbit becomes upset that the apparently haughty Tar-Baby wouldn't even say "howdy" to him: "'I'm gwineter larn you howter talk ter 'specttobble people[22] ef hit's de las' ack,' sez Brer Rabbit, sezee. 'Ef you don't take off dat hat en tell me howdy I'm gwineter bus' you wide open,' sezee." Naturally, the Tar-Baby says nothing, while Brer Fox "he lay low," and watches the rabbit attack, then become entangled in the mound of tar, an easy prey for the fox. But then Harris abruptly ended the tale. As with the folktales, the cliffhanger is typical of trickster tales, for it forces the audience to eagerly anticipate yet another tale. Harris did not disappoint his readers.

Two weeks later, with the readers demanding to know if the rabbit ever escaped, the *Constitution* published the second half, the fourth of the Uncle Remus tales, "Showing How Brer Rabbit was too Sharp for Brer Fox."[23] But this time, Brer Rabbit, Harris's trickster in more than half of his 185 Uncle Remus tales,[24] fools the fox into throwing him into a brier patch where he was able to escape the tar and the frustrated fox, who could not pursue his dinner.

The reprinting of the Uncle Remus tales in northern newspapers, especially the influential *Springfield Republican* and the *New York Evening Post*, established Harris as the leading writer of dialect folklore. In a letter to the editor of the *Evening Post*, which had reprinted several of the tales that first appeared in the *Constitution*, Harris said that had the *Evening Post* had not reprinted the Uncle Remus tales, "his legends would have attracted little or no attention."[25]

For his entire career, Harris would insist he was merely the compiler and editor of the tales others spoke. "All I did was to write out and put into print the stories I had heard all my life," Harris later recalled.[26] Harris may have merely "compiled" the tales, but without the presence of Uncle Remus—and of Harris's own views—the tales would never have had the respect they generated, nor the power others ascribed to them. By the end of the year, the Uncle Remus stories, collected in another medium, would become the most popular stories in America.

---

[1] The five cycles of American Black English, as developed in a comprehensive theory by Walter M. Brasch, are the Colonial-Revolutionary Cycle (about 1765-about 1800, with a pre-cycle of about 85-100 years), Antebellum Cycle (about 1820-1860), Reconstruction Cycle (about 1867-1902), Negro Renaissance Cycle (about 1915-1940), and Civil Rights Cycle (about 1958-1990). Each cycle lasted about twenty-five to forty years, with a peak somewhere near its middle, and was larger than the previous cycle in quality and quantity of materials; each cycle was followed by an intercycle of about a decade or two. For further information, see Brasch's *Black English and the Mass Media* (1981).

[2] Joel Chandler Harris, letter, *The Atlantic Monthly Supplement* (December 1882): 13. Harris says he first read the book in 1862. Harris many times referred to the book, pointing out that Uncle Tom, having escaped a brutal Simon Legree, and having experienced freedom, still wanted to return into the safety that slavery provided. He

would develop the theme more fully in his short stories, "Daddy Jake the Runaway" and "Blue Dave."

3 Joel Chandler Harris, introduction to *Christmas-Night in the Quarters and Other Poems*, Irwin Russell, x-xi.

4 [Joseph Addison Turner], *The Countryman*, 22 December 1862, 6.

5 Quoted by Paul M. Cousins in *Joel Chandler Harris*, 95, and based upon an interview by Cousins with Clark Howell who was at the meeting with his father, Evan Howell, and Harris.

6 The literary device of the foil (also known as the alter ego) has been used by humor and satire journalists to set up "straw-men" for verbal sparring and to project ideas for the "straight man," the actual writer. Joel Chandler Harris probably became familiar with the literary nature of the foil because of its use by Joseph Addison Turner who created Aunt Sally Poke in 1854. Other authors who used foils included Charles Farrar Brown (Artemus Ward) and David R. Locke (Petroleum V. Nasby) in the nineteenth century; Don Marquis (Archy) in the early twentieth century; and in the latter twentieth century, Walt Brasch (Marshbaum), Mike Royko (Slats Grobnik, Dr. I.M. Kooky), and Jimmy Breslin and Art Buchwald (numerous individuals).

7 Joel Chandler Harris, "The Night Before Christmas," 412-13.

8 Sam W. Small, "Story of the *Constitution*'s First Half-Century of Service to the City, State and Country," 24.

9 Julia Collier Harris, *The Life and Letters of Joel Chandler Harris*, 143.

10 Quoted in James B. Morrow, "Joel Chandler Harris Talks of Himself and Uncle Remus," 5.

11 Quoted in William Malone Baskervill, "Joel Chandler Harris," 67.

12 C. Alphonso Smith, "Joel Chandler Harris," 145.

13 Sam W. Small, *Atlanta Constitution*, 20 April 1879, 5.

14 [Joel Chandler Harris], "Uncle Remus Succumbs to the Epidemic," *Atlanta Constitution*, 3 May 1878, 2.

15 Julia Collier Harris, *The Life and Letters of Joel Chandler Harris*, 137.

16 See the letters collected in Hugh T. Keenan, editor, *Dearest Chums and Partners: Joel Chandler Harris's Letters to His Children: A Domestic Biography* (Athens: University of Georgia Press, 1993), a collection of 280 of Harris's letters to his children.

17 Hugh T. Keenan, in *Dearest Chums and Partners*, notes that Harris occasionally used Black language to write to his children after they had moved away from home.

18 [Joel Chandler Harris], review, *Constitution*, 21 November 1877, 2. Harris was inaccurate in attacking Owens for using the word "Buh." Among the major variants were "Br'er," "Bruh," and "Buh." The word, "Brer," as written by Harris, a rough translation of "brother," was meant to be pronounced as "bruh." The postvocalic /r/, common in many American dialects, especially in the South, is not only silent, but changes the exact pronunciation of the previous vowel.

19 Although Brer Rabbit tales appeared in other English language publications, it is doubtful that Harris had read them.

20 Dennis F. Brestensky, "Uncle Remus: Mere Buffoon or Admirable Man of Stature?" 54-55, 57.

21 For a fuller discussion of tar-baby variants and origins, see Adolf Gerber, "Uncle Remus Traced to the Old World," *Journal of American Folk-Lore* (October-December 1893); Aurelio M. Espinosa, "A Folk-Lore Expedition to Spain," *Journal of American Folk-Lore* (April-June 1921); W. Norman Brown, "The Tar-baby Story at Home," *Scientific Monthly* (September 1922); A. M. Bacon and Elsie Clews Parsons, "Folk Songs from Elizabeth City County, Va.," *Journal of American Folk-Lore* (July-September 1922); Newbell Niles Puckett, *Folk Beliefs of the Southern Negro* (1926); Ruth Cline, "The Tar-Baby Story," *American Literature* (March 1930); and "A New Classification for the Fundamental Elements of the Tar-Baby Story on the Basis of 267 Versions," *Journal of American Folk-Lore* (January-March 1943). The primary work on African origins is Frances Baer's *Sources and Analogues for the Uncle Remus Tales* (1980).

22 In a revision for the first book of Uncle Remus stories, Harris changed the phrasing to, "I'm gowinter larn you howter talk ter 'spectubble fokes...

23 For the first book collection of Uncle Remus stories, Harris changed the title to "How Mr. Rabbit Was Too Sharp for Mr. Fox."

24 The number may be as high as 263 tales. However, the definitive collection of the tales, *The Complete Tales of Uncle Remus*, compiled by Richard Chase for publication in 1955, includes only 185.

25 Joel Chandler Harris, letter to the editor, *New York Evening Post*, 19 May 1880.

26 James B. Morrow, "Joel Chandler Harris Talks of Himself and Uncle Remus," 5

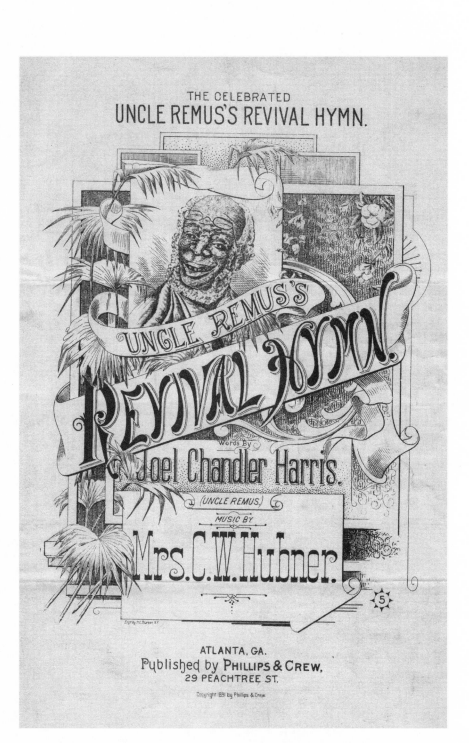

Chapter 4

'A Deep and Wide Influence'

In an itinerant profession, Joel Chandler Harris had been at the *Constitution* four years. In spring 1880, Harris had sent a letter to Stilson Hutchins,[1] owner of the pro-Southern *Washington Post*, hoping to improve both his working conditions and salary. His letter is a revealing insight into his professional and personal life:

> Nothing would please me better than to accept a position on The Post, and I think my knowledge of Southern affairs and my capacity for hard work would be of great advantage to you. I am not a drinker, not a Bohemian, and my whole mind, time and ambition are utterly wrapped up in the newspaper business. My daily average of editorial matter for the Constitution is about two columns.
>
> Whatever may be said, The Post by its position is bound to be the representative of southern democrats, and I can be of great service to you (I believe) in that direction.
>
> ...I am in no sense of the word a Bohemian, have no ambition outside of my newspaper work, and have nothing to do with politics save in the way of a professional journalist—though, personally, I am an uncompromising state rights democrat. By taking the lead in southern politics, The Post can not only make itself popular in this section, but absolutely control southern representatives.
>
> To recapitulate: 1. I am comparatively young (thirty.)[2] 2. I am a hard worker. 3. I like The Post. 4. You know my style and specialties.
>
> Make me an offer.[3]

In late June, Harris covered the Democratic National Convention in Cincinnati, possibly as a cover to talk with Hutchins. However, Hutchins apparently either forgot or deliberately avoided a previously-arranged appointment with him. The creator of the Uncle Remus tales followed up with a friendly letter that again reiterated not only his desire to work for the *Post*, but also revealed a lot about the nature of his personality, personal habits, and ethics, as well as the nature of American journalists and journalism at the time:

> ...As a newspaper man I am entirely docile. I have no friends to puff, no axes to grind, no pet theories to advance, no private interests to forward, no opinions to insist upon. I do my work as a journalist and not as a politician. I am wholly absorbed in my profession, and I would not accept a position where the meagerness of the salary, so to speak, would compel me to do outside work.... I would not accept a political place of any sort, or place myself under obligations to office-holders for quadruple the salary you could afford to pay me. I am aware that this borders on eccentricity, but I cannot help that. I am also eccentric enough to keep sober at all times and to enjoy hard work, provided it is not the mere drudgery of routine. I have done so much of that in my time that the bare thought of it fills me with dismay. If I were on the Post, you would merely have to give me a verbal outline of your views upon any question to have them elaborated into an article or series of articles; and I have come to the conclusion that my supply of paragraphs, such as they are, is inexhaustible. I have morbid views in regard to permanence, and that is one reason why I hate to break my Atlanta connections. My situation here is permanent under any and all circumstances, and to me that is its chief attraction. I have no vanity of any kind or degree, and I have long ago learned that one

man cannot make a newspaper. I know well enough that the only merits I have as a newspaper man are a reasonable capacity for hard and continuous work, and complete sobriety. I have written much more freely than I could have talked, and I believe I have given you a fair idea of my disposition. As to my work, I daresay you have a better opinion of it than I have myself, for I am free to say it is never quite satisfactory to me. In other words I am more puzzled than flattered at its popularity. I know I could not make myself indispensable at the Post, but in the treatment of a certain class of questions, in the discussion of the Southern situation, (which will long remain a factor in our politics and may be made the source of some profit to a leading newspaper) and in the matter of paragraphing I feel that I could earn a reasonable salary on the Post....[4]

Two weeks later, Hutchins wrote Harris a cordial letter, noted how busy he was, that he was the "lineal descendant of the [Wandering] Jew, or have at least inherited his curse," and unequivocally stated he wanted to hire the journalist who could bring a stronger dimension to the *Post*'s Southern coverage:

> I think you will do well and like it here, and I can assure you that I know that no man ever worked for me or with me who did not feel pleased to stay or come back.... I want a first rate staff, and am sure that with you to fill it out we will be all right. Shall be glad to have you come when you can, when you can naturally and easily. We can wait a week or a month if convenient, but want to settle the matter as definite.[5]

Terrified that Harris would leave, if not for the *Post*, certainly for some other newspaper, the *Constitution* increased his salary. An insightful decision for the

No. 4906 L.

Library of Congress,

Copyright Office, Washington.

To wit: **Be it remembered,**

That on the ....29th........ day of March................., anno domini 1880,

............Joel C. Harris...

............Atlanta Ga............, has deposited in this Office the title of a

............Book... the title or description of

which is in the following words, to wit:

> Uncle Remus.
> Mythology of the old Plantation.
> Comprising the wonderful adventures
> of Brer Fox, Brer Rabbit, Brer Wolf
> and Brer Terrypin.
> By Joel C. Harris

the right whereof ....he..... claims as Author. Proprietor...................
in conformity with the laws of the United States respecting Copyrights.

Librarian of Congress.

Copyright for Harris's first book. (Note original title.)

Constitution, the salary increase gave Harris the assurance that he was important to the newspaper while giving the newspaper the respect that would come a few months later from having a best-selling author on its staff.

Joel Chandler Harris had begun thinking about collecting the folktales into a book, and had even secured a copyright on 27 March 1880, for an unpublished collection he called *Uncle Remus, Mythology of the Plantation*. However, he fully expected his reputation to be made solely by his newspaper work, not by book publication. A Northern publisher changed all that. James C. Derby, one of the nation's most respected editors, had read Harris's dialect stories in the *New York Evening Post*. In the spring of 1880, returning from a visit in Biloxi, Mississippi, where he had been negotiating with Jefferson Davis for a book about the Confederacy, Derby stopped in Atlanta to persuade the man who believed himself "a cornfield journalist" of the value of a bound collection of Uncle Remus tales. "I was astonished," said Harris several years later, "but he [Derby] seemed to be in earnest, and so we picked out of the files of the *Constitution* enough matter for a little volume."[6] However, Harris was still a newspaperman who preferred "Uncle Remus in a modest corner of the newspaper to Uncle Remus in a book."[7] Working primarily from published clippings, D. Appleton Company published *Uncle Remus, His Songs and His Sayings; the Folk-Lore of the Old Plantation* in November 1880,[8] adding Harris to its list that included Noah Webster, Charles Darwin, Lewis Carroll, and William Cullen Bryant.

Most of the book was illustrated by nationally-acclaimed artist Frederick S. Church from rough sketches by James Henry Moser, an itinerant illustrator whom Harris had known and admired a decade earlier in Atlanta. Harris had sent Moser's rough sketches of Uncle Remus to Church, telling him that Moser's "conception of the negro is perfect, whatever technical defects there may be about it";[9] Moser's interpretation of Uncle Remus would appear on the title page.

"If you will bear in mind that the stories are perfectly sane and serious—that they are related by the southern negroes with all the sincerity," Harris had written to Church, "you will have no difficulty in catching the curious idea that underlies the legend."[10] However, Church's final pen-and-ink illustrations of the tales portrayed the animals as caricatures, and Uncle Remus as a comical darky, contradicting Harris's own literary portrait of a man whose life spanned all human emotion. Harris was unwilling to criticize either artist in public, but he wasn't satisfied with the results. Two months prior to publication, he had written a private letter to an artist whom he believed would have done a better job of illustrating the book: "The animal illustrations of the folk-lore are made by F. S. Church, and they are good as to artistic execution, but uniformly bad as to spirit and intention. The illustrations of negro character are by Mr. Moser of this city, and while the spirit is good, the art is crude."[11] Harris was worried that the caricatures, especially of Uncle Remus, and the publisher's placement of it as a work of humor would detract from the stories. In the book's introduction, Harris told his readers: "I am advised by my publishers that this book is to be included in their catalogue of humorous publications, and this friendly warning gives me an opportunity to say that however humorous it may be in effect, its intention is perfectly serious; and, even if it were otherwise, it seems to me that a volume written wholly in dialect must have its solemn, not to say melancholy, features."[12]

Harris had originally wished to call his first collection *Uncle Remus's Folk-Lore*, before yielding to the publisher's demands for *Uncle Remus, His Songs and Sayings*. In the book's introduction, Harris discussed not only how he collected the tales, but why he put them into print:

> With respect to the Folk-Lore series, my purpose is to present the legends themselves in their original simplicity, and to preserve them permanently to the quaint dialect—if, indeed, it can be called a dialect—through the medium of which they here become a part of the domestic history of every Southern family; and I have endeavored to give it to the whole a genuine flavor of the old plantation.
>
> Each legend has its variants, but in every instance I have retained that particular version which seemed to me to be the most characteristic, and have given it without embellishment and without exaggeration.[13]

Although Harris rightly claimed, in response to questions from the critics, that the tales were "uncooked" —not made up—the reality is that all oral folktales reflect the personalities of whomever is telling them. Some are minimalist—just the basics, possibly told by someone who has little command of the complexities of language; some are broad, profuse tales, dynamic with the inflections of language. "Jocular storytelling may be judged by how quickly and fluently the talk of the characters can be rendered and how many ranges of voice the taleteller can draw upon," says folklorist Roger D. Abrahams, who explains that in Afro-American folk tales "the trickster himself is often portrayed as having a lisp; other animal characters have their own characteristic way of producing their talk, so that a master storyteller may scream, laugh, shout, rasp, whisper, and imitate in some equally stretched manner the way an animal, devil, witch, or ghost might talk."[14] Another element is the repetitive nature of oral folklore because, says Abrahams, "unlike the reader, the listener can hardly

go back to a previous page."[15] The stories, says Abrahams, are already well-known by the audience, and the "performance becomes at once overly allusive (narrative detail is decreased) and too concrete (extraneous social detail is increased)." The storyteller's commentary, thus, "has little to do with the action, but a great deal to do with how the audience interprets the story and enjoys the performance."[16]

In the Black African and Afro-American oral folklore tradition, says Harris, the audience interacts with the storyteller, encouraging him, laughing, interrupting, adding new information, and several interjections, such as "Dar now!" "He's a Honey, mon!" and "Gentermens! git out de way, an' gin 'im room!"[17] Harris heard the tales, probably several versions of each, kept the essential elements, and recast the oral folklore into his own personality and into the written medium, thus giving it a lineal continuity unlike the oral medium. Although Harris explained the difference between a written and oral folklore medium, White Americans began to believe there was only one version, the one they had read. By writing down the tales, Harris locked into a literary frame an oral folklore that was constantly changing.

Among the tales told by Uncle Remus were several based upon folktales told in other cultures, including some recorded by France's La Fontaine, and "The Awful Fate of Mr. Wolf," a precursor to what became the Disney version of "The Three Little Pigs." However, Harris gave innumerable hints that the tales he had heard from the slaves were distinctly African in origin.

As was the custom with African stories, in each succeeding generation the tales were retold, embellished and modified. From the folk tales of Uncle Remus we realize, perhaps for the first time, that the life, culture, and languages of the American Black were distinctly African in origin, as subsequent analysis of their origins proved. Yet,

UNCLE REMUS

HIS SONGS AND HIS SAYINGS

THE FOLK-LORE OF THE OLD PLANTATION

By JOEL CHANDLER HARRIS

*WITH ILLUSTRATIONS BY FREDERICK S. CHURCH AND
JAMES H. MOSER*

NEW YORK
D. APPLETON AND COMPANY
1, 3, AND 5 BOND STREET
1881

Frontispiece, *Uncle Remus, His Songs and Sayings*

Harris was careful to tell his readers that Uncle Remus and his stories were only one part of Black folklore and language, and not meant to be representative of an entire race.

The academic folklorists and the mass media's "conventional wisdom," while praising the stories, discounted African origins, believing the slaves first heard the tales in America then twisted them into their own patterns of "primitive English." However, folklorist Thomas F. Crane, for a review-essay in the 18 April 1881, issue of the mass circulation *Popular Science Monthly*, discussed the Uncle Remus parallels with folktales of other cultures and concluded the tales were "a valuable contribution to comparative folklore. [N]ot only is the representation of the dialect better than anything that has heretofore been given, but [Harris] has shown himself a master in the difficult art of collecting popular tales. A glance at the variants of these stories published elsewhere will show the vast superiority of Mr. Harris's."[18]

Crane's academic essay also stirred what would be an almost-century long debate about whether the folklore—and, thus, the language—of the American slaves originated in Africa and was brought with the slaves to America, whether they were European tales that were later intermixed with the slaves' own views of life, or if they had origins among Native Americans.

The Smithsonian's J. W. Powell had praised Harris's recordings of the Negro folktales but argued that there were similar tales among both Native American and African tribes, and that the Uncle Remus tales may have been "borrowings" from Native American folklore. Folklorist Heli Chatelain disagreed:

> The myths and tales of the negroes in North, Central, and South America are all derived from African prototypes, and these can easily be traced in

collections… Through the medium of the American negro, African folk-lore has exerted a deep and wide influence on the folk-lore of the American Indians; and that of the American white race itself bears many palpable signs of African inroads.[19]

A decade after publication of the first collection of Uncle Remus tales, folklore scholar Adolph Gerber compared the tales with those of other cultures and concluded that "The majority of those tales was imported from the Old World."[20] But the folklore community continued the debate, with many of the scholars praising Harris's recording but discounting his analysis of origins. It was not until the publication of *Sources and Analogues of the Uncle Remus Tales* (1980) by Florence Baer, a century after publication of *Uncle Remus, His Songs and Sayings*, that the debate finally subsided under a burden of proof as to the African origins of the Uncle Remus tales.

The second story of the book, the direct derivative of a West African folktale, was a reworking of "Brer Rabbit, Brer Fox and the Tar-Baby," first published more than a year earlier in the *Constitution*, and now retitled "The Wonderful Tar-Baby Story." As with the newspaper story, this one also ends with the rabbit entangled with the tar-baby, and the little boy wanting to know what happened. Two tales later, Uncle Remus completed the story. In the newspaper article, Harris had written: "'I gotter go home en bresh up fer Sunday, Brer Fox," sezee, 'but I'll see you later. So long, Be sho' en save me some er dat calamus root,[21] 'sezee, en wid dat he skipt out des ez lively ez a crickett in de embers." Possibly aware that the newspaper ending was too "soft," and that readers might not understand why Brer Rabbit was able to escape the tar and brier-patch, Harris changed the conclusion for the book, and in so doing made the rabbit even sassier. Sitting "cross-legged on a chinkapin log koamin' de pitch outen

his har wid a chip," and a far distance from Brer Fox, Brer Rabbit "he holler out": "'Bred en bawn in a brier-patch, Brer Fox—bred en bawn in a brier-patch!' en wid dat he skip out des ez lively ez a cricket in de embers."

The stories of rabbits and tar-babies, of foxes, bears, and turtles, are interesting and enjoyable. Yet when the surface is peeled away, universal truths about people and their behaviors emerge, the tales becoming nothing less than powerful allegories of human life with all its frustrations, joys, and sorrows. In *Going to the Territory* (1986), novelist Ralph Ellison explains, "Aesop and Uncle Remus had taught us that comedy is a disguised form of philosophical instruction; and especially when it allows us to glimpse the animal instincts lying beneath the surface of our civilized affectations."[22]

In contrast to the stories of the Little Boy and Uncle Remus, the folk tales told by Uncle Remus show the undercurrent of mistrust, hostility, and rebellion by the weaker animals, especially the wily rabbit who constantly evaded the believed superiority of the stronger animals; however, as Brer Fox pointed out to Brer Rabbit, it was Brer Rabbit who deliberately chose to become entangled in the tar-baby while the fox "he lay low." Nevertheless, it was the Tar-Baby story that set the pattern of the weak using cunning intelligence and deception to manipulate the strong.

"Though the rabbit is a shy, small, and humble creature," wrote critic J. V. Nash, "the Negro imagination finds no difficulty in transforming him into a personage of importance, shrewdness, and wit, which makes him the sovereign of his little world."[23]

Brer Rabbit, wrote folklorist A. M. H. Christensen in 1892, "represents the colored man." The rabbit of the tales, she pointed out, "is not as large nor as strong; as swift, as wise, nor as handsome as the elephant, the alligator, the bear, the deer, the serpent, the fox, but he is 'de mos' cunnin' man dat go on fo' leg.'—and by this cunning he gains success. So the negro, without education or wealth, could only hope to succeed by strategem."[24] As historian Wayne Mixon noted:

> The tales themselves, in which the weak constantly triumph over the strong, provide wish fulfillment for Remus much as they did for real blacks. Just as Remus's stories undercut claims of slavery's benevolence, so do his songs, with their references to blacks' making the crops and the whites' receiving the money, to promises made and broken by whites, to backbreaking labor in the summer sun, to avoiding slave patrols, and to the necessity of secrecy, deception, and never losing hope.[25]

An anonymous reviewer for London's *Spectator*, a few months after the book was published, discussed some of the psychology within the Remus tales:

> What strikes us most, perhaps, is the curious simplicity of the trickery which is supposed to win the victory over the superior force. The rabbit, who is always, or almost always, the negro's hero amongst animals—sometimes the terrapin, a kind of freshwater tortoise, we believe, takes his place—gets out of his scrapes by the sort of inventiveness which, if it were conceivable at all, would be not so much an evidence of his superior cunning, as of the infinite and immeasurable gullibility of the fox, or wolf, or bear with whom he has to contend. And evidently the imagination of the negro delighted itself more in grotesquely exaggerating in every way the gullibility of the stronger races, than even in dwelling upon the cunning of the weaker races. These legends embody better the contempt of the weak for the humorously exaggerated stupidity of the strong, than their delight in the astuteness of the weak.[26]

Donald J. Fay noted the conflict between child and adult: "The tales that applaud the trickster Br'er Rabbit's victories over stronger animals serve that same psychological function of releasing a child's anger toward powerful adults that Bruno Bettelheim—in *The Uses of Enchantment*—found in the European folk and fairy tales that parents have used for generations."[27]

In all of the tales of the anthropomorphic cigar-smoking, tobacco-chewing Brer Rabbit—sometimes known by his given name as Riley Rabbit—only the weaker terrapin and crow would beat the cunning rabbit who falls prey to his own believed superiority.

Just as the tales showed the cunning intelligence of the Blacks to escape, or at least modify the behavior of their White captors, the tar-baby tale may also have been an allegory about sectional differences. Literary critic Hugh Keenan believes the tale "shows the rabbit (a wily unreconstructed South) escaping the entanglement of the tar-baby (the Negro Question) by deluding the North (represented by the predatory fox) into letting the South handle its own race relations.[28]

"It needs no scientific investigation to show why he (the negro) selects as his hero the weakest and most harmless of all animals, and brings him out victorious in contests with the bear, the wolf, and the foe [fox]," said Harris. "It is not *virtue* that triumphs, but *helplessness*; it is not *malice*, but *mischievousness*."[29] Although Harris may have wished the rabbit to be merely mischievous, he was by White American standards also amoral and malevolent, traits within the tales from West African folklore. Unlike the animated cartoon characters more than a half-century later, Brer Rabbit was more scoundrel than lovable trickster. According to Robert B. Downs:

Brer Rabbit is a thoroughly amoral creature. He willingly cheats and lies, and he has cruel, savage traits in his character. He scalds the wolf to death, makes the innocent Possum die in a fire to cover his own crimes, tortures the Bear by setting a swarm of bees on him, and after causing the fatal beating of the Fox, carries the victim's head to Mrs. Fox and her children, trying to trick them into eating it in their soup. Uncle Remus's reply to the little boy, when questions are raised about such behavior, was that creatures should not be judged by human moral standards.[30]

Author/critic Julius Lester further explains:

Trickster keeps us in reality. And this is where Trickster's amoral morality is superior to our own moral posturing, our certitude that we know, absolutely, what is right and what is wrong. The more we are alienated from Trickster, the more likely we are to believe the inflated ideas we have about ourselves. Notice in the Brer Rabbit stories how often he exploits the other animals' images of themselves. Brer Rabbit appeals to their vanity, their pride, their posturing egos, and invariably they believe him. The instant they do, they are in Brer Rabbit's power and lost to themselves.

...Whether we are black or white, slave or free, child or adult, Brer Rabbit is us.[31]

Pop culture critic Bernard Wolfe observed:

The world, in Brer Rabbit's weary eyes, is a jungle. Life is a battle-unto-the-death for food, sex, power, prestige, a battle without rules. There is only one reality in this life: who is on top? But Brer Rabbit wastes no time lamenting the mad unneighborly scramble for top position. Because it is by no means

ordained that the Weak can never take over. In his topsy-turvy world, to all practical purposes, the Weak *have* taken over.[32]

Wolfe added another dimension that may or may not have been in Harris's mind when he wrote the tales:

> Food-sharing, sex-sharing—the Remus stories read like a catalogue of Southern racial taboos, all standing on their heads. The South. wearing the blinders of stereotype, has always tried to see the Negro as a 'roaringly comic' domestic animal. Understandably; for animals of the tame or domestic variety are not menacing—they are capable only of mischief, never of malice. But the Negro slave, through his anthropomorphic Rabbit stories, seems to be hinting that even the frailest and most humble of 'animals' can let fly with the most bloodthirsty aggressions. And these aggressions take place in the two most sacrosanct areas of Southern racial etiquette: the gastronomic and the erotic.
>
> The South, with its "sanctions of fear and force," forbids Negroes to eat at the same table with whites. But Brer Rabbit, through an act of murder, *forces* Brer Fox and all his associates to share their food with him. The South enjoins the Negro, under penalty of death, from coming near the white man's woman—although the white man has free access to the Negro's women. But Brer Rabbit flauntingly demonstrates his sexual superiority over all the other animals and, as the undisputed victor in the sexual competition, gets his choice of *all* the women.[33]

The public loved the folktales. However, Samuel L. Clemens in a letter to Harris, said they were merely "alligator pears—one merely eats them for the sake of the salad dressing." The more important work, the dressing, said Clemens, was the characterization of Uncle

Remus.[34] Uncle Remus's character, said literary analyst Donald J. Fay, is the "idealized parent who always has a ready story, who entertains the child as he instructs him in the ways of the world, and who listens to a child's questions."[35] In "Uncle Remus Initiates the Little Boy," Harris set up the continuing story of the love of a young White boy, the son of plantation owners, for an older Black slave, yet another layer of the hoped-for reconciliation of diverse social classes. In his relationship with the Little Boy, Remus is the wise and compassionate teacher who, on the surface, appears to be completely loyal and subservient to his former masters.

Hugh Keenan pointed out:

> On the one hand, Northerners were impressed by the warm, human, family-like relationships between blacks and whites as evidenced by Uncle Remus and the little boy. They were encouraged to see the black man as the instructor of the New South. On the other hand, Southerners could identify with the paternalism of the little boy, who brings food to the old man as he visits him almost daily. This kind of noblesse oblige flattered the aristocratic pretensions of the middle-class New South. And blacks could regard the story as a capsule history of black-white relations, wherein the black man constantly had to use guile to get around the white one.[36]

"In the dialogues with the little boy," said historian Wayne Mixon, "Remus frequently puts whites in their place by disparaging their genteel values and demonstrating his superior knowledge of the things that count, such as the workings of nature and the right way to raise children."[37]

The folktales, surrounded by the stories of Uncle Remus and the Little Boy, had excited the nation. But it was the base of American Black English which gave the tales their credibility. In the book's introduction, Harris explains why the language was so important to an understanding of the culture:

> The dialect, it will be observed, is wholly different from that [of] the intolerable misrepresentations of the minstrel stage, but it is at least phonetically genuine.
>
> The difference between the dialect of the legends and that of the character-sketches, slight as it is, marks the modifications which the speech of the negro has undergone even where education has played no part in reforming it. Indeed, save in the remote country districts, the dialect of the legends has nearly disappeared.
>
> Nevertheless, if the language of Uncle Remus fails to give vivid hints of the really poetic imagination of the negro; if it fails to embody the quaint and homely humor which was his most prominent characteristic; if it does not suggest a certain picturesque sensitiveness—a curious exaltation of mind and temperament not to be defined by words—then I have reproduced the form of the dialect merely, and not the essence, and my attempt may be accounted a failure. At any rate, I trust I have been successful in presenting what must be, at least to a large portion of American readers, a new and by no means an unattractive phase of negro character...[38]

Harris's concern about the acceptability of his dialect-writing may have forced him to be more accurate than his contemporaries in order to avoid negative comments about him, the dialect of the stories, or of the Blacks. Certainly, among White writers, he was among the best recorders of any of the variations of American Black English. Mark Twain, one of Harris's greatest admirers and a close professional colleague, said that "Mr. Harris ought to be able to read the negro dialect better than anybody else, for in the matter of writing it he is the only master the country has produced."[39] Sidney Lanier—one of the nation's outstanding poets and dialect writers, whose dialect poems in 1875-1876 remain among the outstanding examples of the genre—pointed out the Uncle Remus tales are "real negro talk, and not that suposititions [sic] negro-minstrel talk which so often goes for the original. It is as nearly perfect as any dialect can be."[40]

Editor-publisher Walter Hines Page even remarked that Harris had told him, "he can *think* in the negro dialect. He could translate even Emerson, perhaps Bronson Alcott, in it, as well as he can tell the adventures of Brer Rabbit."[41] Author/critic James Wood Davidson, in a letter to Harris, praised the language as "the only *true* negro-dialect I ever saw printed. It marks an era in its line—the first successful attempt to write what the negro has actually said, and in his own peculiar way."[42]

However, just as Harris usually rewrote the Uncle Remus tales several times, modifying narration to make them seem more natural, he also modified the language. Seven decades after Harris's first book was published, dialectologist Sumner Ives would correctly argue that the author of literary dialect tales may exaggerate the language because he:

> ...will notice...peculiarities more readily than he will notice usages that may sometimes appear in his own speech. Hence, the literary dialect may justifiably contain more socially disapproved, old-fashioned or local pronunciations than are present in the speech of any member of the actual group.... [T]he literary dialect is a composite, a compilation of features found in the speech of some members of the dialect group

and associated with that group by others. It does not follow that any one member of the dialect group will have exactly the same features in the same words as he is represented to have in the literary dialect. Hence, an author may without consciously wishing to deceive, exaggerate slightly the frequency of "dialectal" features.[43]

Using a more rigorous paradigm for analyzing written language, Lee Pederson argued a century after the publication of *Uncle Remus, His Songs and Sayings* that although the representation of American Black English was "phonetically genuine," the sentence structures were distinctly more literary creation than accurate transcriptions. In his analysis of the first sentence of the first tale in the book, Pederson concluded:

> No field investigator of American English ever recorded and reported such a sentence from the conversation of a folk speaker, black or white. For that matter, Boswell gives us no evidence that even Dr. [Samuel] Johnson produced a sentence of this Ciceronean girth in his remarkable conversations. Certainly no dialect writer ever endowed a black folk speaker with the linguistic competence to generate such a string.

With Remus's first sentence, Harris pulled all the stops in a highly stylized set piece. Such deliberate use of literary devices recurs in the introductory lines of works deemed important by their authors, from the epic poetry of Vergil and Dante to the tortured syntax of Cotton Mather in his opening paragraphs of *Magnalia Christi Americana*. In his own way, Harris was more successful with this than any of his predecessors. No other sentence in his first book matches the elaborate craft of that initial sentence, and he brought it off in language that his readers accepted as "real Negro-talk," a down-home example of the classical dictum *Ars est artum [sic: artem] celare*. [44] [loosely translated as "it takes a skill to hide a skill."]

Pederson believed that Harris probably synthesized three cultures—the Afro-American tradition, the "rural tradition of Middle Georgia," and the "classical tradition of English prose." Although Harris may have created "art" from speech, the language of Uncle Remus, as read in innumerable sentences, shows a definite Hamito-Bantu language base that no American author could have created without understanding the language and culture of the American slave during the Antebellum and Civil War eras and the newly-freed slaves of the Reconstruction.

The emergence and expansion of regional and national magazines following the Civil War, and a newly-discovered interest in the lives of emancipated slaves, assured Harris recognition well beyond what he had already received in Georgia. From throughout the nation came critical praise for Harris's accurate and honest recordings of Black life and language. "After so many dead failures by a hundred authors to write thus, and after the pitiful *niaiseries* of the so-called negro minstrels," wrote author/critic James Wood Davidson in a letter to Harris, "'Uncle Remus' is a revelation." [45] *Harper's* called the tales "among the best, if not the best, that the South has contributed to our 'cullud' literature since the war." [46] *Literary World* added additional prestige, stating that the Uncle Remus collection was "a really valuable contribution to the literature of the negro character." [47] The *New York Times* pointed out, "in preserving certain quaint legends, and giving us exactly the sounds of the negro dialect, [Harris] has established on a firm basis the first real book of American folk lore." [48] The *New Orleans Daily Picayune* praised Harris for preserving "the genuine flavor of the old plantation." [49] *Scribner's*

Monthly, one of the premiere general circulation magazines, declared:

> ...Mr. Harris has given us...the best sustained and most elaborate study which our literature possesses, or, in all probability, ever will possess, of a type familiar to us all—the old plantation negro. It is a character, now almost a tradition, that has been sketched in song and story; but that will never find a more faithful or sympathetic delineator than the creator of "Uncle Remus."[50]

Spurred by innumerable favorable newspaper and magazine reviews, the public made Harris's compilation of thirty-four legends, nine songs, twenty-one sayings, and one story—most of which first appeared in the *Constitution*—into a best seller, matching the sales of Emile Zola's *Nana* and Lew Wallace's *Ben Hur*. Two weeks after publication, James C. Derby wrote to Harris: "We have sold two editions [printings] of 1500 each [at $1.50 per copy], and the third edition of 1500 more will be in on Friday. Of these, some 500 are ordered. Mr. Chas [Charles] A. Dana [editor of the *New York Sun*] told me in my office last week as follows—'Derby, Uncle Remus is a great book. It will not only have a large, but a permanent, and enduring sale.'"[51]

Within six months, the public bought about 10,000 copies. By the middle of 1881, the tales were being read in England. Rudyard Kipling, who admired Harris's work, later wrote to him that the tales "ran like wild fire through an English public school.... [W]e found ourselves quoting whole pages of Uncle Remus that had got mixed in with the fabric of the old school life."[52] Later, Kipling wrote that he read Uncle Remus stories to his daughter, and thus "my debt to you is two generations deep."[53] During the century following publication, at least a million copies were printed, many of them pirated editions. The publication of the book not only established standards for folklore, dialect writing, and literature itself, it established a future for children's books in America. "[B]efore the publication of *Uncle Remus*...there was nothing like, and for fifty years after there was little else of note in make-believe but the *Uncle Remus* order of serial adventures in the countryside," noted John Goldthwaite, respected children's literature analyst, reflecting upon the history of American children's literature.[54] Indeed, literary analyst Robert B. Downs in 1977 placed *Uncle Remus: His Songs and Sayings* as one of the twenty-five most influential books that changed the South. [55]

In the 30 November 1879 issue of the *Constitution*, Harris had complained about the state of Southern literature, arguing in one of his more forceful editorials that "the stuff we are in the habit of calling Southern literature is not only a burlesque upon true literary art, but a humiliation and a disgrace to the people whose culture it is supposed to represent." Joel Chandler Harris, said novelist Thomas Nelson Page, "unlocked with his genius the fast closed doors of the Magazines and Publishing Houses which hitherto had been as tightly sealed to those who wrote sympathetically of the South as the lost tombs of the Pharaohs."[56] Less than a year after publication of the first Uncle Remus book, *Scribner's Monthly* shocked the staid literary critics by proclaiming that Southern literature defined a new literary era, replacing the dominance of New England regionalism, and cited the Uncle Remus tales for being "as artistic in [their] execution as [they are] characteristic in [their] humor."[57] The words of Joseph Addison Turner, whose letter to his printer's assistant two decades earlier predicting the emergence of Southern literature, had finally come true.

[1] Hutchins, founder of the *Post*, was owner from 1877 to 1889.

[2] He was actually thirty-two years old if we accept his birth date of 1848, thirty-four or thirty-five if we accept his more probable birth in 1845 or 1846.

[3] Letter from Joel Chandler Harris to Stilson Hutchins, 2 April 1880.

[4] Letter from Joel Chandler Harris to Stilson Hutchins, 28 June 1880.

[5] Letter from Stilson Hutchins to Joel Chandler Harris, 10 July 1880.

[6] Quoted in James B. Morrow, "Joel Chandler Harris Talks of Himself and Uncle Remus," 5.

[7] Quoted in Joseph M. Griska, Jr., "Selected Letters of Joel Chandler Harris," 66.

[8] The title page carries the date of 1881, but the book was published in November 1880. To keep a book as current as possible, thus increasing sales, many publishers will increase the publication date if publication falls during the last quarter of a year. Magazine publishers often put publication dates one or two months after the magazine is available on newsstands, believing this keeps the magazine "fresher" in the public's mind.

[9] Letter from Joel Chandler Harris to Frederick S. Church, 11 June 1880.

[10] Letter from Joel Chandler Harris to Frederick S. Church, 17 May 1880.

[11] Letter from Joel Chandler Harris to [Miss] Franklin, 18 September 1880. Quoted in Joseph M. Griska, Jr., "Selected Letters of Joel Chandler Harris," 64.

[12] Joel Chandler Harris, *Uncle Remus, His Songs and Sayings*, 3.

[13] Joel Chandler Harris, *Uncle Remus: His Songs and Sayings*, 3-4.

[14] Roger D. Abrahams, *Afro-American Folklore*, xvii.

[15] Roger D. Abrahams, *Afro-American Folklore*, xviii.

[16] Roger D. Abrahams, *African Folktales, Traditional Stories of the Black World*, xvi.

[17] Joel Chandler Harris, *Nights with Uncle Remus*, xiii.

[18] Thomas F. Crane, "Plantation Folk-Lore," *Popular Science Monthly* (18 April 1881): 824, 825.

[19] Heli Chatelain, *Folktales of Angola* (Houghton, Mifflin 1894), 22-23.

[20] A. Gerber, "Uncle Remus Traced to the Old World," 245.

[21] The calamus root, foreshadowed in an earlier tale, spices up the chicken soup.

[22] Ralph Ellison, *Going to the Territory* (New York: Random House, 1986) 146-49.

[23] J. V. Nash, "Joel Chandler Harris, Interpreter of the Negro Soul," 108.

[24] A. M. H. Christensen, *Afro-American Folk Lore*, xi-xii.

[25] Wayne Mixon, "The Ultimate Irrelevance of Race: Joel Chandler Harris and Uncle Remus in Their Time," 471.

[26] Review, *Spectator*, 2 April 1881, 445.

[27] Donald J. Fay, review, 45.

[28] Hugh Keenan, "Joel Chandler Harris," 227-28.

[29] Joel Chandler Harris, *Uncle Remus, His Songs and His Sayings*, 9.

[30] Robert B. Downs, *Twenty-Five Books That Changed the South*, 160.

[31] Julius Lester, *More Tales of Uncle Remus*, xii-xiii, viii.

[32] Bernard Wolfe, "Uncle Remus and the Malevolent Rabbit," 34.

[33] Bernard Wolfe, "Uncle Remus and the Malevolent Rabbit," 34.

[34] Letter from Samuel L. Clemens to Joel Chandler Harris, 10 August 1881.

[35] Donald J. Fay, review, 45.

[36] Hugh Keenan, "Joel Chandler Harris," 227-28.

[37] Wayne Mixon, "The Ultimate Irrelevance of Race: Joel Chandler Harris and Uncle Remus in Their Time," 471.

[38] Joel Chandler Harris, *Uncle Remus, His Songs and Sayings*, 3-4, 11.

[39] Mark Twain, *Life on the Mississippi*, 317.

[40] Sidney Lanier, "The New South," 847.

[41] Quoted in Julia Collier Harris, *Life and Letters of Joel Chandler Harris*, 164.

[42] Letter from James Wood Davidson to Joel Chandler Harris, 14 December 1880.

[43] Sumner Ives, "A Theory of Literary Dialect," 147.

[44] Lee Pederson, "Language in the Uncle Remus Tales," 294, 298.

[45] Letter from James Wood Davidson to Joel Chandler Harris, 14 December 1880.

[46] Review, *Harper's Magazine* (February 1881): 479.

[47] Review, *Literary World*, 26 March 1881, 118.

[48] "Negro Folk-Lore," *The New York Times*, 1 December 1880, 3.

[49] Review, *New Orleans Times-Picayune*, 19 December 1880.

[50] Review, *Scribner's Monthly* (April 1881): 961.

[51] Letter from James C. Derby to Joel Chandler Harris, 8 December 1880.

[52] Letter from Rudyard Kipling to Joel Chandler Harris, 6 December 1895.

[53] Letter from Rudyard Kipling to Joel Chandler Harris, [n.d.].

[54] John Goldthwaite, "The Black Rabbit: Part One," 92.

[55] Robert B. Downs, *Books That Changed the South*, 160.

[56] Thomas Nelson Page, "Introduction" to 40th year anniversary edition of Joel Chandler Harris's, *Uncle Remus: His Songs and Sayings*, vii.

[57] "Topics of the Times: Southern Literature," *Scribner's Monthly* (September 1881): 786

Wren's Nest, Master Bedroom

Joel Chandler Harris, about 1882

Chapter 5

'Very Close to the Untutored Spirit of Humanity'

Almost-instant national fame did not change the shy and humble journalist. He was still Joe Harris to his friends and colleagues, almost divorcing himself from the literary fame others tried to burden him with. In September 1881, Walter Hines Page, then a twenty-six-year-old writer who would become one of the nation's most influential editors and eventually ambassador to Great Britain, visited Harris in Atlanta:

Entering a dingy doorway and ascending two flights of more dingy stairs, I entered a still more dingy room, on the door of which a dingy red placard was stuck, with this information: "Editorial Rooms." And there I found a dingy-looking individual apparently at sea in an ocean of [newspaper] exchanges, but quite calmly smoking a cigar, with the air of a man who owns the whole day and has no need of haste. I thought he must be the [printer's] "devil" of the office, who was amusing himself with yesterday's papers before the gentlemen came down.

"Is Mr. Harris in?"

"Yes."

"I should like to see him."

"My name is Harris."

"I mean Mr. Joel Chandler Harris, one of the editors of the *Constitution*."

A sly twinkle came into the fellow's eyes as he arose and asked, "What may I do for you?"

"Are you the author of 'Uncle Remus'?"...

A little laugh bubbled up inside of him, he extended his hand, offered me a seat and looked as confused as I felt. I must have said something about how much delight Boston people had got from "Uncle Remus"; for he said with a blush and much confusion, "They have been very kind to 'Uncle Remus.'"[1]

Harris would consider himself a part of the working class his entire life, modestly unable to accept whatever accolades he received; he was just Joe Harris, illegitimate son of a seamstress, printer's devil to a plantation owner, and most importantly, a newspaper journalist. He would write about Uncle Remus and of Brer Rabbit, of moonshiners and laborers, because he identified with and understood the lives of those who did not live in the "Big House."

In its February 1881 issue, *The Critic* published "How Mr. Fox Failed to Get His Grapes," the first Uncle Remus tale to be published in a general circulation magazine. Two months later, it published "How Mr. Fox Figures as an Incendiary." However, for several years, *The Critic* would be shut out as a medium for subsequent Uncle Remus tales.

Four months after the publication of *Uncle Remus, His Songs and Sayings*, Richard Watson Gilder, who had recently succeeded Josiah Holland as editor at *Scribner's Monthly*, wrote to Harris, praised his work, and asked to see whatever Harris wished to submit.[2] The following month, *Scribner's Monthly* published "A Song of the Mole," a light verse. *Scribner's Monthly*, in its June, July, and August issues, published fourteen tales under the general heading "A Rainy Day With Uncle Remus." During the next six years *Century Illustrated Monthly Magazine*,[3] which succeeded *Scribner's* in 1881—and would reach the largest circulation in the country of about 225,000—would publish sixteen more Uncle Remus tales, as well as five of what would become recognized as Harris's finest short stories.

"Uncle Remus was a lucky accident, and perhaps I can do nothing else as well,"[4] Harris explained to Robert Underwood Johnson, assistant editor at *Century*. But he had to find out. He would write light verse and try to concentrate upon stories of lower-class Georgian Whites and of racial and class distinction, heeding Mark Twain's suggestion that he should not give the public too many Uncle Remus tales, or else their value would diminish.

Almost two years after the Uncle Remus collection first appeared, Harris completed "Mingo," a character sketch of the relationship of a poor White Middle Georgian "family with a well-bred" freed slave who is bound by a moral conscience and sense of duty to the orphaned child of his former owners. "Mingo" is not only "one of Harris's most sensitive portraits of the black man,"[5] wrote Bruce Bickley in 1978, but also "an intriguing anticipation of Faulkner's studies in black endurance and strength of character."[6]

Harris's next major short story was "At Teague Poteet's," the story of a fiercely independent pro-union mountain family that became moonshiners to pay for their daughter's education, and how their lives were affected by federal agents. Harris, the consummate journalist, had based the story upon the trial of two federal agents charged with killing a moonshiner; like all good writers, Harris brought into the story his own views, values, and life experiences, including an underlying theme that moral law may sometimes transcend the written law.

Harris told James R. Osgood that said he liked this new story "a great deal better than I do Mingo, but that may mean that it is worse."[7] The story, Harris wrote to Robert Underwood Johnson, "doesn't satisfy me, but I

have come to the conclusion that I can't satisfy myself."[8] Submitting the manuscript to *Century*, the always-insecure and self-deprecating Harris was unsure about the quality of the story, or even if the magazine would publish it: "Enclosed you will find a sort of whatshisname. I'm afraid it is too episodical to suit serial publication—but after all, life itself is a series of episodes. Perhaps something else is the matter. If you don't find it available, you can at least give me some helpful suggestion."[9]

Century editor Richard Watson Gilder, whom Harris relied upon and readily acknowledged as a master editor for his works, not only disagreed with Harris's self-effacing view but had suggested that "At Teague Poteet's" should be promoted in his magazine as a "novelette." Harris modestly suggested that the appellation was much too pretentious. Gilder replied, "I am afraid that in your modesty you think I am not sincere in what I have said of the merits of the piece.... As I think over the story I find it has left a very definite impression and a very agreeable human feeling."[10] However, after praising Harris's characterization of the Poteet family, Gilder gently added, "The [manuscript] is not a 'failure'; it is definitely accepted in its present shape, in the belief that you can easily strengthen it."[11] Harris appreciatively, but somewhat reluctantly, accepted many of the editorial suggestions of Gilder and Robert Underwood Johnson.

"At Teague Poteet's: A Sketch of the Hog Mountain Range" was published as a two-part serial, and not as a novelette, in the May and June 1883 issues of *Century*, receiving both popular and critical acclaim. James C. Derby, whose opinion was respected throughout the publishing industry, said he considered "At Teague Poteet's" to be "the very best description of the 'Moonshiners' and other kindred characters which has yet been written."[12]

Literary critic and biographer Paul M. Cousins suggests:

[Harris] was most successful in his delineation of the middle-class Georgians, because he knew them as thoroughly as he did the plantation Negro. He was on sure ground when he set forth their humor and integrity, their independence and common-sense, and the force of their vernacular speech. And with equal sureness, he realistically brought to life the poor whites. In his realistic emphasis upon the middle and lower classes and the Negroes rather than upon the planters, Harris departed from the romantic pattern which the serious writers of Southern antebellum fiction had followed. His own boyhood of poverty and misfortune had given him a sympathetic insight into the mind and heart of the poor, the lowly, and the unfortunate.[13]

"Blue Dave"—"so-called because of the inky blackness of his skin"—is the story of a slave's seven-year escape from a brutal owner, and the legend of the man who was "swifter than the wind and slicker than a red fox." However, Blue Dave trades his limited freedom for protection and a life with relatively few worries about food and housing when a kindly plantation owner agrees to buy him.

"A Piece of Land"—weaker than "Mingo," "At Teague Poteet's," and "Blue Dave"—is the story of how greed destroys families. Although editors expected Harris to constantly question the literary worth of his stories and were ready to praise him, Harris was unusually harsh about "A Piece of Land." In a letter to his editor, Harris was discouraged by what he had written: "[It is] crude

and amateurish. I'm disgusted with myself, and I've no doubt you are disgusted with me. I'm very unhappy about it, and sincerely trust you have been put at no serious disadvantage by my lack of art. I am convinced that what I send is trash, and I'm in that condition that the very thought of it is offensive to me."[14]

Although the public liked Harris's short stories, they demanded more Uncle Remus. For his second book, Harris would compile stories which had originally appeared in the *Constitution*, *The Critic*, *Scribner's Monthly*, and *Century*, and make minor revisions to many of them. Although published in one of the South's leading newspapers and the nation's leading literary magazines, Harris still could not understand his fame. The first compilation was published at $1.50 a copy. Osgood wanted to publish the second collection for $3.00 a copy. "This won't do," Harris demanded, stating, "The public may stand for $2 for the trash, but I doubt it."[15] Then the sly Harris, always capable of getting the best for his works, snuck in the "however" clause—unless you make the cover "devilish interesting and romantic."[16] *Nights With Uncle Remus: Myths and Legends of the Old Plantation*—with a rather "devilish" and "romantic" cover—was published in November 1883. The illustrations, by Frederick S. Church and William Holbrook Beard, were better than the first compilation of tales, but Harris was still dissatisfied with them.

Harris structured the time frame of his second Uncle Remus collection from early fall through Christmas, and set the stories not during the Reconstruction of the first collection but in the Antebellum era, a time when, as Harris stated early in the book, Uncle Remus "belonged" to Miss Sally. Biographer Paul M. Cousins observed that if Uncle Remus "had an instinctive desire to be free, he gave no outward indication of it, and his personal difficulties came upon him in freedom, not in slavery." [17]

Library of Congress,

No. 7.9.6.3.0.   Copyright Office, Washington.

To wit: Be it remembered,

That on the 30: day of April, anno domini 1883, Joel Chandler Harris, of Atlanta Ga, has deposited in this Office the title of a Book the title or description of which is in the following words, to wit:

Nights with Uncle Remus
Myths and Legends of The Old
Plantation
By Joel Chandler Harris.
(All Rights Reserved)

New York:
Century Magazine
Boston:
James R Osgood & Co
1883 – 1884

the right whereof he claims as Author in conformity with the laws of the United States respecting Copyrights.

Librarian of Congress.

Copyright for Harris's second book

In this second collection, Harris wove three additional narrators into the stories—Daddy Jack, an elderly Gullah Black who had been brought to the Sea Islands aboard a slave ship; the house servant Tildy; and the cook Aunt Tempy—and had them tell some of the same tales so the reader could see the language variations.

The Gullah spoken by Daddy Jack, like the Middle-Georgia American Black English spoken by Uncle Remus, is a creole, a combination of at least two languages that over time have become a separate language; a creole then becomes a speaker's first language. In the folk tale about the rabbit and the alligator, the difference in the two languages is apparent. Both characters appear in "Why the Alligator's Back Is Rough"—originally published in the August 1883 issue of *Century Illustrated Monthly Magazine*—each one telling the tale from a different perspective.

When Harris had begun compiling and writing the folklore of the plantation, he knew little about the systematic study of language and folklore. But with an intellectual and journalistic curiosity, he studied the basics of the two emerging disciplines, slyly conceding "to know that you are ignorant is a valuable form of knowledge, and I am gradually accumulating a vast store off it."[18] The thirty-one page introduction of the second volume of Uncle Remus tales, however, reveals that the inquisitive Harris had learned as much about language and folklore as many academics, and was still concerned about public acceptance of a book of dialect:

> In the Introduction to the first volume of Uncle Remus, a lame apology was made for inflicting a book of dialect upon the public. Perhaps a similar apology should be made here; but the discriminating reader does not need to be told that it would be impossible to separate these stories from the idiom in which they

have been recited for generations. The dialect is a part of the legends themselves, and to present them in any other way would be to rob them of everything that gives them vitality.[19]

Harris did not need to worry about the quality of his transcriptions nor of the public acceptance. The reviews were as strong for Harris' second compilation as for his first. After an introductory statement that Harris's "mastery of the negro dialect and skill as a story-teller placed him in the front rank of American writers," *The Nation* asserted that compared to his critically-acclaimed first compilation of tales, even with the tar baby story, "this work more than holds its own, and indeed, regard being had to the literary skill displayed in setting so large a number of stories, must be thought an extraordinary *tour de force*."[20] The *New York Times* called the book "a delightful work" and stated that not only was Harris "an admirable raconteur" but that his ability to differentiate the languages of his characters made him "a philologist of no small merit."[21] *Dial*, a mass circulation magazine, noted, "The skill with which the tales are introduced, the descriptions of the old man's demeanor, and his by-talk with the little boy, all show a high degree of dramatic power."[22]

"Marse Henry" Watterson, one of the nation's most respected journalists, and editor of the *Louisville Courier-Journal*, praised Harris shortly after his second book was published for his "genius for subtle observation, and a thorough sympathy for this theme." The Uncle Remus tales, said Watterson, are "in all respects, in graphic power and in spirit, tone, and color, the best picture of negro life and character which has yet appeared in any language."[23]

Like his first collection of tales, *Nights With Uncle Remus* was also a critical and commercial best-seller, with

sales of 24,890 through twenty-five printings; a 1904 edition subsequently sold 81,563 books in thirty-four printings.[24] But sales were definitely lower than for the first book. It sent Harris deeper into a depression of self-deprecation that hovered over his life as he continually doubted the value of his works. "I realize the fact that *Nights With Uncle Remus* is a failure," a brooding Harris wrote to Benjamin H. Ticknor at Osgood, "I judge of these things by the returns, and not by the criticisms of the press."[25] James R. Osgood replied he did not "consider the book a 'failure' in any sense, although they have not as yet done what we all had a right to hope." He explained that he believed *Nights With Uncle Remus* was "much hurt" by the list price of $1.50 which did not yield enough gross income and, thus, royalties. Harris, of course, had strongly urged a $1.50 price against Osgood's $3.00 original list price. In his letter to Harris, Osgood now casually slipped in his original desire of having "strongly advocated dividing the matter and making two books at $1.50" each.[26]

Harris had begun a serialized novel of Georgian life in 1878 but suspended it before the first episode appeared in the *Constitution* because of the developing popularity of the Uncle Remus stories. With two Uncle Remus books on the market, Harris convinced James R. Osgood to publish a compilation of four stories that did not include animal folktales. "No novel or story can be genuinely American unless it deals with the *common people*, that is, *country* people," Harris wrote in a letter-to-the-editor of the June 1884 issue of *Current* magazine.

Mingo and Other Sketches in Black and White (1884)—composed of "Mingo," "At Teague Poteet's," "Blue Dave," and "A Piece of Land"—was Harris's attempt to break free of Uncle Remus and the tar-baby. *Mingo and Other Sketches*, said Harris, "is intended to please the aged and half wits of our time—those who are suffering for want of sleep."[27] The critics, some perhaps surprised Harris could write more than newspaper stories and Uncle Remus tales, disagreed. "In these stories [Harris] shows a true dramatic force," the *New York Times* noted.[28] *Harper's* concluded, "It will not be easy to find in our home literature four more perfect or more thrilling stories than those of Mr. Harris's telling."[29] The *New York Daily Tribune* pointed out, "in the 'poor whites' of Georgia, [Harris] has found material as fresh and picturesque as anything in the delightful experiences of Uncle Remus, and he has handled it with the ease, mastery, and the grace of a natural artist."[30]

The Nation, one of the more influential news and literary magazines in the late nineteenth century, although reflecting a little of the language and racial stereotypes of the age, nevertheless declared:

> [Harris] is very close to the untutored spirit of humanity. He discriminates nicely between natural emotions in the widest sense and those which are a class inheritance. He uses rude or corrupt language to express only primitive passion and thought—fierce hatred, unreasoning love, a dog's gratitude for kindness, a savage's impulse toward revenge; he never offends or weakens by palpable incongruity between idea and form. In this respect his perception is subtler and more truthful than Bret Harte's, with whom he may be legitimately compared. Both authors have keen instincts and insights, but Harris's are the finer and deeper. Harte's characters are by far the more picturesque, his incidents are more thrilling, but Harris's people wind themselves about our hearts and owe little to circumstance.[31]

However, sales were only 3,000 in eight printings.[32] Although Harris, like most authors, questioned his publisher's marketing campaign, he undoubtedly

wondered—and perhaps became depressed about—why a nation that so loved the books about Uncle Remus refused to buy what he considered to be the more powerful stories of society.

Even more powerful than his characterizations in "Mingo," "At Teague Poteet's," and "Blue Dave" is Harris's tragic portrait of "Free Joe," a freed slave, which first appeared in the November 1884 issue of *Century*; the magazine paid Harris $100 for the serial rights, $20 less than *Harper's* had paid for "Mingo."[33] The short story became the anchor of *Free Joe and Other Georgian Sketches*, published by Charles Scribner's Sons in 1887. Three of the stories in the collection had been published in magazines earlier that same year.[34] Their rapid appearance in a collection suggests that Harris recognized that for greater readership, he needed to put "Free Joe" into a collection, but had not yet developed enough short fiction to fill out a full collection.

Based upon the life of a free slave Harris had known, "Free Joe" is the Antebellum tragedy of an emancipated slave who lived well, but whose wife, Lucinda, was owned by a kindly judge. Upon her master's death, the wife becomes the property of the judge's vindictive and spiteful half-brother who forbids her from ever seeing her husband again. But, every night beneath a poplar tree, they secretly meet until the owner finds out and sells her to a distant plantation. Free Joe, unaware of the transaction, with his dog waits beneath that tree every night thereafter. Soon, he realizes he will never see his wife again. As Harris explained, Free Joe was:

> ...a black atom, drifting hither and thither without an
> owner, blown about by all the winds of circumstance
> and given over to shiftlessness.

He realized the fact that though he was free, he was more helpless than any slave. Having no owner, every man was his master.... [A]ll his efforts were in the direction of mitigating the circumstances that tended to make his condition so much worse than that of the negroes around him—negroes who had friends because they had masters.

So far as his own race was concerned Free Joe was an exile. If the slaves secretly envied him his freedom (which is to be doubted, considering his miserable condition), they openly despised him, and lost no opportunity to treat him with contumely. Perhaps this was in some measure the result of the attitude which Free Joe chose to maintain toward them. No doubt his instinct taught him that to hold himself aloof from the slaves would be to invite from the whites the toleration which he coveted, and without which even his

Illustration of Free Joe from Century Magazine.

miserable condition would be rendered more miserable still.[35]

Although it may seem that Harris was again telling the world that life on the plantation was not all that bad, and that ex-slaves were trapped by their freedom, the reality is that Harris humanized one former slave in order to tell a nation that it could not just eliminate the evils of slavery by setting people free then expecting them to survive in a society they never understood. Harris's condemnation, thus, was not of Free Joe or of freedom, but of society itself.

At the end of the story, Free Joe returns to the woods where he had met his wife. In the woods, Micajah, an elderly impoverished White who had befriended Free Joe, tries to awaken his friend whom he thinks is only sleeping. Harris explains:

> Receiving no response [he] went to Free Joe and shook him by the shoulder; but the negro made no response. He was dead. His hat was off, his head was bent, and a smile was on his face. It was as if he had bowed and smiled when death stood before him— humble to the last. His clothes were ragged; his hands were rough and callous; his shoes were literally tied together with strings; he was shabby in the extreme. A passer-by, glancing at him, could have no idea that such a humble creature had been summoned as a witness before the Lord God of Hosts.[36]

It was as strong an indictment of slavery and society as any of the abolitionist writings.

"In writing it," Harris told Robert Underwood Johnson at *Century*, "I have striven merely to recall to the memory of some of my friends the unhappy environment of one of the Lord's creatures—the whole being a figment of the brain except that portion which seems most imaginative."[37] But, Harris, the persuasive journalist knew he could structure a story to make it seem as if he were merely telling the facts, the circumstances—"the memory" of others—yet still carry forth a social message by what he chose to include and—more importantly—*how* he structured the story.

The critics and the public cried at the plight of Free Joe, and praised the writing of its creator. "We know of no story which for simple pathos equals 'Free Joe,'" stated the *New York Times*.[38] "Nowhere has the helpless wretchedness of the dark side of slavery been more clearly recognized or more powerfully depicted," literary analyst William Malone Baskervill pointed out in 1897. "Harris had once again gone outside himself and entered into the heart and soul of a plantation Negro who was at the opposite end of the social structure of plantation Negroes from Uncle Remus and Mingo," wrote biographer Paul M. Cousins who noted that Harris "portrayed him as a warmly appealing human being caught in a mesh of unhappy circumstances from which he could not free himself."[39] Theodore Roosevelt, shortly after becoming president in 1901, wrote Harris that he doubted, "there is a more genuinely pathetic tale in all our literature than 'Free Joe.'"[40] Unfortunately, even with strong reviews, sales of the book the first year of publication were only 3,200,[41] again causing Harris to wonder about his own value as a writer.

Two years after giving the nation the character of Free Joe, Harris told the story of Daddy Jake, a slave who escapes when he thinks he has killed a brutal white overseer. At the time, as Harris explained, "a negro who struck a white man was tried for his life, and if his guilt could be proven, he was either branded with a hot iron and sold to a speculator, or he was hanged."[42] If there was brutality to Blacks in one of Harris's stories, it was often by an overseer. In *The Bishop and the Boogerman*, Harris

had one of his characters talk about "Old Tuttle," a White overseer who "had no niggers of his own, and he took his spite out on other people's niggers."[43]

In "Daddy Jake," two children—Lucien and Lillian, named for Harris's children—set out to find their companion Daddy Jake, are trapped by the river, rescued by Daddy Jake and other runaways, and hear a Brer Rabbit tale told by Crazy Sue. The children convince Daddy Jake to return to the plantation because the foreman was only injured. As with many of Harris's slave characters, Daddy Jack was happy to be back on the plantation among his friends. Freed slaves after the Civil War returned for any of a number of reasons, including the revelation that being free did not mean that Whites—in both the North and South—would accept them as anything more than slaves.

Although Harris was a man of sensitivity who abhorred violence and abuse of all forms, he also believed in slavery during the Antebellum era and segregation during Reconstruction. As strong as were his very human portraits of Mingo, Free Joe, and Daddy Jake, Harris's themes for his portraits of Blacks were not unlike that of other White authors. For a December 1888 article in the general circulation magazine, *Forum*, social critic Albion Tourgee explained the two major roles in which writers had placed the American Black:

In one he figures as the devoted slave who serves and sacrifices for his master and mistress, and is content to live or die, do good or evil, for those whom he feels himself under infinite obligation for the privilege of living and serving. There were such miracles, no doubt, but they were so rare as never to have lost the miraculous character. The other favorite aspect of the Negro character from the point of view of the Southern fictionist, is that of the poor "nigger" to whom liberty has brought only misfortune, who is relieved by the disinterested friendship of some white man whose property he once was.... About the Negro as a man, with hopes, fears, and aspirations like other men, our literature is very nearly silent.[44]

"Little Compton" is the story of a respected New Jersey merchant who relocated to Georgia in 1850, and was tormented by his loyalties and beliefs as war approached. With the opening of the Civil War, he returns North to serve in the Union army and loses an arm at Gettysburg while shielding Captain Jack Walthall, a fellow Georgian serving in the Confederate army. After being taken prisoner, Compton returns to Georgia where the people continue their friendship with him, although he still wears his uniform. Their love for the Northern soldier from Georgia is rewarded when, running "hither and thither," he convinces "small parties of foragers" from Sherman's main army on its "march to the sea" to spare the town. Once again, Compton saves Walthall, this time from a German mercenary, perhaps not unlike the Pennsylvania Dutch that Harris himself had first seen on the Turnwold plantation in 1864. As the Union troops marched through town, they saw "the tall Confederate, in his uniform of gray, [resting] his one hand affectionately on the shoulder of the stout little man in blue, and on the bosom of each was pinned an empty sleeve." The sight prompted the Union commander to stop; Little Compton told his story of war and comradeship. Harris concludes his story:

> "Well, you know this sort of thing doesn't end the war, boys," [the general] said, as he shook hands with Walthall and Little Compton; "but I shall sleep better to-night."

Perhaps he did. Perhaps he dreamed that what he had seen and heard was prophetic of the days to come, when peace and fraternity should seize upon the land, and bring unity, happiness, and prosperity to the people.[45]

"Little Compton" was one of Harris's most powerful tales and most representative of his hopes for reconciliation following the war. Harris had trouble with the story, mostly because of the volume of political writing he was doing at the *Constitution* during an election year. The first draft was rejected by the *Century*'s Richard Watson Gilder who made several suggestions. "Your letter in regard to its weak points paralyzed me," Harris wrote to Gilder, "but I have tried hard to profit by every suggestion you made. I know that it is much better now... It still seems to be desperately thin."[46]

The story *was* "thin," reflective of a writer burdened by too much work, and not enough time to reflect upon any of it. The story was also burdened by the author reporting the events of a part of history, but never having had battlefield experience. A month after receiving the second draft, Gilder made additional suggestions, including a request to modify the opening and to strengthen the ending; Gilder also included suggested dialogue, but was careful to praise Harris and the story, well aware of the author's sensitive nature.[47] The third draft was significantly better than the first draft, but Gilder still had "one further suggestion" about the conclusion, and a concern about a minor character. "Little Compton" became one of the nation's most beloved stories, and is often included on lists of America's best short fiction.

"Azalia"—a typical Harris plot that involved class distinction, Reconstruction, and a romance between a Northerner, in this case a Boston woman, and a Southerner, this time a former Confederate general—

underwent fewer revisions. "It seems to me, on the whole, the best first draft of a story you have sent here except 'Trouble on Lost Mountain,'" wrote Richard Watson Gilder, who also noted that Harris's latest story "has not the complete dramatic unity of that story, but it is much better in that respect than the first draft of 'Little Compton.'"[48]

Authors and editors often have different opinions about a manuscript. A good editor, like Gilder, will significantly improve the work, while resisting making changes just because his ego suggests he can; a good author, like Harris, may sometimes be upset by the suggestions, but will recognize that these suggestions are often made not by frustrated writers who cannot create anything original, but by editors who care about the editorial quality of what they publish. "I have written all my books on the spur of the moment, not for money or notoriety, but because it gave me pleasure to write them,"[49] Harris once wrote, humbly explaining that he was merely an observer of life.

> I have tried to keep Joel Chandler Harris as much out of my works as possible...[W]hat I have written was for its own sake, and not for money nor for the glorification of the man who was accidentally behind it all. And yet the man is there somewhere—standing for lack of cultivation, lack of literary art, and lack of all the graces that make life worth living to those who affect culture; but I hope that honesty, sincerity and simplicity are not lacking.[50]

Like all authors, Harris had a fierce determination to be read, but also knew that increased readership also means increased income. The author and publisher are often in conflict about the promotion of a book. The

author often believes the publisher is not devoting enough time, energy, or money into promoting a certain book. The publisher's response is usually that not only does the public, not the publisher, determine the sales, but that the publisher has many authors needing attention and must allocate resources in varying amounts to all of them. Harris was no different from any author wanting readership and sales. His first book had been published by D. Appleton, which had sought him out and made him a nationally-acclaimed author. Shortly after that book was published, Harris asked Samuel L. Clemens for advice about publishers, and Clemens strongly recommended James R. Osgood of Boston whom he said could give Harris better direction and sales. Clemens arranged for Osgood to be in New Orleans in May 1882 for what would be Harris's aborted lecture tour with Twain and George Washington Cable.[51] In September 1883, Osgood offered Harris a royalty of twenty percent of the list price for his *Nights With Uncle Remus*, then less than seven months later offered twenty percent for *Mingo*, although the standard author royalty was ten to fifteen percent of list price. At the time, Osgood was routinely offering the higher royalties to lure the better writers to his company.

During his three-decade literary career, Harris would switch publishers a number of times, staying the longest with Houghton, Mifflin. "I have no favorites among publishers," Harris wrote to his agent in 1904, "but have tried to keep on good terms with all of them."[52] Moving among publishers was strictly a business decision. Harris may have been shy, not easily accepting accolades, but like most writers he wanted his work to be easily available to the public, to be read, to be something that stirred their imaginations, their enjoyment, and their intellect. Like Mark Twain, he placed as high a demand upon his publisher to deliver his work to the people as he placed upon himself to produce good work.

Although Harris always believed he needed the extra income from his book royalties—to give his family security, to expand his home or to fix up the "farm"—he wasn't absorbed by money. "The happiest people are those who never try to be rich, and I thank heaven that I never had any desire for riches," Harris once wrote to one of his children, suggesting that the purpose of having money might be "to help the unfortunate."[53] The purpose of his writing would be to bring some laughter, some enjoyment, and some insight into the human condition to the people of the country.

---

[1] Descriptive letter written by Walter Hines Page, 28 September 1881. Published in Burton J. Hendrick, *The Training of an American*, 148-49.

[2] Letter from Richard Watson Gilder to Joel Chandler Harris, 10 March 1881.

[3] *Century Illustrated Monthly Magazine* will be referred to simply as *Century* in subsequent references. *Scribner's Monthly* died with the change of ownership and title. Six years later, Charles Scribner's Sons, which had begun *Scribner's Monthly*, and had long been a leading book publisher, began publishing *Scribner's Magazine*.

[4] Letter from Joel Chandler Harris to Robert Underwood Johnson, 25 January 1882.

[5] R. Bruce Bickley, Jr., *Joel Chandler Harris*, 106

[6] R. Bruce Bickley, Jr., *Joel Chandler Harris*, 107.

[7] Letter from Joel Chandler Harris to James R. Osgood, 4 October 1882.

[8] Letter from Joel Chandler Harris to Robert Underwood Johnson, 7 November 1882. Quoted in Robert Underwood Johnson, *Remembered Yesterdays*, 380.

[9] Letter from Joel Chandler Harris to Richard Watson Gilder, 1882. Quoted in Julia Collier Harris, *The Life and Letters of Joel Chandler Harris*, 201.

[10] Quoted in Julia Collier Harris, *The Life and Letters of Joel Chandler Harris*, 202.

[11] Ibid.

[12] J. C. Derby, *Fifty Years Among Authors, Books and Publishers*, 434.

[13] Paul R. Cousins, *Joel Chandler Harris*, 135.

[14] Letter from Joel Chandler Harris to Benjamin H. Ticknor, 24 April 1884.

[15] Letter from Joel Chandler Harris to Benjamin Holt Ticknor, 23 August 1883.

[16] Letter from Joel Chandler Harris to Benjamin Holt Ticknor; August 23, 1883. Quoted in Griska, p. 125.

[17] Paul M. Cousins, *Joel Chandler Harris*, 133.

[18] Joel Chandler Harris, *Nights With Uncle Remus*, viii.

[19] Joel Chandler Harris, *Nights With Uncle Remus*, xxxii.

[20] Review, *The Nation*, 15 November 1883, 422.

[21] "Negro Folk-Lore," *New York Times*, 20 November 1883, 2.

[22] "Briefs on New Books," *Dial* (December 1883): 195.

[23] Henry Watterson, *Oddities in Southern Life and Character*, 304.

[24] William Bradley Strickland, *Joel Chandler Harris: A Bibliographic Study*, 38.

[25] Letter from Joel Chandler Harris to Benjamin H. Ticknor, 29 July 1884.

[26] Letter from James R. Osgood to Joel Chandler Harris, 29 September 1884.

[27] Letter from Joel Chandler Harris, July 1884. Quoted in Julia Collier Harris, *The Life and Letters of Joel Chandler Harris*, 203.

[28] "Southern Sketches," *The New York Times*, 16 June 1884, 3.

[29] "Editor's Literary Record," *Harper's* (September 1884): 641.

[30] "New Publications," *New York Daily Tribune*, 6 July 1884, 8.

[31] Review, *The Nation*, 7 August 1884, 116.

[32] William Bradley Strickland, *Joel Chandler Harris: A Bibliographic Study*, 43.

[33] Until the early part of the twentieth century, most magazine publishers paid authors by word count, with ten cents a word being a solid payment for a better author. Harris usually commanded more than that. The practice of paying by word is still used by some magazines today, although most pay a flat fee.

[34] Other stories in the collection were "Little Compton," first published in the April 1887 issue of *Century*; "Aunt Fountain's Prisoner," first published in the March 1887 issue of *Scribner's Magazine*; "Trouble on Lost Mountain," first published in the January 1886 issue

of *Century*; and "Azalia," serialized in the August, September, and October 1887 issues of *Century*.

35 Joel Chandler Harris, "Free Joe and the Rest of the World," *Century* (November 1884): 117, 120.

36 Joel Chandler Harris, "Free Joe and the Rest of the World," 123. Literary critic Jerry Allen Herndon in his 1966 doctoral dissertation at Duke University notes the similarity of the deaths of Free Joe and Uncle Tom.

37 Letter from Joel Chandler Harris to Robert Underwood Johnson, 21 July 1884.

38 "Uncle Remus's Sketches," *The New York Times*, 15 January 1888, 14.

39 Paul M. Cousins, *Joel Chandler Harris*, 147.

40 Letter from Theodore Roosevelt to Joel Chandler Harris, 12 October 1901.

41 William Bradley Strickland, *Joel Chandler Harris: A Bibliographic Study*, 46.

42 Joel Chandler Harris, *Daddy Jake the Runaway*, 6.

43 Joel Chandler Harris, *The Bishop and the Boogerman*, 127.

44 Albion Tourgee, "The South as a Field for Fiction," 409.

45 Joel Chandler Harris, "Little Compton," *Century* (April 1887): 856.

46 Letter from Joel Chandler Harris to Richard Watson Gilder, 22 July 1886 [Virginia].

47 Letter from Richard Watson Gilder to Joel Chandler Harris, 21 August 1886. [Virginia]

48 Letter from Richard Watson Gilder to Joel Chandler Harris, 14 December 1886.

49 Letter from Joel Chandler Harris to William Baskervill, 15 April 1895.

50 Letter from Joel Chandler Harris to William Baskervill, 18 March 1895.

51 See chapter 7.

52 Letter from Joel Chandler Harris to Paul R. Reynolds, 10 June 1904. [Virginia.]

53 Quoted in Julia Collier Harris, *The Life and Letters of Joel Chandler Harris*, 253

Joel Chandler Harris

Chapter 6

'Mow Down the Old Prejudices That Rattle in the Wind'

Since 1876, Henry W. Grady and Joel Chandler Harris had been colleagues and friends who bounced ideas off of each other. In the first ten to fifteen minutes of each day's 9:00 A.M. editorial meeting, Grady, Harris, and the rest of the staff joked with each other, sometimes getting personal with their insults to loosen themselves for the day's pressures. Together, Harris and Grady had forged an editorial policy that had stressed the vigorous pursuit of both news and justice, emphasizing the development of the South as a major force in American industry and politics and the necessity to reunite the country while protecting the rights of all people.

Grady "understood human nature perfectly, and knew how to manage men,"[1] wrote Harris, who explained why the *Constitution* was developing a national reputation:

[Grady also] had an instinctive knowledge of news in its embryonic state; he seemed to know just where and when a sensation or a startling piece of information would develop itself, and he was always ready for it. Sometimes it seemed to grow and develop under his hands, and his insight and information were such that what appeared to be an ordinary news item would suddenly become, under his manipulation and interpretation, one of the first importance. It was this faculty that enabled him to make the *Constitution* one of the leading journals of the country in its method of gathering and treating the news.[2]

Much of the success of the *Constitution*, according to journalist-historian Raymond B. Nixon, writing in the mid-1930s, was because "Grady was a great reporter and master news executive" who took journalism into a new era:

> Just as in his public policies Grady belongs to the New South rather than to the Old, so in his journalistic methods he exemplifies not the personal journalism which the Civil War rendered obsolete, but the modern era, with its emphasis upon the gathering and interpreting of news. The South, certainly, has never seen his like as one...who could picture even the most difficult of subjects in colorful strokes that caught the public fancy.[4]

Like Horace Greeley, who had given the *New York Tribune* an editorial voice to make it the most influential American newspaper of the Antebellum and Civil War eras, the senior editors of the *Constitution* during Reconstruction also recognized that the soul of a newspaper was its editorial pages.

"I am not a politician. I am a Democrat on election day, but that is as far as I go," Harris once noted.[5] However, his writings challenged that belief. In both his fiction and newspaper editorials, Harris was a feisty crusader for social justice and the end of sectionalism, a populist who was cynical of big business and the government. He believed that financiers, usually of the Republican party, controlled the political process at the expense of the working class, identified as being of the Democratic party. During the 1877-1881 administration of Rutherford B. Hayes, Harris regularly attacked the Republicans and "the partisan depravity of the Republican newspapers of the North."[6]

The Compromise of 1877 had allowed the Republicans to take the presidential election from Samuel Tilden, who had a 250,000 vote plurality of the 8.3 million votes cast. In the electoral college, Tilden had 184 votes to Hayes's 165. To gain twenty disputed electoral votes from Oregon, South Carolina, Florida, and Louisiana, and a one-vote victory, the Republicans, with an 8-7 majority on a special elections commission appointed by Congress to decide the disputed votes, gave Hayes all twenty votes and that one-vote electoral college victory. The compromise was that in exchange for the block of votes, the Republican administration would pull federal troops out of the South, thus ending Reconstruction. Although Harris believed in reconciliation and in the South's self-determination, he wrote against the compromise, and of a developing Republican plan not to challenge Democrats in the South. Thus, with the South's own ways of not allowing Blacks to vote, and the Republicans' agreement not to oppose Democrats for local office, Blacks, more likely to vote for Republicans, were effectively disenfranchised. The Northern Republicans, in a brilliant political move, then used the almost inconsequential voter turn-out by Blacks as proof that the South suppressed voting rights. Harris, however, believed that Blacks were better off if the radical Republicans had not interceded in their behalf, and if the South was allowed to solve its own problems. The radical Republicans, said Harris, were responsible for planting the seeds of open hostility and revolution into the minds of the freed Blacks so that the resulting chaos in the South would allow the Republicans to harvest political gain. Reflecting the Reconstruction era, Harris wrote:

> No doubt some injustice would have been done to individuals if the North had permitted the negroes

to work out their political salvation alone, but the race itself would be in better condition every way than it is to-day; for outside interference has worked untold damage and hardship to the negro. It has given him false ideas of the power and purpose of government, and it has blinded his eyes to the necessity of individual effort. It is by individual effort alone that the negro race must work out its destiny. This is the history of the white race, and it must be the history of all races that move forward.[7]

Howard W. Odum, professor of sociology at the University of North Carolina, pointed out in 1925 that by these editorials, "[Harris hoped to] dissipate sectional jealousy and misunderstanding, as well as religious and racial intolerance. He longed for the people of his own state and section to conquer their sensitiveness to rational censure and to cultivate the tonic of habit of self-criticism, for he realized that until their intelligence reached this level no real progress was possible."[8]

In one of the great ironies of his own career, Harris, who like most Confederates loathed Abraham Lincoln, now praised him as one of the greatest Americans in history, and attacked the invective of separation that Jefferson Davis continued to preach.[9] For a 14 January 1882, editorial in the *Constitution*, Harris had lashed out against Davis and those who believed that the South "shall rise again":

> ...[T]here are men, living and dead, whose connection with the late war is both historic and heroic, but Mr. Davis's connection with the cause is historic merely. His [Davis's] restless petulance and his ridiculous rhetoric do not commend him to the admiration of those who from first to last were as true to the confederacy and who, to-day, are as true to its memories as Mr. Davis can possibly be. He had an opportunity

to become the one figure around which all these memories would gather and cluster, but he has lost no opportunity to destroy the grace and harmony of his position. He is no longer the central figure, and he no longer has the authority to represent anybody or anything save his own splenetic passions....

...[I]nstead of following the example of General [Robert E.] Lee, he has chosen to display the temper of a disappointed politician. When he says that "the cause is not lost, but only sleeping," he utters what every sensible Southern man knows to be veriest bosh. Mr. Davis should either put himself in sympathy with the South of to-day. or he should hold his piece.... [I]f Mr. Davis or anybody else dreams that slavery is to be, or can be, revived, he is, indeed, demented. If the cause to which he alludes is the cause of constitutional liberty, we can say to him that the people of the South have just as much constitutional liberty as they had before the war. With slavery out of the way Georgia has no more interest in the dogma of state sovereignty than has Massachusetts, perhaps not so much. We have no doubt Mr. Davis believes the South is in chains, but everybody else knows she is freer and more prosperous in all directions than when slavery was part of the environment.[10]

Many of Harris's short stories included marriages between Yankee soldiers and Southern women, another layer in his lightly disguised allegories for what he had hoped would be a reconciliation between the North and South, for love among all peoples no matter who they were or what they may have done.[11] Even two decades earlier, Harris had established the direction for almost all of his subsequent writing: the seventeen-year-old printer's devil for *The Countryman* wrote that one of the greatest ambitions is "to be a peace-maker on earth and

to be kind and charitable to our fellow-mortals."[12] His editorials, essays, and stories carried forth that belief. In "A Story of the War," first published in the *Constitution*, Harris had Uncle Remus kill a Yankee sharpshooter who was taking aim at Mars Jeems, Uncle Remus's benevolent master and Miss Sally's father. In a revision for his first book, Harris had Uncle Remus wound the Yankee; the wound and subsequent infection caused the Yankee's arm to be amputated. Sally and Uncle Remus then nursed him back to health. The Yankee, John, married Sally; their child became the Little Boy of the tales. Five years after the war, John's sister visits them in Atlanta and hears Uncle Remus tell her how they had met:

> "But you cost him an arm," exclaimed Miss Theodosia.
> "I gin 'im dem," said Uncle Remus, pointing to [Sally], "en I gin 'im deze"—holding up his own brawny arms. "En ef dem ain't nuff fer eny man den I done los' de way."[13]

Most of the *Constitution* editorials during the 1880s and 1890s focused upon the hope that the "New South" would arise from its ruins, and that the country would reunite in mutual tolerance: "We do not regard this question of sectionalism as at all political in the usual acceptance of the term. We look upon it as a disaster of the most deadly aspect—a disaster that slays the social instincts of the people and destroys commercial enterprise and national progress. We have protested against it, not as Georgians, or as Southerners, but as Americans."[14] In articles, essays, editorials, and even the dialect tales, Howell, Grady, and Harris each spoke out for the rights of the South and of ways to rebuild the economy, while arguing that both North and South needed each other to survive. Correctly, they pointed out that the problem of reconciliation did not derive solely from the South's bitterness. However, like most Southerners, they also believed that one of the major problems preventing reconciliation was that the North flooded the South with carpetbaggers and political cronies who profited from the subjugation of a defeated people. Nevertheless, Harris and Grady also recognized that many of the South's problems had their origins at home, and tried to get the people to understand what it would take for the New South to emerge.

Grady, whose father was a Confederate officer killed during the war, proudly told about the "New South" and pleaded for the nation to again unite. That speech, delivered at the New England Society in New York on 22 December 1886, and reprinted throughout the country helped both North and South better understand the problems that followed the Civil War and established Grady as the most influential spokesman of the South. Sitting near Grady was Gen. William T. Sherman whose "march to the sea" destroyed a wide path of Georgia, and was as hated in Georgia as was Lincoln. Of Grady, Harris would write: "[He] never bore malice. His heart was tender and his nature too generous.... His first thought was always for the destitute and the lowly."[15] But Grady was not alone at the *Constitution* in those sentiments. Although Grady did love humanity and deplored violence, it was Harris who used the editorial pages to attack those who participated in mob violence or the occasional lynching. Calling vigilante justice "a disgrace to this country," and a "dangerous and demoralizing species of barbarism," Harris editorialized that "Judge Lynch...should have no more excuse to show his head in Georgia, one of the original thirteen, than in England or in any other civilized state."[16] In subsequent articles and essays, Harris wrote that many of the lynchings were because Whites believed Black men had raped White

women—he didn't say much about White plantation owners raping Black slave women—but that the actions of a few, whether White or Black, should never justify the destruction of a society based upon law.

In writings and speeches, Grady called for the continuance of segregation, and had no question about what he believed was the genetic superiority of the Caucasian race. George Washington Cable, author of several best-selling novels about the creoles of New Orleans, had continually called upon the South to yield to federal and moral laws and give equality to the Blacks; if the South would not do it, he demanded that the federal government again intercede. "In Plain Black and White," published in the April 1885 issue of *Century*, in rebuttal to Cable's commentary in the January issue, Grady argued that the federal government had abolished slavery—"for this, all men are thankful"—and ordered Blacks to be allowed to vote. For these two points, wrote Grady, "The North demanded it; the South expected it; all acquiesced in it." But the third point, one argued by Cable for full equality and integration, Grady opposed categorically:

> [T]he South will never adopt Mr. Cable's suggestion of the social intermingling of the races. It can never be driven into accepting it. So far from there being a growing sentiment in the South in favor of indiscriminate mixing of the races, the intelligence of both races is moving farther from the position day by day…Neither race wants it. Deplore or defend as we may, an antagonism is bred between the races when they are forced into mixed assemblages. This sinks out of sight, if not out of existence, when each race moves in its own sphere… [With integration] the lower and weaker elements of the races would begin to fuse and the process of amalgamation would have begun. This would mean the disorganization of society. An

internecine war would be precipitated. The whites, at any cost and at any hazard, would maintain the clear integrity and dominance of the Anglo-Saxon blood. They understand perfectly that the debasement of their own race would not profit the humble and sincere race with which their lot is cast, and that the hybrid would not gain what either race lost....

The South must be allowed to settle the social relations of the races according to her own view of what is right and best. There has never been a moment when she could have submitted to have the social status of her citizens fixed by an outside power. She accepted the emancipation and the enfranchisement of her slaves as the legitimate results of war that had been fought to a conclusion. These once accomplished, nothing more was possible. "Thus far and no further," she said to her neighbors, in no spirit of defiance, but with quiet determination.[17]

Harris agreed with Grady about the South solving its own problems, but his views about race relations reflected those of his first mentor, Joseph Addison Turner. Less than a year after the end of the Civil War, and shortly before his newspaper folded, Turner argued: "If the negro is forced upon us as a citizen, we stand for educating him, inducing him to accumulate property and to do other things which will make him a good citizen. In his attempt at elevating himself he should receive all the aid and encouragement in the power of our people to give him."[18]

In one of his most forceful editorials, published in the *Constitution* of 11 May 1883, Harris struck out against racism, arguing, "There is no reason why any Southern man, woman or child should have any prejudice against the negro race. There is no ground for it, no excuse for it.... The Southern editor who makes the discussion of this problem [reconstruction] an excuse for attacking

and abusing the negroes grossly misrepresents his readers and the people of his section."

Against opposition from the people of the South, and in direct conflict to Grady, Harris, although believing in segregation, hoped it would one day end; he called for a repeal of numerous Jim Crow laws, once writing that the role of the journalist is to "[mow] down the old prejudices that rattle in the wind like weeds." If anything, Harris was naive, unable to realize that just because he believed in equality and respected other people did not necessarily mean that others did. In an unsigned editorial in the *Constitution* of 16 April 1878, but which Harris probably wrote, the issues of equality, segregation, and states' rights were fused:

> We should, of course, prefer to see a full white delegation sent to Atlanta from the northern states [for a national Sunday School convention]; if, however, one or two of them should send a negro delegate, there would be no disposition here to either refuse him his seat, or frighten him into not claiming it. The south has, in all honor and sincerity, agreed, if left to herself, to guarantee to the negro, his fullest rights...
>
> We desire to put the northern delegates present upon notice, that they will find no illiberation here. They will find that the negro is fairly and honestly treated. He is not admitted to that social equality which his condition does not justify, his welfare demand, or his comfort suggest, and which is denied him in the north. But for all practical purposes of life, he is given and guaranteed a legal chance with the white man.[19]

In his folklore, in articles, and in editorials, Harris deplored the belief, advanced by the science of the day and advocated by Grady, that Blacks were genetically inferior to Whites. He argued that Blacks were only at a more "primitive" stage of development and that many Blacks could easily match the best White minds. He argued that when environmental factors were removed, Blacks were just as capable as Whites, not only of completing a college education but in helping to shape the country during its second century. He argued that Blacks may not be ready for higher education just yet, but there would come a time in their natural progression when they should be admitted into all colleges. He often cited Dr. Booker T. Washington as an example of "an orator of great power, a writer of unusual ability, and an extraordinary administrator of large and complicated interests."[20] Others claimed that if Washington was their intellectual equal—or better—it was because of his White blood. Harris asked why it could not be because of his Negro blood. However, in one of the greater contradictions of his editorial voice, while Harris believed that Blacks with White ancestors would rise to leadership in all facets of society, he opposed miscegenation.

Other than the issue of racial superiority and segregation, Harris and Grady differed on only one other major issue. Grady called for the urbanization of the South; Harris wanted to preserve the rural, agrarian tradition, upset by the materialism developing within the "New South." Grady believed that the South needed its agricultural base, but it also needed to develop an industrial economy to allow it to develop and, perhaps, become self-sufficient. Nevertheless, even with their disagreements, the two friends helped the nation to better understand the problems of the South and the need for a reconciliation on all levels of society.

At the end of 1889, suffering from a lingering cold but compelled to honor previously-scheduled commitments, Henry Grady toured New England to speak about "The Race Problem in the South," and to argue against a pending civil rights bill in Congress. Grady had believed

the bill's enactment into law would inflame the nation's passions of sectional mistrust and undo whatever progress had been made in race relations following the Civil War. He argued that the race problems of the South should be solved within the South, not by congressional mandate. In Atlanta, two weeks after delivering the keynote address at the Merchants Association in Boston, Grady died from pneumonia. He was thirty-nine years old.

From throughout the nation had come praise for the spokesman of the New South, but the finest tribute was written by Joel Chandler Harris: "Here was a life that has no parallel in our history." Later, in a seventy-page eulogy for a memorial book, Harris would write that Grady "died the best beloved and the most deeply lamented man that Georgia has ever produced, and to crown it all, he died a private citizen, sacrificing his life in behalf of a purpose that was neither personal nor sectional, but grandly national in its aims."[21]

Tragedy continued in the life of one of the nation's leading humorists. Less than a year after Henry Grady died, Linton Harris, a gentle soul who had shared his father's love of roses, died from complications of diphtheria at the age of seven; Mary Harris, who had lived with her son and his family since 1877, died six months after Linton, at the age of seventy-five. Mary, an independent woman, had been Harris's standard and, until he had married, the most stable element in his life. Added to never-ending sorrow over the deaths of Joseph Addison Turner in 1868 and Evan Harris in 1878, the loss of three of the closest people to him sent Harris into a depression that may have been alleviated only by an overwhelming passion to write—and the love of his home.

Mary Harris

[1] Joel Chandler Harris, *The Life and Works of Henry W. Grady*, 56.

[2] Joel Chandler Harris, *The Life and Works of Henry W. Grady*, 62-63.

[3] Julia Collier Harris, *Joel Chandler Harris: Editor and Essayist*, 48.

[4] Raymond B. Nixon, "Henry W. Grady, Reporter," 343.

[5] Julia Collier Harris, *Joel Chandler Harris: Editor and Essayist*, 48.

[6] Joel Chandler Harris, *Atlanta Constitution*, 14 December 1879.

[7] Joel Chandler Harris, *Stories of Georgia*, 310-12.

[8] Howard W. Odum, *Southern Pioneers in Social Interpretation*, 153.

[9] Harris's other heroes were Robert E. Lee and "Stonewall" Jackson.

[10] "Mr. Davis and the South," *Atlanta Constitution*, 24 January 1882, 2.

[11] Among the stories that include North-South marriages are "An Amuscade," "At Teague Poteet's," "Rosalie," "Trouble on Lost Mountain," and the novelette *Azalia*.

[12] J. C. Harris, "Ambition," *The Countryman*, 14 April 1863, 11.

[13] Joel Chandler Harris, *Uncle Remus, His Songs and Sayings*, 185.

[14] "An Important Admission," *Atlanta Constitution*, 6 December 1879.

[15] Joel Chandler Harris, *The Life and Works of Henry W. Grady*, 14, 22.

[16] [Joel Chandler Harris], "The Gallows in 1879," *Atlanta Constitution*, 4 January 1880, 2.

[17] Henry Grady, "In Plain Black and White," *Century* (April 1885): 910-11, 916.

[18] [Joseph Addison Turner], "What is to become of the Negro?" *The Countryman*, 13 February 1866, 17.

[19] [Joel Chandler Harris], "Brother Whitley vs. Brother Arnett," *Atlanta Constitution*, 16 April 1878, 2.

[20] Quoted in Julia Collier Harris, *Joel Chandler Harris, Editor and Essayist*, 143.

[21] Joel Chandler Harris, *The Life and Works of Henry W. Grady*, 9

The Wren's Nest, West Parlor

Joel Chandler Harris, 1890s

Chapter 7

'His Habits are Simple
...His Wants are Few'

In the summer of 1881, Joel Chandler Harris rented a six-room house in "ramshackle condition...full of rat holes, and almost hidden from view by a crop of giant ragweeds"[1] on 5.23 acres of land in West End, a small unincorporated village of middle-class and upper-class Whites near Atlanta.[2] Among Harris's neighbors in the village were former governors, prominent business executives, and his close friend Evan P. Howell who had urged the Harrises to move into West End.[3] The following year, Harris hired an architect and contractor who transformed the farmhouse into a Queen Anne style Victorian house, believed to be the first of its kind in Atlanta.

The house soon became known as "The Sign of the Wren's Nest" for a pair of wrens which had taken refuge in the mail box in a battle against a superior force of sparrows, and had made the letter-box their home. Harris, who loved birds and the symbolism for things that endure, never took down that letter box:

> The letter-box [is] an eyesore. Over and over, Sophia[4] has protested against the unsightly thing by wondering what the neighbors think of it. A hundred times she has exclaimed, "If you were a man of any energy, Cephas, or a man of any taste, you wouldn't have such a thing as that in the very eye of the public, where everybody can see it. It is a blot on the landscape. Why, people will think—"
> But the Farmer [Harris] has never been able to discover what the people will think about the old letter-box, for Sophia

enters her protest only when she issues forth from the house to take the trolley-car, and, as she is always a trifle late for it, the verdict of the neighborhood population is a sealed one, so far as the Farmer is concerned.

But even to him the old letter-box is a mystery. He could not tell you why such an unsightly thing has been allowed to remain in such an prominent position; it is rickety and ridiculous; it is everything it should not be in this spic and span generation…. A word to the yardman would have sent it to the limbo of the trash pile long ago, but the word has never been spoken. There the old box stood while the birds were wrangling over it, and there it stands today, nailed to a tree, now that the gatepost has disappeared, with the disappearing fence. It has been exposed to wind and weather all these years and yet it is practically intact.[5]

Just as he saw no reason to dispose of the old letter box, Harris saw little reason to cast aside furniture, just because it was no longer in style or a little ragged:

> "[N]either carpets nor furniture, no matter how new and fine, could be arranged so as to make a home. Old carpets and furniture have much the character of old friends and they suit the Farmer to a T….
>
> The finest things in the world are as cheap as dirt when they are not subordinate to something else. They cannot make a home if the spirit of the home be not in those who inhabit the house. It is bred in the air, it is borne on the breeze, and is so insistent that no one can mistake it.[6]

"He didn't like the new smell," said Essie Harris, "and was glad when it wore off; he liked things that had served us; wanted things to stay put."[7] When forced to buy new furniture, like any middle-class family during the late

STATE OF GEORGIA, *Fulton* **County.**

This Indenture, made this *fourth* day of *October* in the year of our Lord One Thousand Eight Hundred and *Eighty three* between *Benjamin H. Broomhead* of the County of *Fulton* of the one part, and *The Constitution Publishing Company* of the County of *Fulton* of the other part.

Witnesseth, That the said *Benjamin H. Broomhead* for and in consideration of the sum of *Twenty five hundred* Dollars, in hand paid, at and before the sealing and delivery of these presents, the receipt whereof is hereby acknowledged, ha$ granted, bargained, sold and conveyed, and by these presents doe$ grant, bargain, sell and convey unto the said *The Constitution Publishing Company, their* heirs and assigns, all that Tract or Parcel of Land, situated lying and being in

Land Lot number One hundred and eighteen (118) in the fourteenth (14th) district of originally Henry now Fulton County, known as lot number Sixteen (16) in Langston Crane & Hammock's subdivision or survey, and containing Five and twenty three one-hundredth $\langle 5\frac{23}{100} \rangle$ acres, more or less.

To Have and to Hold the said *bargained premises* with all and singular the rights, members and appurtenances thereof, to the same being, belonging, or in any wise appertaining, to the only proper use, benefit and behoof of *them* the said *The Constitution Publishing Company, their successors* heirs, executors, administrators and assigns, in Fee Simple;

And the said *Benjamin H. Broomhead his* heirs, executors, and administrators, the said *bargained premises* unto the said *The Constitution Publishing Company, their successors* heirs, executors, administrators and assigns, against the said *Broomhead and his* heirs, executors, and administrators, and all and every other person or persons, shall and will warrant and forever defend, by virtue of these presents.

In Witness Whereof, the said *Benjamin H. Broomhead has* hereunto set *his* hand and affixed *his* seal the day and year first above written.

Signed, sealed and delivered in presence of

W. D. Luckie

J. W. Jenie (?)

B. H. Broomhead (SEAL)

(SEAL)

Notary Public Fulton Co. Ga.

Deed to Harris's first house in Atlanta

The Wren's Nest, with Joel Chandler Harris standing on the porch

nineteenth century, he shopped in the Sears, Roebuck catalogue.

Although Harris helped fixed the house which always seemed to need repair, it was Essie who made sure it was a home by her unconditional love for her husband and children, and by her concern for the house itself. "The average man thinks a beautiful house is something external, but there is no genuine beauty in any house or in any place that is not put into it from the depths of somebody's soul,"[8] said the Reverend James Lee, pastor of the Park Street Methodist Church, and a close friend. "[A] gentle but positive influence in our home was father's philosophy of life which was exemplified by his kindly nature, and his affection," said Evelyn Harris, "but mother was with us every hour of the day and night."[9] If

Harris had any defect as a parent, it may have been, as Hugh Keenan observed in *Dearest Chums and Partners*, that he was too controlling of the lives of his boys, even into adulthood, while being gentler with his girls. Although Harris himself was a stern task-maker who "was liberal in his practice of this theory that...to spare the rod was to spoil the child," it was Essie's "tender heart and her protective spirit [that] impelled her often to endeavor to lighten the punishment," Evelyn Harris remembered.[10] It was she who took care of the children while their father worked; it was she who made sure the repairs to the house were done; it was she who made sure the house was clean.

"Mother was an exacting house-keeper," said Evelyn Harris, and "Father was miserable when the normal routine was disturbed, and walked around like a lost pet if he happened to appear on the scene when house cleaning was in progress."[11] As a result of Essie's concern and her husband's devotion to his family, the Wren's Nest was "the most beautiful home in Atlanta, and people from all over the country make pilgrimages to see it," said Reverend Lee.[12]

Behind the house was the garden, a place for Harris to retreat and restore his wonderment of nature. During the mid-1880s, Harris informally named the "estate" Snap-Bean Farm, a playful jab at the Sabine Farm estate of *Chicago Daily News* humorist and poet Eugene Field, author of "Sharps and Flats," a daily 2,000 word column of paragraphs. Harris and Field had exchanged numerous humorous broadsides in a journalistic "feud" that lasted several years, but the respect Harris and Field had for each other became evident when Harris wrote the introduction to Field's novel *The House* (1896).[13]

At Snap-Bean Farm Harris was, by his own desire, a middle-class "Farmer" who grew several dozen varieties of roses in the front yard, raspberry and strawberry vines in the back yard, and vegetables in the fields. The farm, said Forrest Adair, one of his closest friends and son of one of the principal developers of the West End, "kept him in touch with nature—with country life."[14] For the Sunday *Constitution*, and in seeming antithesis to his hard-driving editorials about politics, Harris wrote dozens of essays about nature, plants and animals, always referring to himself as the "Farmer."

Harris spent most of his time either at the *Constitution* or at his home and garden. He usually left the house to go to work about 8:30 A.M., took the twenty-minute trip by mule cart, an early form of the streetcar, returned for a noon dinner—often consisting of bacon or other pork, collard greens, cornpone-bread, and pot-liquor (the left-over juices of meats and vegetables) —returned to the newspaper for the rest of the afternoon, then left in late afternoon or early evening for his home. During the four trips by mule cart, he chatted with the residents from the West End who worked in Atlanta, and often took the reins for a few blocks to give the driver a break to eat lunch. Harris loathed the introduction of the electric streetcars in 1889; they made travel faster, more efficient, there was less time to chat with the driver and passengers—and he could not take the reins.

At the Sign of the Wren's Nest, "his habits are simple in the extreme. His wants are few," wrote his friend John Henderson Garnsey in 1896, elaborating that Harris wanted "plenty to eat, large quantities of water to drink, plenty of heat in the cold winter, plenty of light, by day and night, on the funny little square table at which he writes, seated in a little square-backed rocking chair— these make up the sum and substance of his desires."[15] But Garnsey neglects one of Harris's wants: the presents of animals. As a youth, Harris had pet dogs and a pet horse; at Turnwold, he spent parts of every day watching birds, squirrels, and other wildlife. As a youth, he befriended innumerable stray cats and dogs, his mother once told Essie Harris. It never occurred to Harris not to have animals around him. At the Wren's Nest, he and his family were constantly surrounded by animals, primarily cats, dogs, and Essie's canaries. But, they also made pets of ducks, chickens, rabbits, guinea pigs, pigeons, donkeys, horses, cows, and whatever animals wandered onto the farm. "I have often been perplexed to know what to do with our excess of kittens," said Essie Harris who remembered her husband "was always finding another puppy and bringing it home."[16] Harris especially loved birds, even refusing to trim the hedges because he believed it would frighten them.[17] "He was an authority on all varieties of Southern birds," wrote his friend Forrest Adair, "and his study of the mocking bird...is a prose poem

'His Habits are Simple...His Wants are Few'

Wren's Nest, Master Bedroom

[that] would have made his literary reputation if he had written nothing else."[18]

But, children and dogs were his primary love. "I am merely a simple-minded old fellow who is very anxious for a few chosen friends to like him," Harris wrote to a friend late in life, noting, "Many children and a great many dogs are fond of me, and that is a good test."[19]

Seldom would Harris leave his family and Georgia. "I prefer to stay where I can see the lawn and the flowers, and hear the birds, and run the chickens out, and chunk old Ovid [his dog] out of the flower beds," Harris once explained.[20] Perhaps he stayed in Atlanta because he was terrified that he would stammer and embarrass himself in front of strangers. Perhaps it was because he feared the crowds of authors, publishers, and the public who would try to entice him into various dinners in his honor, to become a part of the aura he believed he never had; he believed he was, after all, merely a "cornfield journalist." Perhaps it was because of his numerous small illnesses, many brought about by overwork, that he was terrified at leaving the comfort and security of the Wren's Nest and Atlanta. Whatever the reasons, Harris stayed in Atlanta, living a simple life protected by the anonymity given by a career on a newspaper, Harris was comfortable. He "never liked to talk about anything he had written, and never liked to hear anyone else talk about it," wrote Don Marquis, his friend and colleague from the rival *Journal*.[21]

However, Samuel L. Clemens believed he might change that. In 1881, Clemens, by his strong praise of the Uncle Remus tales, had helped establish Harris as a major writer, and almost guaranteed that his works would be treated with respect. The following year, with the Uncle Remus tales known throughout the country—and a favorite of his own daughters—Clemens had urged Harris to join him for a series of public readings in New Orleans the first week of May. Clemens knew Harris was shy and afraid to perform in public, but wrote to Harris that he had "thought out a device whereby I believe we can get around that difficulty. I will explain when I see you."22

Harris did join Clemens and novelist George Washington Cable, author of the popular *Old Creole Days*, in New Orleans and surprised many Southerners by attending Sunday services in a Black church. The next day, Clemens, as Mark Twain—he was careful to separate his personal and literary selves—and George Washington Cable delighted their audience with discussions and readings from their books. Harris, however, still could not break his torment enough to read from his own works. In *Life on the Mississippi* (1883), Twain wrote about what happened that day in New Orleans:

[Harris] is a shy man. Of this there is no doubt. It may not show on the surface, but the shyness is there. After days of intimacy one wonders to see that it is still in about as strong a force as ever. There is a fine and beautiful nature behind it, as all know who have read the Uncle Remus book; and a fine genius, too....

He deeply disappointed a number of children who had flocked eagerly to Mr. Cable's house to get a glimpse of the illustrious sage and oracle of the nation's nurseries. They said—

"Why, he's white!"

They were grieved about it. So, to console them, the book was brought, that they might hear Uncle Remus's Tar-Baby story from the lips of Uncle Remus himself—or what, in their outraged eyes, was left of him. But it turned out that he had never read aloud to people, and was too shy to venture the attempt now. Mr. Cable and I read from books of ours, to show him what an easy trick it was; but his immortal shyness was proof against even this sagacious strategy; so we had to read about Brer Rabbit ourselves.23

On 2 May, before the tour ended, Harris returned to Atlanta. At the end of the year, Harris and Cable light-heartedly dueled in print about the banjo—Cable claimed Blacks played the banjo, Harris claimed they did not; Cable was proven to be correct.

Between 1881 and 1885, Harris and Twain exchanged six letters, each praising the other, each probably written as much out of friendship and professional respect as to influence a nation that the other was a major writer.[24] But they would meet only once more after the lecture tour. In spring 1883, Harris finally accepted Twain's invitation to come to Hartford, Connecticut.

In 1884, Harris rejected a tour with journalist-novelist Thomas Nelson Page. The next year, James B. Pond, agent for some of the nation's leading writers, including Twain and Cable, begged Harris, "the people—including the children—are calling for you, and that has not happened to any author of late years. *No* will not do for an answer."[25] Harris answered "no." With a fee of $10,000 proposed—at a time when the average household income in the country was about $800 a year—Harris refused to go on a lecture tour with Twain and James Whitcomb Riley. Harris remarked, "I would not put on a dress-suit every night in the winter for $10,000, much less go on a stage and make a fool of myself."[26] Several years later, Harris even bowed out of a speech he was scheduled to deliver at a country fair in his home town. According to the *Eatonton Messenger*: "After [Henry] Grady had concluded an eloquent oration, Harris was introduced to an eager audience. He made the statement that he could never make a speech without a drink of water and as he left the stands the crowd cheered and laughed. They knew he would not be back for any speech-making."[27]

Harris's shyness among strangers even extended to his literary colleagues. Among the better mid-nineteenth century writers who lived in Georgia were Harry Stilwell

Edwards, A. B. Longstreet, Richard Malcolm Johnston, William Tappan Thomson, and Francis O. Ticknor. But Harris barely spoke with them. "Perhaps his reluctance to do so grew out of his natural shyness and his consciousness of his humble origin and lack of formal education," wrote biographer Paul M. Cousins.[28] No matter how much money, fame, or "social status" Harris achieved, he still saw himself as part of the working class, deliberately placed his own stature well beneath that of his contemporaries, and felt uncomfortable dealing with those whom he saw to be of a "higher class," no matter how friendly and respectful they were. Indeed, in most situations, he was the Uncle Remus to the master.

Writing to nationally-known illustrator Arthur Burdett Frost in 1886, the forty-year-old Harris apologized profusely for what he believed was a case of bad manners when Frost had visited the Wren's Nest. The letter, however, reflects not a case of bad manners, but an insight into Harris's life and personality:

> "I really hope I didn't make an unfavorable impression on you by reason of any lack of conversational tact, and my general awkward lack of fluency. I have no social accomplishments whatever, and avoid society in all of its shapes and forms as one would shun the plague. The knowledge of this deficiency— or, rather, of these deficiencies embarrasses me to an extent beyond description."[29]

Essie "understood his diffidence and respected it without encouraging it," Evelyn Harris remembered, and it was she who "entertained and charmed the visitors and 'explained' father's absence while he spent miserable moments in some remote, secluded spot on the place."[30]

Ironically, it was among Blacks that Harris could often feel at ease. In one instance, Harris encountered

Joel Chandler Harris and James Whitcomb Riley, early 1900s

three dozen Black railroad workers sitting outside the Norcross, Georgia, train station in the summer of 1882. Harris, who was waiting for a train to Atlanta, sat with some of them and began to tell the tar-baby story. "I have found few negroes who will acknowledge to a stranger that they know anything of these legends," Harris wrote in the introduction for *Uncle Remus; His Songs and Sayings*, "and yet to relate one of the stories is the surest road to their confidence and esteem."[31] Charles Colcock Jones in 1842 had cautioned: "Persons live and die in the midst of Negroes and know comparatively little of their real character... They are one thing before the whites, and another before their own color. Deception towards the former is characteristic of them, whether bond or free, throughout the United States."[32] Whether free or enslaved, Blacks had a well-founded mistrust and suspicion of Whites and had no reason to allow them into their culture. If Blacks did tell stories to Whites, it was often tales they thought Whites wanted to hear and in the stereotyped manner Whites expected Blacks to tell such tales. Yet, the railroad workers in Norcross not only listened attentively to what Harris was telling, and how he was telling it, but enthusiastically told their own stories, with Harris laughing, enjoying, and learning with them. It was, says Bruce Bickley, one of Harris's main chroniclers, "a rare moment of relaxation [with Harris becoming as] unselfconscious among these Negroes as he had been with the blacks on Turner's plantation twenty years earlier."[33]

As Joel Chandler Harris, literary writer and folklorist, he was awkward and shy; as Joe Harris, journalist and community resident, however, he was witty, charming, and relatively outgoing. Among small groups of people he knew well, especially among children who visited him at the Wren's Nest, Harris seldom stammered and projected himself into the storyteller. For a profile in the *Methodist*

Messenger, Forrest Adair wrote about Harris the Storyteller: "When interested and in the mood, he is a capital talker, full of good stories and reminisces, and bubbling over with quaint humor.... When a child, a countryman or a good, old-fashioned darky comes along, the busy journalist and story writer throws off the cares and business of the moment, and his jolly optimism is contagious."[34]

Following a most-enjoyable two-week visit by James Whitcomb Riley to the Wren's Nest, Riley's long-time companion John M. Dickey wrote to Harris: "To bring home money is one thing, but to bring home the memory of *love* and *laughter* is another thing,—and vastly superior. And it is this dear memory of you and your home that Mr. Riley has now to enrich his daily life. He has in his possession the *true* friendship of that 'peculiar man' down south and this possession is his new fortune."[35]

Harris was an active participant in the community, even enthusiastically participating in annual Summer fairs on his front lawn which raised funds for the church; both he and Essie gave freely to almost every charity or person with a sob-story. His wife would shield him from the curious, yet Harris invited numerous persons into his home, enjoyed lawn games with his friends, and easily carried on conversations. "[T]he house and grounds were constantly filled with noisy, happy boys and girls," Evelyn Harris remembered.[36] John Henderson Garnsey, who spent numerous evenings at the Wren's Nest, revealed:

> [Harris] lives his simple life, unmolested by the busybodies of the world. ...[To] the person who gushes at him, or seems visibly impressed by him, [he] is more reserved than the proverbial oyster.... It is in the darkness of a summer evening, on the great front porch of his home... that the man breaks forth into conversation. I have had in these rare twilight hours

the plot of a whole book unfolded to me,—a book that is yet in the dim future, but which will make a stir when it appears; I have heard stories innumerable of the old plantation life and of happenings in Georgia during the war; and I have heard through the mouth of this taciturn and un-literary looking man more thrilling stories of Colonial life in the South than I had believed the South held. At these times, the slight hesitancy that is usually apparent in his speech disappears; his thoughts take words, and come forth, tinged by the quaint Georgia dialect, in so original a shape and so full of human nature that one remembers these hours long afterwards as times to be marked with a white stone.[37]

[1] Julia Collier Harris, *The Life and Letters of Joel Chandler Harris*, 174.

[2] Atlanta would annex West End in 1894.

[3] The street was originally named Lickskillet Street, renamed Gordon Street for a Confederate general after the Civil War, then renamed Ralph David Abernathy Boulevard in 1991. The house on Gordon Street had been built for the Muse family as a three-room farmhouse about 1870; three more rooms were added in 1873. George Muse, owner of Muse's Men's Clothing, soon to become one of the region's largest clothiers, sold the house in 1878 for $3,300 to Benjamin H. Broomheard, a speculator who had rented it to several transient families. By 1881, when he rented the house to the young Harris family, it had been in disrepair for several years. Two years later, Broomheard sold the house and land for $2,500 to Howell's Constitution Publishing Company; concurrently, Harris took out a $2,500 mortgage to repay the company.

[4] Harris playfully referred to his wife as Sophia, she called him Cephas, short for Josephus. Harris used these names not only in non-fiction essays by "The Farmer," but also in fiction, notably his semi-autobiographical novel, *Gabriel Tolliver*. In public, Essie called her husband, "Mr. Harris"; when she was mad or upset with him, it was "Joel."

[5] Joel Chandler Harris, "The Old Letter-Box," *Uncle Remus's Magazine* (July 1907): 9.

[6] Joel Chandler Harris, "Houses and Homes," *Uncle Remus's Magazine* (October 1907): 5.

[7] Esther LaRose Harris, quoted in Myrta Lockett Avary, *Joel Chandler Harris and His Home*, 15.

8 James W. Lee, "The Character of Joel Chandler Harris," 111.

9 Evelyn Harris, A Little Story, 42.

10 Evelyn Harris, A Little Story, 23.

11 Evelyn Harris, A Little Story, 49.

12 James W. Lee, "The Character of Joel Chandler Harris," 111.

13 Sabine Farm, named after the stories written by Horace, was formalized in Field's poem, "My Sabine Farm," published in the Chicago Daily News, 1 August 1885, four years after Harris had moved into The Sign of the Wren's Nest.

14 Forrest Adair, "Joel Chandler Harris—Master Builder," 6.

15 John Henderson Garnsey, "Joel Chandler Harris: A Character Sketch," 66.

16 Esther LaRose Harris, quoted in Myrta Lockett Avary, Joel Chandler Harris and His Home, 5.

17 Mrs. M. F. Merriam, "At Snap Bean Farm," Southern Ruralist, 15 October 1913, 22.

18 Forrest Adair, "Joel Chandler Harris—Master Builder," 6.

19 Mrs. L. H. Harris, "The Passing of Uncle Remus," 191.

20 Quoted in Julia Collier Harris, Life and Letters of Joel Chandler Harris.

21 Don Marquis, "The Farmer of Snap Bean Farm," 7.

22 Letter from Samuel L. Clemens to Joel Chandler Harris, 2 April 1882.

23 Mark Twain, Life on the Mississippi, 471-72.

24 See Mark Twain to Uncle Remus, 1881-1885, compiled by Thomas H. English, Emory University Publications, 1953.

25 Letter from James B. Pond to Joel Chandler Harris, 9 April 1885.

26 Quoted in Julia Collier Harris, The Life and Letters of Joel Chandler Harris, 214.

27 W. W. Walker, "The Story of Joel Chandler Harris...," 1.

28 Paul M. Cousins, Joel Chandler Harris, 94.

29 Letter from Joel Chandler Harris to A. B. Frost, 19 March 1886.

30 Evelyn Harris, A Little Story, 45.

31 Joel Chandler Harris, Uncle Remus, His Songs and Sayings, 10.

32 Charles C. Jones, The Religious Instruction of the Negroes in the United States, 110.

33 R. Bruce Bickley, Jr., Joel Chandler Harris, 44.

34 Forest Adair. "Stories and Incidents in the Life of Georgia's Best Known Writer," 1.

35 Letter from John M. Dickey to Joel Chandler Harris, 8 May 1900.

36 Evelyn Harris, A Little Story, 33.

37 John Henderson Garnsey, "Joel Chandler Harris: A Character Sketch," 66

Study, The Wtren's Nest

Joel Chandler Harris, 1890

Chapter 8

'Distorted Words and Illiterate Grammar'

With America's "Manifest Destiny" shaping a nation that had spread between the two oceans, the major American newspapers experienced huge circulation increases, and the number of magazines increased from 700 before the Civil War to almost 4,000 by the end of the century. Following the Civil War and the beginning of the Reconstruction Cycle, Americans realized that no part of the country could exist in isolation, and that each had a unique contribution to make. Among the more significant writers were Thomas Dunn English, Sidney Lanier, Irwin Russell, Harry Stilwell Edwards, George Washington Cable, Lafcadio Hearn, Thomas Nelson Page, Mark Twain, and, of course, Joel Chandler Harris—all of them White, each of whom attempted to accurately portray the South and all of its people, each of whom used variations of American Black English in their dialect verses, short stories, and novels.

The success of the Uncle Remus stories had spurred a proliferation of dialect tales and book compilations. Alcée Fortier, of Vacherie, Louisiana, during the 1870s had collected French Creole folktales from slaves at the local plantations, and wrote of Compair Lapin (the rabbit) and Compair Bouki (the stupid hyena, originally a Wolof word.) Fourteen of his tales, including "Piti Bonhomme Godron" (the tar baby), were published in 1888 in the academic journals *Transactions of the Modern Language Association of America* and *Journal of American Folk-Lore*. The following year, ten of them were collected for *Bits of Louisiana*

Folk-Lore. In 1895, the American Folk-Lore Society commissioned Houghton, Mifflin (which published many of Joel Chandler Harris's works) to publish Fortier's *Louisiana Folk-Tales in French Dialect and English Translation*, a collection of folktales told in Creole with English literary translations. At the time, Fortier was president of the American Folk-Lore Society and a dean at Tulane University.

Many of the eighteen animal tales in Gullah compiled by A. M. H. Christensen, and which appeared in the nationally-recognized *Springfield* (Mass.) *Republican* and *New York Independent*, actually preceded Harris's stories, but it was not until the Uncle Remus tales became popular that the public responded to her stories which were finally collected and published in 1892.

In the introduction to *Negro Myths From the Georgia Coast Told in the Vernacular* (1888), Charles Colcock Jones, Jr. readily acknowledged Harris's work, and explained the differences in language and cultural observations of Uncle Remus and Daddy Jack to those of the Blacks in his sixty-one tales from the Georgia swamplands, most of whom spoke Gullah.

In Charleston, South Carolina, Ambrose Gonzales wrote the first of a dozen "Kinlaw Tales" in 1886. Six years later, while editor-publisher of *The State*, South Carolina's leading newspaper, Gonzales would write fourteen "Silhouettes," each one mixing humor and tragedy to help readers better understand the mind of the South and of its Gullah people. The final "Silhouette" appeared in the 22 May 1892, issue of *The State*; with a few minor exceptions, it would be almost three decades before Gonzales again used the Gullah language in his stories.

Other major White writers during the late nineteenth century who essentially understood elements of American Black English and African-American folklore, and whose works usually appeared first in newspapers before being collected into books, were Katherine Sherwood Bonner MacDowell, whose first collection, *Dialect Tales* (1883), was published the year of Harris's *Nights With Uncle Remus*; Emma M. Backus, whose folk tales appeared in the *Journal of American Folk-Lore*; Harry Stilwell Edwards, editor of the *Macon Telegraph* from 1881 to 1887; poets Thomas Dunn English, Sidney Lanier, and Irwin Russell, whose dialect verses, published in the major American magazines, exposed the humor and tragedy of the Black in the Civil War and Reconstruction South; Lafcadio Hearn and George Washington Cable, newspaper reporters in New Orleans who individually would become two of the nation's most acclaimed literary writers during the late nineteenth century; and, of course, Joel Chandler Harris and Mark Twain. But, all were White, writing from White perspectives.

A few Black journalists—among them Paul Laurence Dunbar, James D. Corrothers, James Edwin Campbell, and Charles Waddell Chesnutt—who were never allowed to work on the staffs of White-owned newspapers—gave perspectives that few Whites could understand. Chesnutt's first major folktale, "The Goophered Grapevine," published in the August 1887 issue of the *Atlantic Monthly*, featured Uncle Julius, based upon Uncle Remus but far more militant. Julius would appear in several more tales during the next decade. Typical tales had Whites believing they were superior to the trickster Julius who usually proved his—and the Blacks'—own superiority. In *The Conjure Woman* (1899), a compilation of seven dialect tales that first appeared in magazines, Chesnutt—who had read the Uncle Remus tales to his own children when they were young—directly attacked Harris for how he recorded Black language and for "reinforc[ing] a white supremacist ideology." Chesnutt's last

book, *The Colonel's Dream* (1905), was an impassioned plea for racial tolerance and equality.

However, most writers who used Blacks in their stories portrayed them in comical stereotype, depicting them as being lazy, wide-eyed, nappy-haired creatures who wielded razors, stole watermelons and chickens, and butchered and distorted Standard English in their vain attempts to become like their more gentrified White superiors. These writers, said Thomas Nelson Page, "have supposed that they were writing dialect when they were only writing distorted words and illiterate grammar, not knowing that the master here [Harris] has used the vehicle [dialect] only to carry the thought, and that the secret of his craft lies not in the manner so much as the matter."[1] During this era, innumerable businesses, restaurants, and products (including dolls, gardening supplies, and foods) featured comical Black motifs, with the names of Sambo, Rastus, and Uncle Remus and Brer Rabbit.

Poet-journalist James Whitcomb Riley, one of Harris's closest friends during the first decade of the twentieth century, and who, like Harris, used dialect to enhance characterization, pleaded:

> Let [the writer of dialect] be schooled in dialect before he sets up as an expounder of it.... The real master not only knows each varying light and shade of dialect expression, but he must as minutely learn the inner characteristic of the people whose nature native tongue it is, else his product is simply a pretense—a wilful [sic] forgery, a rank abomination....
>
> [D]ialect means something more than mere rude form of speech and action—that it must, in some righteous and substantial way, convey to us a positive force of soul, truth, dignity, beauty, grace, purity, and sweetness, that can touch us to the tenderness of fears.[2]

Harris himself had numerous times spoken out against the inaccurate depictions of American Blacks and their languages, but the proliferation of dialect tales continued.

The introduction of *Uncle Remus and His Friends* (1892) shows Harris still concerned about acceptance of American Black English, and painfully aware that thousands of ignorant and racist writers had bastardized the Black language in order to justify not only cheap humor but their own sense of intellectual superiority:

> Naturally, these stories are written in what is called negro dialect. It seemed to be unavoidable. I sympathize deeply and heartily with the protest that has been made against the abuse of dialect. It is painful, indeed, when the form of the lingo trails on the earth, and the thought flies in the air. I had intended to apologize for the plantation dialect, but a valued correspondent in "The Flatwoods" assures me that "old man Chaucer was one of the earliest dialect writers," and I have recent seen (in the "New York Independent") an essay by Professor March, in which there is a perfectly serious effort to rival the phonetics employed by Uncle Remus.
>
> The student of English, if he be willing to search so near the ground, will find matter to interest him in the homely dialect of Uncle Remus, and if his intentions run towards philological investigations, he will pause before he has gone far and ask himself whether this negro dialect is what it purports to be, or whether it is not simply the language of the white people of three hundred years ago twisted and modified a little to fit the lingual peculiarities of the negro. Dozens of words, such as *hit* for *it*, *ax* for *ask*, *whiles* for *wiles*, and *heap* for *a large number of people*, will open before him the whole field of the philology of the English tongue. He will discover that, when Uncle Remus tells the little boy that he has a "monstus weakness fer cake

what's got *reezins* in it," the pronunciation of *reezins* uncovers and rescues from oblivion Shakespeare's pun on *raisins*, where Falstaff tells the Prince, "If reasons were as plentiful as blackberries, I would give no man a reason on compulsion."[3]

In July 1892, Harris had announced that a series of tales, beginning in the 24 July issue of the *Constitution*, would be the last he would tell using Uncle Remus. Although the announcement spread quickly within the publishing community and the South, it was not until December, with the compilation in book form, that the entire nation finally understood that Harris would no longer write about the plantation philosopher and the tales he told the Little Boy. In a tightly worded conclusion to *Uncle Remus and His Friends*—consisting of the twenty-four tales from the *Constitution* which were published between 23 July and 6 November, plus sixteen songs and thirty-one sketches—the creator of the Uncle Remus tales declared:

> [T]he old man will bother the public no more with his whimsical stories.... No doubt there is small excuse for such leave-taking in literature. But there is pretense that the old darkey's poor little stories are in the nature of literature, or that their re-telling touches literary art at any point. All the accessories are lacking. There is nothing here but an old negro man, a little boy, and a dull reporter, the matter of discourse being fantasies as uncouth as the original man ever conceived of. Therefore, let Uncle Remus's good-by be as simple as his stories; a swift gesture that might be mistaken for a salutation as he takes his place among the affable Ghosts that throng the ample corridors of the Temple of Dreams.[4]

Undoubtedly, Harris was tired of the proliferation of poorly-written dialect tales, combined with the development and acceptance of the grotesque distortion in caricature,[5] the "intolerable misrepresentations" that surrounded the depiction of American Blacks, possibly afraid that his accurate renditions of the language and reliable retelling of the African-American folk-tales would not only be tainted by what else appeared in print, but cause further proliferation.

Bruce Bickley suggests one of the reasons for cutting off the Uncle Remus tales may have been because Harris "had become somewhat fatigued by the flurry of folkloristic commentary that his stories had generated," and that Harris, now well-entrenched in metropolitan life, may have exhausted the material he had learned while in rural Putnam County.[6] However, there could be another explanation. *Uncle Remus and His Friends*, with sales of 56,866 in forty printings,[7] again established Harris as a best-selling author after several books without the tales sold less 3,000-8,000 copies each. Like his rabbit, Harris had been trapped by his own tar-baby, and the more he tried to pull away, the more he was bound to it, possessed by the hope to write a novel. He wanted—needed—to be a novelist. But as Julia Collier Harris observed, he "had a deep-seated conviction that the handling of a sustained plot would be beset with difficulties; and in his lack of self-confidence, doubtless the difficulties magnified themselves mightily."[8]

He complained about, but enjoyed, the work he did in daily newspaper journalism which brought innumerable issues to the public's attention. But Uncle Remus's legacy had bonded Harris to his stories and character portrayal of America's slaves, forcing him to write more and more tales, often at the exclusion of his own desire to concentrate on social issue journalism and class distinction as plots for portrayals of the lower-class

Joel Chandler Harris in *Constitution* office

Whites—and kept him away from the novel. Most of what he wrote for national publication carried the publisher's descriptor, "by the author of Uncle Remus"; for some works, publishers even made the byline of "Uncle Remus" larger than that of "Joel Chandler Harris."

Although vowing to break free of Uncle Remus tales, Harris nevertheless agreed to let D. Appleton Co. reprint *Uncle Remus, His Songs and Sayings* as a fifteenth anniversary edition. But he demanded better illustrations. The *New York Evening Post* of 6 December 1880, had extended Harris's concerns, dismissing the comical illustrations—"The work is humorous to a high degree certainly; but it is not comic"— and praising Harris for understanding the human mind and emotion. Well aware of the grotesque distortion many artists used to portray Blacks, Harris always worried that the artists assigned by the magazine and book publishers did not understand the Blacks well enough to characterize them. For "Azalia," Harris told *Century* editor Richard Watson Gilder that although he did not object to E. W. Kemble, a nationally-respected artist who used the grotesque distortion of caricature, "Pray ask him to treat my decent people decently, and with some refinement... Beg him also to give the old negro man some dignity, and to remember the distinction between the Guinea negro—as he is in New Orleans—and the Virginia negro as he is in Georgia."9

No matter how hard Harris tried to give insight to his artists—and no matter how hard they tried to comply with his wishes—the result was never what Harris wanted. This time, for the fifteenth year commemorative edition of *Uncle Remus, His Songs and Sayings*, Harris insisted upon using A. B. Frost, who had illustrated "Free Joe" in 1884, "Little Compton" in 1887, and *Uncle Remus and His Friends* in 1892, and for which Harris declared the drawings were "perfect." For the fifteenth anniversary edition, Frost contributed 112 illustrations, placing the animals into human clothes. So pleased was Harris with Frost's insights into the characters and the absence of grotesque distortion that he dedicated the book to him, stating that Frost "breathed the breath of life into these amiable brethren of wood and field."

However, the publisher, not the illustrator, reaped the financial benefit from the illustrations. Not only did D. Appleton keep the original illustrations for the fifteenth anniversary edition, it apparently "sold them for *more* than they paid me for making them," Frost wrote more than three decades later, concluding, "It was the most unfortunate business deal I ever made."[10]

Nevertheless, the illustrations enhanced Frost's national reputation—and Harris's admiration. In the introduction to a book of Frost's drawings, Harris not only praised the man who had become the most famous illustrator of the Uncle Remus stories, but also provided an insight into the nature of art and of art as journalism:

> Other artists had tried their hands at it [depicting the Uncle Remus tales], but although they did fairly well, there was something lacking....
>
> The difficulty to be solved was how to interpret these creatures from the viewpoint of the negro's imagination. The result of the artist's effort is a series of drawings which for pure humor have probably never been surpassed. The illustrations rarely approach the comic, but the way in which human nature has been combined with animal nature is deliciously illuminating....
>
> He knows how to deal with all the values necessary to give life and movement to a drawing. Among American illustrators, none has covered a wider field, or given more genuine pleasure and satisfaction to a public that is not quite happy with a book or a magazine unless it is full of pictures that convey a meaning

and give a gratification that is not to be found in the printed matter....

The one characteristic that marks all the work of Mr. Frost, the one quality that stands out above the rest, is its persistent and ever-present humor, which gives it a color and pungent flavor of its own. It represents the artist's way of looking at life, and it is so completely his own way, it is so entirely the result of his own individuality, that most of his drawings have a decided literary touch; that is to say, a literary man, perceiving the verities arranged in postures so sympathetic and illuminating that they tell their own story at a glance, may well envy Mr. Frost the possession of a gift that is capable of looking around and behind what should seem to be commonplace, and of bringing out all that is calculated to relate it to our own personal experiences, whether these last are the result of reflection, observation, or adventure. When this result is produced in a large way, and persistently, the only name we have for it is humor, and it remains humor whether the medium is plastic, pictorial, or purely literary.[11]

The 1895 edition of *Uncle Remus, His Songs and Sayings*, like its first edition, was warmly received by reviewers and the public.

Thomas Nelson Page, whose own compilation of folklore, *In Ole Virginia* (1887), was based upon the Uncle Remus tales but with the focus more to the White slave-owner, praised Harris: "No man who has ever written has known one-tenth part about the negro that Mr. Harris knows, and for those who hereafter shall wish to find not merely the words, but the real language of the negro of that section, and the habits and mind of all American negroes of the old time, his works will prove the best thesaurus."[12]

A review in the *New York Times* pinpointed an historical reason why the Uncle Remus tales were important: "It fixes for us the subtle characteristics of a people who, in the nature of things, must soon pass, and who, but for writers like the historian of Uncle Remus, would be practically unknown to the rising generation: for the educated negro of the coming years is quite another person from his ancestor, who lived 'befo' de wah.'"[13]

A year after the fifteenth anniversary reprint of the first Uncle Remus book, the Century company reprinted the 1889 edition of *Daddy Jake the Runaway, and Short Stories Told After Dark* as a companion volume to Rudyard Kipling's *Jungle Books* stories. The *New York Times* of 24 October pointed out that whereas Kipling saw the nobility of animals, Harris looked at their craftiness, and pointed out that Harris has "behind him the genius of an entire race." The *Chicago Tribune* noted: "Bre'r Rabbit and Bre'r Fox are elder brothers of Baloo, the Bear, and Bagheera, the Panther, despite the fact that the latter were discovered by Mr. Kipling in the hoary jungles of India. And surely Uncle Remus is akin to Mowgli. Like the foundling of the Seeonee Wolf Pack, Uncle Remus knows the master words of the beasts in his domain."[14] Despite such praise, Harris continually wondered if Uncle Remus did not exist whether he would still be taken seriously as a writer.

Harris's first literary work of the decade was the collection *Balaam and His Master, and Other Sketches and Stories* (1891), consisting of "Balaam," the story of a man consumed by gambling, first published in the February 1891 issue of *Century*; "A Conscript's Christmas," the problems of the draft, first published in the December 1890 issue of *Century*; "Ananias," a Reconstruction story, first published in the April 1888 issue of *Harper's Monthly*; "Where's Duncan?" a psychological profile of a

Line illustration by A. B. Frost, 1895

"mixed-blood" woman, previously unpublished; and "The Old Bascomb Place," about the conflict between "Old South" and the emerging "New South" after the Civil War, first published in the August 1889 issue of *Century*.

At the beginning of the decade, largely because of his Uncle Remus tales and a few of his short stories—among them "Free Joe," "Mingo," "At Teague Poteet's," and "Little Compton"—*The Critic* declared Harris was among the top ten "literary immortals."[15] A review in the 15 November 1883, issue of the *Nation*, had suggested that Harris's "accurate and sympathetic observation, his poetic imagination, his strength and tenderness in character drawing, a certain dramatic instinct...show that he may yet make a name in fiction as in folk-lore."[16] But, it was not to happen.

During the 1890s, Harris's fears, inherent in most good writers, enveloped him. He questioned if his writing was really good or merely just popular; with each succeeding editorial, essay, short story, or tale, he became more concerned he would never be able to match his previous efforts; he wondered just when the public would finally detect him to be a "fraud." He constantly needed the reinforcement other journalists could provide to him, assurances that he was a good writer, assistance to make him even better. He knew he could write quickly and ably under deadline pressure, something many writers are unable to do, but he continually questioned the quality of every tale he wrote. A letter he wrote to Edward L. Burlingame, editor of *Scribner's Magazine*, reveals Harris's fears and how they even influenced his decisions:

> The main reason I send most of my available stuff to "Scribner's" is due to the fact that your letters, now and again, seem to breathe a note of appreciation. And though I am old enough to know that such an

expression belongs to the art of editing, and is prompted by a sense of sympathy with a poor provincial, who,
though he has no time to do his best, is doing the best
he can—though I am old enough to know this, yet I
am not too old to feel the need of the encouragement
that frequently takes shape even in your briefest
notes.[17]

Publishers had to constantly explain to Harris that he
was a good writer, that his views were substantial and
important. "We had confidence in Harris," wrote Robert
Underwood Johnson in his memoirs, "and—perceiving
that he had little in himself—we expressed it."[18] But no
matter how much assurance he received, every review,
even those praising him, left him still doubting his own
talent.

To add to his torment, the reviewers, while praising
his folklore stories, were often unkind to his novels, especially the ones that were semi-autobiographical. All good
writers thread their own experiences through their works,
exaggerating, embellishing, modifying, or even diminish-
ing some of the realities to bring stronger characterization
and an exciting plot to their readers. The fiction they
produce is often a catharsis of what they hoped might
have happened. It was no different with Joel Chandler
Harris, whose writings all had the unmistakable shade of
reality. In 1891, Samuel S. McClure paid Harris $2,500
for newspaper syndication rights to *On the Plantation,*
which would become the first of three lightly-disguised
autobiographical novels. The following year, the same
year that Houghton, Mifflin published *Uncle Remus and
His Friends,* D. Appleton Co., which had published the
first Uncle Remus book in 1880, published *On the
Plantation* in book form, forcing Harris to accept E. W.
Kemble as the artist. "For a man who has no conception
whatever of human nature," Harris wrote to A. B. Frost,

"Kemble does very well."[19] D. Appleton, which had disregarded Harris's wishes as to whom should illustrate the book, paid Harris $2,300 for the text, at that time a relatively high advance against royalties.[20]

Harris dedicated *On the Plantation* to Joseph Addison Turner, and created twelve-year-old Joe Maxwell as a substitute for twelve-year-old Joe Harris to tell about his life on a Southern plantation during the Civil War. The war would be only an undercurrent to the novel. As with his other stories, Harris concentrated upon character development, in this instance of a young boy and the people who had helped bring him into adolescence. The novel shows Harris's sympathy for the plantation slave and, contrary to a number of later critics' accusations, his understanding of the problems of slavery. Present throughout the novel are Joseph Addison Turner, his children, the plantation slaves, and both Confederates and Yankees; mentioned only in passing was Harris's mother. The omission probably was deliberate, not because Harris was estranged from his mother but because he respected her far too much to say anything about her or her relationship with her son while she was alive.

The book is an illuminating look into Harris's life and literary career. Written almost three decades after the war, *On the Plantation* reflected not what existed but what Harris may have believed existed and what he may have wished were true. In 1862, Yankees destroyed most of the buildings on Turnwold; in the novel, however, a kindly Yankee officer stops a brutal German mercenary, probably a Pennsylvania-Dutch soldier, from vandalizing the hat factory. The novel, which accented Harris's hope of a national reconciliation, in which all people contribute to society and no one hates anyone else, was truly a "curiously sanitized depiction of the Confederate home front," according to historian John C. Inscoe.[21]

In a brief introduction, Harris explained the merger of history and fiction, challenging readers not to accept everything in the book as factual, but that even those incidents that did not occur may bear more truth than fiction:

> Some of my friends who have read in serial form the chronicles that follow profess to find in them something more than an autobiographical touch. Be it so. It would indeed be difficult to invest the commonplace character and adventures of Joe Maxwell with the vitality that belongs to fiction. Nevertheless, the lad himself, and the events which are herein described, seem to have been born of a dream. That which is fiction pure and simple in those pages bears to me the stamp of truth, and that which is true reads like a clumsy invention. In this matter it is not for me to prompt the reader. He must sift the fact from the fiction and label it to suit himself.[22]

The last sentences of the novel underscored Harris's life and writings: "A larger world beckoned to Joe Maxwell, and he went out into it. And it came about that on every side he found loving hearts to comfort him and strong and friendly hands to guide him. He found new associations and formed new ties. In a humble way, he made a name for himself, but the old plantation days still live in his dreams."[23]

Literary critic William M. Baskervill pointed out that not only was *On the Plantation* "the best account" of Harris's early life, but that it was "a delightful volume [and] one of the more interesting books that Mr. Harris has written."[24]

"[T]hose who never tire of Uncle Remus and his stories—with whom we would be accounted—will delight in Joe Maxwell and his exploits,"[25] the *Saturday Review* stated in one of the book's first reviews. The *Boston Daily*

Preliminary Pencil Sketch, "Money Mint," by A. B. Frost

Advertiser called the book "fascinating," noting it was "full of interest and will not fail to add to the reputation of the author."[26] *The Chataquan*, one of the nation's more influential journals, declared it to be "one of the most charming books imaginable … It is bright, fresh, and radiant with its own peculiar humor."[27] The *Book Buyer* noted "the most entertaining pages…are those devoted to the episodical legends of the old negroes, in the 'Uncle Remus' vein to which the author's fine literary instinct and exquisite sense of humor give much value."[28] The *Critic* called Harris "an epic story teller," stated that the chapter, "Tracking a Runaway," is "a marvelous piece of word-painting, rivalled only by 'A Georgia Fox-Hunt,'" and noted that Harris "reproduces the sentiment of the plantation very perfectly, and recalls it from the dead in a way that makes it live again."[29] The book had crossed the lines between adult and children's literature. The *Chataqua Independent* reported that "grown folk as well as boys may read it with delight."[30] The influential *A Mother's List of Books for Children* (1909) listed three of Harris's books—*Uncle Remus, His Songs and Sayings*; *Nights With Uncle Remus*; and *On the Plantation*. Even nine decades after the book's publication, critics praised Harris's fictionalized autobiography. In the foreword to a reprint edition, novelist Erskine Caldwell noted that not only is it an "interesting and eloquent story," but "has succeeded in surviving the ravages of time."[31]

Sister Jane: Her Friends and Acquaintances (1896), the second of his autobiographical trilogy, was an historical romance that a century later could have been the basis for many television soap operas. The story involved innumerable kinds of love affairs, underscored by infidelity, unrequited love, and characters who exerted control over other people's lives. But most of all, it was a plea for tolerance and compassion. To narrate the story, Harris developed William Wornum, originally a minor character in *The Romance of Rockville*. But, Wornum also had innumerable parallels to Harris's own life and character traits.

Harris folded characteristics of his mother into both Wornum's sister, Jane—"the only mother I had ever known"—and Mandy Satterlee, the central character of the novel, a single mother whose child was born in 1848. Only after his own mother had died could Harris have written Mandy's story. Harris believed the novel was one of his lesser works, and even tried to pull it from publication, possibly because he realized how closely it paralleled the lives of his mother and family, but equally probable because he was sensitive to the comments and editorial "suggestions" from Houghton, Mifflin, that requested rewrites. It never took much to make Harris doubt the quality of his own writing. "I cannot image how I could ever have made the mistake of sending it to you in the first place," Harris wrote to editor Francis J. Garrison, indicating, "If I had the money to pay you for the trouble and expense it has already cost you, I'd recall the stuff and burn it."[32]

Walter Hines Page, at that time editor of the prestigious *Atlantic Monthly*, tried to reassure Harris:

> Early one Sunday morning I took [the manuscript of] Sister Jane out into the Boston Common, and there she proceeded to unfold herself. Except Uncle Remus himself, no Southern characters have walked from life into a book quite so naturally or unblurred, it seems to me, as William Wornum, Sister Jane, and the two old fellows from the country. In answer to your question which you asked me some time ago, namely, What is the matter with the book? let me say that it needs to be put in type and printed.[33]

Despite Page's confidence, *Sister Jane* was published to mixed, occasionally highly derogatory reviews, many of which questioned Harris's ability as a novelist. The *San Francisco Chronicle* called it a "close and loving study";[34] *The Critic* praised Harris for his careful portrayal of the lower-class White culture; and the *Chicago Tribune* believed the book "will raise [Harris] still higher in the estimation of critics and establish him yet more firmly in the hearts of the people."[35] However, the *New York Daily Tribune* called it "a dull book" that is "an amorphous production through which pale, soulless, bodiless personages ramble with scarcely a glimmer of vitality among them all";[36] *Nation*, which praised the Uncle Remus stories, called it "flawed"; and *The New York Times* proclaimed that as good a short story writer as Harris was, he should not have attempted a novel. Wounded by the criticism, Harris returned to collections of short fiction. Nevertheless, largely upon Harris's reputation, the public quickly bought more than 3,000 copies, making it one of the year's more popular books. Total sales, however, were only 6,458 in eight printings,[37] with only eighty-three copies sold during 1900 to 1902.[38]

Contemporary literary critics have also attacked Harris for being "occasionally poignant but rarely profound."[39] Yet as a journalist Harris did not intrude upon the lives of the people he observed and created. His novels, like those written by most journalists, were a series of stories and character sketches, tied together by underlying themes. Briefly reviewing another writer's book, Harris wrote to James Whitcomb Riley, "I find in his work the very kind of weakness that is all through mine—the subordination of the story itself to the characters."[40] Paul M. Cousins, in explaining Harris's strengths as a writer, also explained a little about the nature of the better writers who were also journalists:

> Harris worked on a principle that realistic character delineation in a story was more important than the

167

'Distorted Words
and Illiterate
Grammar'

contrived manipulation of events for the sake of dramatic climax. Consequently, he envisioned his characters clearly, endowed them with life, and rarely ever struck a false note, but he found it difficult to tie together the various strands of a plot in a long story in which there were many characters involved in many incidents.[41]

In contrast, he often left entire sections of plots sketchy, as if he expected the reader to fill in the holes, perhaps overwhelmed by the marathon that becomes a novel. Harris realized his literary strengths were the tales and short stories, which he could adapt to a novel format, but he still believed he needed to write the "classic" novel.

Some critics often claimed that Harris's tragic literary flaw was that he did not revise his writing before sending it to press. Like most journalists, however, Harris made innumerable corrections onto the current draft, sometimes rewrote onto a clean sheet, then, like most newspaper journalists, wadded up and discarded the pages of the previous draft to make sure there would not be any confusion as to which draft was current. Although he kept rough drafts of some of his works, most were thrown out. As a result, it is impossible to determine how many drafts of a story Harris wrote. The demands of journalism, though, made Harris a "fast write" who could often formulate the story in reasonable final draft on paper with minimal need of revision—or, as he had learned while sneaking paragraphs into *The Countryman*—sometimes at the type case with no prior draft. In an autobiographical sketch for *Lippincott's Monthly*, Harris answered his critics: "I am a journalist and nothing else. I have no literary training, and know nothing at all of what is termed literary art. I have had no opportunity to nourish any serious literary ambition, and the probability is that if such an opportunity had presented itself I would have refused to take advantage of it."[42]

More than four decades after first setting type on Turnwold, Harris was still the journalist, observing people and society and trying to get a mass audience to better understand their own lives. Just as he used Uncle Remus to tell stories to the Little Boy on the plantation, he now used Aunt Minervy Ann Perdue, a Black cook—partially based upon both Aunt Betsy Evans from Turnwold, and Chloe, a Black "milker" and cook at Harris's home during the 1890s—to tell stories to a thinly-disguised Atlanta newspaper reporter about Black life and human emotions in the years following the Civil War. Harris's new Black character, a forceful, intelligent woman, had first appeared in seven short stories published in *Scribner's Magazine* during 1899. Like Harris and Uncle Remus, she despised the radical Republicans, and worked to "reform" the state's Republican legislature which included her weak husband, Hamp, whom Minervy Ann believed was being used by the carpet-baggers.

For the illustrations, Harris wanted A. B. Frost, "the only artist that understands American character sufficiently well to be able to represent it perfectly in black and white."[43] By the late 1890s, Harris himself had improved his writing and insight into character so that Aunt Minervy Ann Perdue was far more complicated and complex than most of his previous characters, including Uncle Remus.

Harris also wove into his stories a cross-section of Reconstruction humanity, including former plantation aristocrats, lower- and middle-class Whites, and innumerable variations of emancipated slaves. Harris rewrote the seven previously-published tales, then added another for *The Chronicles of Aunt Minervy Ann*, published as a book by Charles Scribner's Sons at the end of the year.

The reviews for the *Chronicles* were more complimentary than for previous novels, but sales were only about 3,000.[44] The *Independent* praised the novel as "strong, peculiar, full of charming genius," and pointed out that the title character was one "to be framed in the reader's memory. Once known she will never be forgotten."[45] Three weeks later, the mass circulation magazine declared it one of the year's best books, an opinion echoed by most of the literary reviews. "All that is best and worst in the negro character, all that the South knows so well and that the North does not know at all, may be studied to advantage in this vivacious narrative," wrote Agnes Repplier in the 30 September 1899 issue of the *Saturday Evening Post*. The *New Orleans Daily Picayune* of 12 November called it a book "of great strength, power and true genius." The *New York Times* reviewer said the book "is a fit companion to Uncle Remus," and pointed out that *Aunt Minervy* is "line for line, an accurate picture of the defeated but unbroken people of the South and the conditions they had to face during that dark time of reconstruction. The wonderful humor of the book saves it from tragedy.... It is a smile that is very close to tears, for [Aunt Minervy's] artless narrative is full of the pathos of the time." [46]

During the 1890s, while searching to expand his literary range, yet a little afraid to experiment too much, Harris modified the Uncle Remus-Little Boy tales. Instead of the Little Boy, he created seven-year-old Sweetest Susan and eight-year-old Buster John; instead of Remus himself, he had Drusilla, a twelve-year-old Black nanny "who was their playmate—their companion, and a capital one she made."[47] The Sweetest Susan/Buster John stories appeared in six books. In an era of emerging children's fiction, partially ushered in by Harris himself with the publication of the first Uncle

Illustration of "Uncle Remus and The Litte Boy," by A. B. Frost.

Pen-and-ink illustration by A. B. Frost

Remus book, he became one of the most popular writers of books that did not have Blacks as central characters.

If the critics were sometimes unkind toward his later work, especially some of his children's stories, the children themselves loved the tales. Children, wrote Harris, are "persistently misunderstood, misinterpreted, and driven back upon themselves" by adults.[48] "I get down to their level, think with them and play with them. I was a child in feeling when I began to write for other children, and haven't grown up yet," Harris told *Boston Daily Globe* reporter James B. Morrow. He explained that it may not have been his innate shyness nor his life-long stammer that led him not to tell his stories to the children. "I don't even read or tell stories to the children whom I know," said Harris. "I might not be afraid of them, but don't you see they would begin to look up to me, and instead of being their playmate I should be an old man."[49]

Little Mr. Thimblefinger and His Queer Country (1894)—a series of stories featuring Drusilla and the two White children who are led by a four-inch tall man into a magical world beneath a spring where they meet a human-sized Miss Meadows and Mr. Rabbit—was a critical failure but a commercial success, with sales of more than 20,000 copies in twenty-five printings.[50] The theme of the sequel, *Mr. Rabbit at Home* (1895)—which sold more than 14,000 copies in twenty printings[51]—was a storyteller contest that threaded its way through the twenty-four tales, fifteen of which had first appeared in the *Constitution* between 2 December 1894 and 10 March 1895.

In many of his books, Harris found ways not only to tease the reader with "inside information," but also poked fun at himself. In *Little Mr. Thimblefinger and His Queer Country*, not only does Harris introduce Mr. Thimblefinger to the startled children as "the queerest little man they had ever seen or even heard of except in make-believe story-books," he had Mr. Rabbit mistake Drusilla for a tar-baby. In the sequel, he had the rabbit, who complained about how dull the stories were that Mr. Thimblefinger told, arguing about how best to tell a story; the scene foreshadowed not only Harris's complaints about the "scientific" value of folklore, which would be more fully developed in *Wally Wanderoon*, but possibly explained Harris's own belief that the stories he mined were drying up.[52]

During the latter part of his life, Harris created numerous White characters as foils, usually discarding them after a couple of appearances when they failed to develop the presence of an Uncle Remus. At the beginning of a new century, he would find his perfect stand-in. To his cast of White characters, Harris now added Billy Sanders, an old but peppery street-corner "philosopher of Shady Dale," to criticize the trusts and greed. Billy Sanders first appeared in "The Kidnapping of President Lincoln," a four-part story in the June 1900 issues of *The Saturday Evening Post*, then republished in the collection *On the Wing of Occasions* (1900), a collection of five stories about Confederate spies. Suggested by an actual plot in 1864, "The Kidnapping of President Lincoln" cast the president and Sanders, an Army private from Middle Georgia, in the same room during the Civil War. At Lincoln's invitation, Sanders was supposed to escort a Confederate spy to the South, but the Confederacy set up a ruse to have him kidnap the president. However, the plot fails when Sanders and his accomplice become enamored with Lincoln's wit and humanity. George Lorimer, editor of the mass circulation *Saturday Evening Post*, one of the nation's largest circulation magazines, told Harris that his story "is the best story that has ever come into this office, and one of the best I have ever read. The picture of Mr. Lincoln and the old spy is simply perfect.... It is a rattling story and a splendid piece of work, and no editor has any business fooling with it or making changes."[53]

Like Harris's other writings, both on the *Constitution*'s editorial pages and in magazine fiction, it was a plea for understanding, compassion, and sectional tolerance. Theodore Roosevelt, a social reformer whose presidential administration paralleled the muckraking era, appreciated Billy Sanders' attacks against the trusts and corruption. But, he also appreciated Harris's campaign to end sectional hatreds. Shortly after becoming president in 1901, Roosevelt wrote to Harris:

> ...I have felt that all that you write serves to bring our people closer together. I know of course the ordinary talk is that an artist should be judged purely by his art; but I am rather a Philistine and like to feel that the art serves a good purpose. Your art is not only...an addition to our sum of national achievement, but it has also always been an addition to the forces that tell for decency, and above all for the blotting out of sectional antagonism.[54]

By the end of the decade of the 1890s, Joel Chandler Harris had written only a scattering of dialect tales, but he had also written four books of local color stories, three novels, a book of sketches of Georgia history, six children's books—and a book-length translation, assisted by Essie Harris, from the French folktales of Count Ortoli. *Qua: A Romance of the Revolution*, based upon the true story of an African prince who was made a slave during the American Revolution, was unfinished; a play in two acts, *Herndon Wood: A Plantation Comedy*, possibly written in the late 1880s or early 1890s and reflecting events in 1869 Georgia, was unproduced. Although sensitive to criticism, Harris still wrote what he wanted to write, bringing forth issues he wanted the people to know.

[1] Thomas Nelson Page, "Immortal Uncle Remus," 644.

[2] James Whitcomb Riley, "Dialect," *Forum* (December 1893): 466.

[3] Joel Chandler Harris, *Uncle Remus and His Friends*, viii-ix.

[4] Joel Chandler Harris, *Uncle Remus and His Friends*, x-xi.

[5] See Walter M. Brasch, *A ZIM Self-Portrait* (1990).

[6] R. Bruce Bickley, Jr., *Joel Chandler Harris*, 87.

[7] William Bradley Strickland, *Joel Chandler Harris: A Bibliographic Study*, 65.

[8] Julia Collier Harris, *The Life and Letters of Joel Chandler Harris*, 340 [Virginia].

[9] Letter from Joel Chandler Harris to Richard Watson Gilder, 26 May 1887. [Virginia.]

[10] Letter from A. B. Frost to Miss Jamison, 11 December 1927.

[11] Joel Chandler Harris, "Introduction," A. B. Frost, *Book of Drawings*, ix, v, vi.

[12] Thomas Nelson Page, *Book Buyer* (December 1895): 645.

[13] Review, *New York Times*, October 10, 1895, 16.

[14] "Seven Fanciful Christmas Books Dedicated to Young Readers," *Chicago Tribune*, 29 November 1896, 43.

[15] "Nine New 'Immortals,'" *The Critic*, 19 July 1890, 33.

[16] Review, *The Nation*, 16 November 1883, 422.

[17] Letter from Joel Chandler Harris to Edward L. Burlingame, 4 November 1898.

[18] Robert Underwood Johnson, *Remembered Yesterdays*, 378.

[19] Letter from Joel Chandler Harris to A. B. Frost, 7 June 1892.

[20] Letter from D. Appleton & Co. to Joel Chandler Harris, 19 May 1891. *The Romance of Rockville*, a serialized novel published by the *Constitution* in 1878 was Harris's first novel. However, it was not published in book form. Thus, *On the Plantation* is considered to be Harris's first published novel. *On the Plantation*, with an introduction by Erskine Caldwell, was reprinted in 1980 by the University of Georgia Press, and in 1997 by Sergeant Kirkland's Museum Press of Fredericksburg, Virginia.

[21] John C. Inscoe, "The Confederate Home Front Sanitized...," 654.

[22] Joel Chandler Harris, *On the Plantation*, vii.

[23] Joel Chandler Harris, *On the Plantation*, 233.

[24] W. M. Baskerville [sic], "Joel Chandler Harris," 62.

[25] "New Books and Reprints," *Saturday Review*, 2 April 1892, 403.

[26] "Books and Authors," *Boston Daily Advertiser*, 5 July 1892, 5

[27] "Stories and Other Books," *The Chataquan*, 15 June 1892, 387.

[28] "Novels and Short Stories," *The Book Buyer*, June 1892, 212.

[29] "On the Plantation," *The Critic*, 6 August 1892, 65.

[30] Review, *Chataqua Independent*, 12 May 1892, 664.

[31] Erskine Caldwell, Foreword, *On the Plantation*, 1980 reprint, xi

[32] Letter from Joel Chandler Harris to Francis J. Garrison, quoted in Paul M. Cousins, *Joel Chandler Harris*, 168.

[33] Letter from Walter Hines Page to Joel Chandler Harris, 3 August 1896.

[34] Review, *San Francisco Chronicle*, 13 December 1896, 4.

[35] "Uncle Remus's White Sister," *Chicago Tribune*, 5 December 1896, 10.

[36] Review, *New York Daily Tribune*, 20 December 1896, 2

[37] William Bradley Strickland, *Joel Chandler Harris: A Bibliographic Study*, 84.

[38] Letter from Houghton, Mifflin & Co. to Joel Chandler Harris, 18 March 1902.

[39] R. Bruce Bickley, Jr., "Joel Chandler Harris," 191.

[40] Letter from Joel Chandler Harris to James Whitcomb Riley, 30 September 1901. Quoted in Julia Collier Harris, *The Life and Letters of Joel Chandler Harris*, 460.

[41] Paul M. Cousins, *Joel Chandler Harris*, 139.

[42] Joel Chandler Harris, "An Accidental Author," 420.

[43] Letter from Joel Chandler Harris to Edward Burlingame, 10 February 1898.

[44] William Bradley Strickland, *Joel Chandler Harris: A Bibliographic Study*, 92.

[45] Review, *The Independent*, 2 November 1899, 2964.

[46] "New and Notable Fiction," *New York Times*, 14 October 1899, 701.

[47] Joel Chandler Harris, *Little Mr. Thimblefinger and His Queer Country*, 6

[48] Joel Chandler Harris, "Little Children on the Snap-Bean Farm," 5.

[49] James B. Morrow, "Joel Chandler Harris Talks of Himself and Uncle Remus," 5-6.

[50] William Bradley Strickland, *Joel Chandler Harris: A Bibliographic Study*, 69. The 1923 edition went through six printings of 75,000 copies.

[51] William Bradley Strickland, *Joel Chandler Harris: A Bibliographic Study*, 72.

52 See Hugh Keenan, "Joel Chandler Harris," in volume 42 of *Directory of Literary Biography*, 232.

53 Letter from George Lorimer to Joel Chandler Harris. Quoted in Julia Collier Harris, *The Life and Letters of Joel Chandler Harris*, 429.

54 Letter from Theodore Roosevelt to Joel Chandler Harris, 12 October 1901.

A. B. Frost:

Joel Chandler Harris, about 1897

Chapter 9

'The Other Fellow'

Like many writers, Joel Chandler Harris believed he was two selves. One was the journalist; the other was the creative writer of short fiction. Both, Harris believed, were separate personalities. In an especially illuminating letter to John Henderson Garnsey about a year after the publication of *Sister Jane: Her Friends and Acquaintances*, Harris brought forth a reality of the journalist as fiction writer:

> "Sister Jane" is still selling, but Lord! it's poor stuff. No doubt that's because the brother [William Wornum] represents my inner—my inner—oh, well! my inner spezerinktum; I can't think of another word. It isn't "self" and it isn't—oh, yes! it's the other fellow inside of me, the fellow who does all my literary work while I get the reputation, being really nothing but a cornfield journalist…And that's the trouble. I wish I could trot the other fellow out when company comes. But the cornfield journalist pursues me and stays on top.[1]

In one of his innumerable letters to his children, Harris elaborated upon the "other fellow," emphasizing not only his dual personality, but also the nature of the creative process of writing:

> I never have anything but the vaguest ideas of what I am going to write, but when I take my pen in my hand,[2] the rust clears away and the "other fellow" takes charge. He is simply a spectator of my folly until I seize a pen, and then he comes

forward and takes charge. Sometimes I laugh heartily at what he writes. If you could see me at such times, and they are very frequent, you would no doubt say, "It is very conceited in that old man to laugh at his own writing." But that is the very point; it is not my writing at all; it is my "other fellow" doing the work, and I am getting all the credit for it. Now I'll admit that I write the editorials for the paper. The "other fellow" has nothing to do with them, and, so far as I am able to get his views on the subject, he regards them with scorn and contempt; though there are rare occasions when he helps me out on a Sunday editorial. He is a creature hard to understand, but, so far as I can understand him, he's a very sour, surly fellow until I give him an opportunity to guide my pen in subjects congenial to him; whereas, I am, as you know, jolly, good-natured, and entirely harmless. Now, my "other fellow," I am convinced, would do some damage if I didn't give him an opportunity to work off his energy in the way he delights. I say to him, "Now, here's an editor who says he will pay well for a short story. He wants it at once." Then I forget all about the matter, and go on writing editorials…. [P]resently my "other fellow" says sourly: "What about that story?" Then, when night comes, I take up my pen, surrender unconditionally to my "other fellow," and out comes the story, and if it is a good story I am as much surprised as the people who read it.—Now, my dear gals will think I am writing nonsense but I am telling them the truth as near as I can get at the facts—for the "other fellow" is secretive. [3]

The "other fellow's" secretive nature may have been the persona Harris needed to distinguish the shy and reclusive writer of tales who avoided public readings from the more outgoing energetic journalist, the one who chatted with mulecar riders and often took the reins on the way home. Harris, as the literary writer, would use the phrase "scorn and contempt" several times in discussions or interviews about his newspaper career; but the journalist Harris, no matter what he said, still loved the profession and his life as a journalist.

As a journalist writing editorials and essays, Harris maintained a slight detachment to his story; as a journalist writing fiction, however, he was absorbed by the characters and stories. Ray Stannard Baker, one of the nation's leading investigative journalists during the muckraking era, observed that Harris's characters "all became extraordinarily real to him so that he carries on conversations with them as though they were living persons. And they keep clamoring for recognition with him."[4]

The journalist Joe Harris, said Walter Hines Page:

> ...does not appreciate Mr. Joel Chandler Harris. From merely looking at him one must be pardoned for fearing that he could not keenly appreciate anything. A little man...with red, unkempt hair, a fiery half-vicious mustache, a freckled face and freckled hands; and there is nothing striking about him—what strange habitations does genius choose among men! His eyes are all that belong to Mr. Joel C. Harris; all other things, hair, complexion, hands, chin, manner, and clothes are the property of Joe Harris.[5]

At the newspaper, Joe Harris often dressed in baggy, ill-fitting clothes; at other times, especially when he was supposed to be Joel Chandler Harris, he was impeccably dressed. It might seem as if Harris had a dual personality, or a psychological problem in dealing with two different kinds of writing. However, journalists who also write fiction often became two writers, with the fiction writer often taking on the personality and moods of the characters they create before the characters develop their own

lives and take over the story. Less than a decade after Harris told his children about the "other fellow," Konstantin Stanislavsky, who probably never read any of the Uncle Remus stories, began to develop "method acting," in which the actors draw upon their own emotions and experiences to enter the thoughts and feelings of the characters they portray as they search the subtext of the dialogue, essentially becoming that character. Underlying Harris's two selves was the soul of the journalist, and there was little question that it was a journalist who was telling the stories.

During the 1890s, Harris attended the morning editorial meetings at the *Constitution* but returned to the Wren's Nest before noon. Part of his reason for leaving after the morning meetings was to write and to be with his family; part of the reason for being at the *Constitution* only in the morning was to escape the steady influx of readers who dropped by just to say "howdy" to Uncle Remus's creator.

Over the course of that decade, Harris wrote about 3,000 articles and editorials during the day, and twelve books at night. His books were issued by the nation's leading publishers. His newspaper stories were simultaneously published in a mini-syndicate consisting of the *Atlanta Constitution*, *Boston Daily Globe*, *Chicago Inter-Ocean*, *Louisville Courier-Journal*, *New Orleans Times-Democrat*, *New York Sun*, *Philadelphia Times*, *St. Louis Republic*, *San Francisco Examiner*, and *Washington Evening Star*. He led a fight to secure an international copyright law, partly because of his disgust at the proliferation of pirated editions of his own books. Long before William Jennings Bryan crusaded against the gold standard, Harris threw his newspaper's support behind the "free silver" issue, arguing that using only one precious metal as the nation's financial standard benefitted "Big Business" more than the working person. But no issue

The senior editorial staff of the Constitution during the 1890s included Clark Howell Jr., managing editor; Joel Chandler Harris, associate editor (seated); and (standing, left to right) Wallace P. Reed, editorial writer; J. K. Ohl, city editor; and Frank L. Stanton, special writer. On the desk is a photo of Henry W. Grady. Every editor of the Constitution, including Harris and Grady, used the desk between 1880 and 1989.

was as constant throughout his career as his campaigns to end sectional and racial hatreds.

As a journalist, Harris was capable of producing both high quantity and high quality output against deadline pressures. But balancing two successful careers left him not only emotionally exhausted from the researching, writing, reading of galleys and page proofs, and myriad business details associated with writing but also susceptible to innumerable illnesses. "I am lying—or, rather I am telling the truth—flat o' my back at home where I have been for three weeks, the result of pleurisy and overwork on the paper," he wrote to Richard Watson Gilder in September 1886. He was tired, but he continued to combine two jobs. Later that month, Harris finally took a vacation. "The mountain air has revived me, and I have returned to work much improved," he wrote Gilder. He said he even planned to take more vacations: "My experience has taught me that it is best to take a vacation every year—a fact that I have ignored heretofore. Next summer I am going to start early and stay late if the Lord spares me."[6]

But unlike his family, Harris did not take many long vacations. He believed he was trapped in newspaper journalism and needed to keep working his two full-time jobs, perhaps believing that if he could devote his life to his literary writings he might be free. As early as 1882, he had written Mark Twain that he had hoped that the proposed lecture tour worked out so he could "drop this grinding newspaper business and write some books I have in mind."[7]

Four years later, Harris complained to Gilder, "For several months I have been suffering with fatty degeneration of the mind—and local politics… The newspaper grind has been harder than ever, owing to various circumstances."[8] Some of these circumstances surrounded his research and writing of editorials about the state and congressional elections. A slightly sarcastic reply to novelist Ambrose Bierce who, in an article in the *New York Journal* had attacked Harris's writing, reveals not only Harris's fragile sensitivity, but also his insecurity, his desperation to be liked, and his humble view of his own writing:

> I should like very much to know in what way I have unfortunately won your dislike. Perhaps I am wrong in interpreting the statement as personal dislike. Perhaps your dislike applies only to the stuff that has been put in books bearing my name. Such a feeling would be natural enough in a man possessing, as you do both literary art and culture, as well as the gift of style (if it is a gift), and I should be the last to feel or express surprise; but it worries me to have your dislike of my stuff extended to me. The excuse for what I have written lies in the fact that, poor as it is, it is the best I could do. Some of us, you know, are compelled to stay very close to the ground so that when we fall few bones shall be broken....
>
> I am simply a cornfield "journalist," and have never held any higher position, even in that field, than that of writer of political editorials. For twenty years this has been my trade, and has left me small opportunity—none, in fact—to even attempt *literary* work. Even the Remus business is not my own, but is composed of stories originally told to me by negroes....
>
> Dislike my cornfield trash as much as you please, but don't worry me with the suspicion that you dislike me personally. If you knew me, I rather think you'd like me. I'm a great deal less harmless than the stuff I put in books.[9]

It was a thread that underscored not only his life but that of the lives of most journalists, no matter what they choose as their primary medium. They believe they are condemned to sit in the balcony of the literary world, looking at everything, but not allowed the respect of those sitting in the orchestra seats; they accept, even if reluctantly, the public's belief that the ephemera of newsprint is tangential to the esteem American society gives bound volumes of flat sheets. They complain about never-ceasing deadlines, incompetent managers, pettiness and jealousies among the staff, and innumerable unnecessary problems thrust upon them by politicians, businessmen, and the public who never understand the difficulties inherent in their profession. But they are driven to dig for facts and try to uncover truth, their intellectual curiosity fueled by the challenge.

Although magazine stories and books provided a substantial income for Harris, he stayed at the *Constitution*, even refusing a guaranteed annual income from Century in 1885 for his magazine articles and books because the contract also required him to cease regular employment on the newspaper. Perhaps his refusal was because he did not believe his family could survive on the $2,500 a year guarantee from Century, although it was significantly higher than the median family income of the country. The regular paycheck from the *Constitution* provided the base of his living, while the additional income from freelancing helped pay for the extended comfort of his family upon whom he placed almost no spending restrictions. Julia Collier Harris believes her father-in-law rejected the offer because of "his abnormal lack of confidence in himself as a 'literary man.'"[10] All of those reasons may have been part of why Harris refused to leave newspaper journalism. More probably, he rejected the offer because his professional life centered around the companionship and intellectual stimulation of fellow journalists. To give that up, to *not* be a part of the daily news-rush and the knowledge of what was happening throughout the country, would be to abandon the place he was most comfortable outside of his own home. But gnawing at him was his desire to be recognized as a novelist, like Oliver Goldsmith whose work first inspired him, or Alexandre Dumas's *The Count of Monte Christo* (1845), which he believed was the most entertaining adventure novel, or Charles Dickens's *A Tale of Two Cities* (1859), which he said was one of literature's best social issues novels,[11] or the dozens of authors of classics he had read while at Turnwold.

"The Farmer is not a great reader" of contemporary literature, Harris once wrote, explaining that "the things that are old in literature, the books on which several generations have left their stamp of approval, are sufficient for him, though he is not adverse to reading a rattling modern story, as full of the sensational as it can be packed."[12] He liked reading the works of George Eliot, Henry James, Rudyard Kipling, and Mark Twain. Yet, by the end of the nineteenth century, he had recognized that he would not be the novelist he had hoped to become. "I can't write a long story," Harris wrote to his daughter, Lillian, in 1896. "I put all my strength in the episodes and leave the thread of the main story hanging at loose ends."[13]

By the end of the nineteenth century, journalists realized they could go beyond newspapers into magazines, then entering their popular stage, or use books as a medium for expression. In mid-November 1893, responding to a suggestion of *Scribner's* editor Edward L. Burlingame, Harris took a brief leave as the *Constitution*'s chief editorial writer to become a news reporter, covering the aftermath of a devastating 125-mile an hour hurricane in October that had hit the Sea Islands off the South Carolina and Georgia coasts, home of the Gullah Blacks, home of the fictionalized Daddy Jack. The hurricane and subsequent flooding killed almost 2,000, left about 30,000 homeless, and scuttled almost 400 small

vessels. Harris's stories, including eyewitness accounts of the Gullah Blacks, appeared in *Scribner's* February and March 1894 issues. Magazine journalism appealed to Harris: "I wish I was out of the newspaper business so I could devote my whole attention to stories and magazine work."[14] It would not happen for another seven years.

Although Harris probably did not recognize it at the time, a letter from Frank N. Doubleday, one of the nation's more prestigious publishers, may have been what began a one-year transition, ending with his retirement from daily newspaper journalism. In a letter of 28 December 1899, Doubleday proposed that Harris contact Houghton, Mifflin, Charles Scribner's Sons, and D. Appleton, publishers of his previous books, and secure their permission to allow Doubleday to reprint the books and issue them as a boxed set with a uniform binding to be sold by subscription at $20-$30 per set. Doubleday would give the other publishers a 7-1/2 percent royalty, but would make Harris a partner. "We would be willing to advance all the money necessary to do all this work, and to take the risk, and at the end give you half profits," Doubleday wrote.

In early 1900, Doubleday, McClure & Company dissolved. The result was the formation of McClure, Phillips & Company and Doubleday, Page & Company. Samuel S. McClure, editor of *McClure's* magazine, had already begun leading America into the muckraking era that would tear into political and corporate corruption and greed, social issues that had appealed to Harris's journalistic soul; Doubleday, Page would move more into developing a reputation for publishing high quality literary works. McClure took Booth Tarkington and the investigative journalists with him to the new company; Doubleday kept most of the other major literary authors, including Rudyard Kipling and Mark Twain; it would soon sign Arthur Conan Doyle, O. Henry, Joseph

Conrad, and Edwin Markham. The two companies over the next four years would compete for both Harris's fiction and non-fiction.

The opening salvo to get Harris to sign an exclusive contract was fired by Walter Hines Page upon the failure of D. Appleton & Company, publisher of Harris's first book. "I have a feeling that this old publishing house, in the difficulties and mismanagement with which it has struggled for a number of years, has not done everything for the book that should have been done," wrote Page. Page, who had been one of Harris's professional colleagues and friends almost two decades, knew well Harris's insecurities and need for praise, combined with his compulsive need to publish and earn money for his family. He fully intended to bring Harris and the Uncle Remus works into the new publishing house. Page suggested that because of the problems Appleton had during the previous decade, *Uncle Remus; His Songs and Sayings* "has not been made to reach that steadily large sale to which, of course, it is entitled." Praising Harris, he said, in all honesty: "If I had to select only one book of American production that has a closer title to immortality, I should take 'Uncle Remus' without a moment's hesitation. If I am right in this judgment, it is a book that a publisher ought to pay continual attention to and exhaust all his resources and ingenuity in furthering its sale."[15] However, Harris couldn't find the contract with D. Appleton. Disappointed, but not willing to give up, Page wrote back, "I take it for granted that some day when you least expect it, it will turn up somewhere in your house."[16]

In that same letter, Page acknowledged receiving Harris's approval for Doubleday, Page & Company to publish *On the Wing of Occasions*, a collection that included "The Kidnapping of President Lincoln," which was in the current issue of the *Saturday Evening Post*.

Four of the Harris family children, about 1891. Mildred and Joel Jr. (front row); Lillian and Evelyn (back row)

One reason Page became a partner with Doubleday was to fulfill his own hope to edit a major American magazine of social, political, and literary consequence. "We are going to have a magazine," Page wrote to Harris, 2 August 1900, "and if I do say it myself, a bully good one." He then pitched his friend—"Of course I cannot have a magazine without devilling [sic] you about it; and I cannot have a magazine such as I want without getting your help." How Harris could help was suggested by Henry Lanier, one of Doubleday, Page's officers, and son of poet Sidney Lanier. Relaying Lanier's idea, Page suggested:

> Take "Billy Sanders"; he is a genuine man, and he has his own point of view, and he has his own limited knowledge of things, and his absolutely unlimited imagination. Why not put into "Billy Sander's" [sic] mouth an explanation once a month of some great thing that is going on in the world about which he knows nothing, but about which he would be willing to take [talk] like a philosopher? I think that in this way you could find machinery for saying some of the best things that you or anybody else has said. [17]

The magazine became *World's Work*, which for more than three decades would be everything Page had wanted; Billy Sanders appeared in three of the first four issues, discussing business and political issues. Page paid Harris well; however, Harris soon moved Billy Sanders from *World's Work*, and into the manuscript of *Gabriel Tolliver*, which would become the last of his three autobiographical novels.

With assurances from the *Saturday Evening Post* and William Randolph Hearst's *New York Journal* to take his shorter fiction and essays, Harris retired from the *Constitution* on 6 September 1900 to become a full-time freelance writer. The day after Harris announced his retirement, the rival *Atlanta Journal* noted: "In the use of the powerful weapons of satire and ridicule he has few peers, but this power has never been abused by him or prostituted to rough and unkind service. In his writings, as in his life, Mr. Harris is a man whose genial spirit has made him beloved as much as his rare gifts have caused him to be admired." In a five paragraph summary, the *Constitution* informed its readers on 7 September that whenever they detect "a delicate vein of the human nature [they] may know that habit has forced the laborer [Harris] back into the field."

The day he read about Harris's retirement, an ecstatic Walter Hines Page wrote to his friend: "There can be no loss, of course, but gain in every way, except possibly, financial. Whatever we can do to make up the financial deficit—you may be sure that this publishing house has nothing before it that will give it so much pleasure as any task for you." After assuring Harris that advance orders for *On the Wings of Occasions* were "very promising," Page then renewed his pitch to have Doubleday, Page reprint the first Uncle Remus book : "I hope that your daily newspaper labor being ended you will be able to find your old contract with Appleton about the original "Uncle Remus." Send it to me if you can ever lay your hands upon it."[18]

The next day, Henry Lanier, reiterated Page's enthusiasm: "I hope you'll let me say personally that I am delighted to know the *Constitution* will no longer take up the time in which you ought to give to the stories and books."[19] In that letter, Lanier also mentioned that Doubleday, Page had just signed an agreement to publish *Everybody's* magazine, planned a 100,000 circulation run for the already-established weekly, and wanted Harris's writings. He urged Harris to come to New York City for a week at the publishing company's expense.

By now, it was obvious that not only was Doubleday, Page courting Harris, it had every intention of marrying him. But there was still D. Appleton & Company, which had just gone through a reorganization, had made it a priority to pay its authors, and was still selling 3,800-4,000 copies every year of *Uncle Remus: His Songs and Sayings*. Likewise, another publishing giant had been making plans to bring Harris into its literary harem. The socially shy Harris, who was seldom shy at knowing how to work with publishers to gain the best advantage for his works, wrote to Page:

> I have recently received an offer from a firm of publishers which interests me very much. They propse [sic] to handle all my stuff, and pay me a salary of $4,000 a year. They are to make such disposition of the output as will be to the mutual advantage of both parties, and they are to have the privilege of making the stuff into books, on which they pay the usual royalties. Should there be any surplus over and above the $4,000, after the stuff is disposed of, it is to be paid to me. I have not made up my mind in regard to this proposition, but it gets very close to me, as you may imagine. It would enable me to go right ahead with my work without regard to quenseconses, as Mr. Sanders would remark. I believe in my soul that if the chaps had said $4,500, I'd 'a' drapt right at his feet. Sech is life among the common people. Anyhow, I'll be in the throbbin' metropolis along about the23rd [sic] when I hope to fetch some more remarks from the hot an' heavin' bosom of our dear old friend Sanders, and then I'll find out what my market price is, and maybe get some stock issued on me, like the feller in a little tale I was readin' t'other day. It's a great scheme in a big an' growin' country like our'n.

Well, I jeef drapt in for to see how you-all was
gittin' along, an'pass the time of day. I reckon they aint
no need to tell you that I'm e'en about. [20]

Within two weeks, still in shock there was someone else,
Page took the hint for a $4,500 guarantee:

When you let drop the remark the other day in
your letter that you had an offer for $80. a week for
your whole literary product (and more, if it yielded
more—the $80. a week being a guarantee), we real-
ized how slow we are! For we wish you [to regard us]
as your publishers and as your friends wholly at your
service—for any arrangement that was businesslike,
that you would like best and that would bring the best
results to you. It is an advantage, if a publisher serves
you well, to keep him constantly employed, and to
keep your literary enterprises together. We have *On
the Wing of Occasions*; we have your promise of your
historical novel; we have Mr. Billy Sanders (the second installment has come) [for *World's Work*
magazine]; and we have in a way taken it for granted
that we were yourn and you were ourn. [21]

Well aware that although Harris retired from daily
newspaper journalism, he had not retired from journalism, Page sweetened the offer, asking Harris to become
editor of *Everybody's*. Page noted that although the magazine had published several outstanding writers, it was
still one of twenty-seven ten-cent monthlies "and it has
not had much to distinguish it hitherto from the rest,"
except for one thing—the magazine was secretly owned
by Philadelphia's retailing giant John Wanamaker who
was also the nation's largest book retailer. Wanamaker,
wrote Page, "had the trade and the money and the business organization; but he didn't have the editorial
equipment." *Everybody's*, with Harris as editor, "would

give it literary prominence over every other prominent magazine." Page, whose own contribution to Doubleday, Page was to bring editorial excellence to the company, wrote to Harris, "We can spend a sufficient sum on authors and artists to get the best." Knowing Harris hated to travel, Page said that the magazine could be edited from Atlanta, and Harris would not have to go to New York City except "when you feel disposed to do so." Page again begged Harris to come to New York City "before it gets cold. Come and spend a week with us—with me. We'll do our best to give you a bully good time."[22]

During the mid- and late-1890s, Harris and Sam McClure had developed a mutual respect, with McClure publishing a few of Harris's stories, and encouraging him in his book publishing. McClure, Phillips, now sensing it could sign Harris to an exclusive contract, matched the book offer, told Harris he could write "at his own pace,"[23] gave him assurance of publication in McClure's magazine, and sweetened the offer with a guarantee of newspaper syndication. On 1 November, at Harris's request, Walter Hines Page sent a preliminary agreement and reiterated the basic terms that guaranteed Harris forty dollars a week as non-resident editor of Everybody's, plus lucrative book and magazine terms. But such was not to be. Sometime during the next week, Harris signed with McClure, Phillips for an eighty dollars a week guarantee that included newspaper syndication and book publishing, but no responsibility as a magazine editor.

"I need not say that we (and I personally in particular) are heartily sorry to hear of your decision," Henry Lanier wrote to Harris, carefully reiterated that Harris had previously committed a book to Doubleday, Page—"We have been counting on this for so long that it would break all our hearts to think that it was going somewhere else!"—and asked Harris to consider sending short stories, to Everybody's.[24] As much as he personally liked and admired Frank N. Doubleday, Walter Hines Page, and Henry W. Lanier, he was committed to Samuel S. McClure and John S. Phillips. For almost three years, Phillips would continually keep Harris informed about manuscripts, production, and royalties. Harris had written at least one, often two, editorials a day, then another 500-1,000 words on unprinted newsprint at night at home. Now "retired," his production, now with a typewriter, would increase to about 2,000 words a day."[25]

Journalism, said Harris, speaking from the weariness of having spent almost four decades in the profession, "is a good deal like pourin' water in a sieve. It's the most thankless, perishable kind of head work, I reckon. I thought I couldn't quit, but I've never regretted quittin'. In fact, I haven't got over my surprise that I can feel so good out of the harness."[26] But, Harris could not just stay at home and write. Writers need the social, intellectual, and emotional stimulation of being with people, of seeing things, of getting ideas. As much as others believe writing is a "lonely life," as much as writers humbly say they are uncomfortable with strangers coming up to them in public, they truly enjoy meeting their readers, even if some hang on a little longer than comfortable. It was no different with Harris. Even after retirement from the *Constitution*, he took the street car to and from the *Constitution*, chatted with drivers and riders, and attended morning editorial meetings at the newspaper, enjoying the companionship of people he had worked with for two decades. No matter how much he moaned, the love of his calling had been so embedded within him that he continued to write editorials for the newspaper, and essays and features for magazines.

It was daily newspaper journalism that had provided the base for Harris's ability to write quickly and efficiently, to develop the skills he needed as a writer. His retirement from the *Constitution* merely meant that he traded expression in one medium of journalism for another. He recognized that his life was that of a journalist, possibly unable to realize that through that profession he contributed far more to others' understanding and enjoyment of life than he ever could as a novelist. Underlying Harris's fiction was still the journalist/narrator skillfully weaving a story. As Anthony Burgess seventy years later would say of Daniel Defoe, "[He] was our first great novelist because he was our first great journalist, and he was our first great journalist because he was born not into literature but into life."

Nevertheless, striving to be a "literary" writer, Harris would devote most of his writing time to fiction in the last decade of his life. After leaving the *Constitution*, he wrote four novels, five books for children, and two collections of short stories, most of them best-sellers, none of them distinguished, but all of them based upon his observations of life. Julia Collier Harris, who for most of her own life was a journalist, suggested several years after her father-in-law's death: "Perhaps if [he] had felt it possible to give up his editorial work years before he did, in a more abundant leisure he might have developed his art at the point where he felt it weakest, thus gaining that mastery in craftsmanship which the novelist must possess."[27]

It is probable that with fewer daily demands, Harris would have had the time to think through and revise most of his fiction, rather than be compelled to maintain the pace in literary fiction as he did in newspaper journalism. But the base of his "day job" had provided the techniques, stimulation, and opportunities for his literary "night job." To have cut away his work at the *Constitution* would have compromised his literary career. Nevertheless, when his son Julian had begun a career as a journalist, then was promoted quickly to managing editor of the *Constitution* at the age of 24, Joel Chandler

Harris, as his daughter-in-law Julia Collier Harris later wrote, "realized, perhaps with regret, that the executive talents of his eldest son would probably turn him aside indefinitely from the development of any literary gifts he may have had."[28]

For more than a decade, Joel Chandler Harris had done little with Black folklore. He had wanted to break free of the bonds of the Uncle Remus stories, to write about the greater social issues and present solutions to a nation at the beginning of its second century, yet he knew that his national fame was based upon those allegorical folktales about rabbits, foxes, and bears. But, there was a more compelling reason to break from the plantation stories. In response to George Lorimer who had wanted sketches for the *Saturday Evening Post* and was willing to pay the industry's top rates, Harris declared: "I could furnish you with some Uncle Remus sketches on various topics, but my supply of folklore has run out; the field seems to be exhausted; and it would be useless to try to invent this sort of thing. The forgery would stare one in the face. A piece of fiction is easily invented, but an individual cannot compete with long generations in building up a fable."[29]

As associate editor of one of the nation's finest newspapers, as a best-selling author, and as a resident of an affluent suburb, Harris was a long way from the plantation of Joseph Addison Turner—and the stories of its slaves. For his next major book, *Gabriel Tolliver: A Story of Reconstruction*, Harris would again recycle his life. In this third of Harris's semi-autobiographical novels, Cephas, a fortyish writer reminisces about his life twenty-five years earlier. The opening of *Gabriel Tolliver* is possibly the most compelling insight into the writer-journalist's conflicting personalities.

For several years Sophia had listened calmly to my glowing descriptions of Shady Dale[30] and the people there. She was patient, but I could see by the way she sometimes raised her eyebrows that she was a trifle suspicious of my judgment, and that she thought my opinions were unduly coloured by my feelings. Once she went so far as to suggest that I was all the time looking at the home people through the eyes of boyhood—eyes that do not always see accurately. She had said, moreover, that if I were to return to Shady Dale, I would find that the friends of my boyhood were in no way different from the people I meet every day. This was absurd, of course—or, rather, it would have been absurd for any one else to make the suggestion; for at that particular time, Sophia was a trifle jealous of Shady Dale and its people. Nevertheless, she was really patient. You know how exasperating a man can be when he has a hobby. Well, my hobby was Shady Dale, and I was not ashamed of it. The man or woman who cannot display as much of the homing instinct as a cat or a pigeon is a creature to be pitied or despised.[31]

Harris's mind may have been set in the rural and the nurturing atmosphere of the plantation, of the small and isolated town where he grew up, but his professional life was in the metropolis. Several years earlier, when it appeared that Julian, then sixteen years old, might stay longer than a summer with his maternal grandparents in rural Upton, Quebec, Harris cautioned him, "No youngster who has any promise of a career can afford to bury himself in Upton, or in any other country place."[32]

Gabriel Tolliver was first serialized in the January through November issues of *The New Era*, a Philadelphia mass circulation magazine, before publication at the end of the year by McClure, Phillips. In a letter to James Whitcomb Riley, for whom the book is dedicated, Harris

wrote: "When I decided to quit newspaper work, I turned to this work, and, when I began it, I determined to write it in my own way, without regard to models, standards, or formalism of any kind. I determined to write something to please myself. The result is what you have. It is mine; it is *me*.... I mean by this that I surrendered myself wholly to the story and its characters."[33] The novel's dominant theme was the arrest and false imprisonment of a Georgian who was suspected of killing a carpetbagger, underscored by several romances. But the book was a study of Reconstruction, a probing look at the relationships between the newly-freed Blacks and the now-impoverished Whites, and included a subplot about two children—one White, one Black—who were restricted by society from becoming friends. Although the "dialect portraits in *Gabriel Tolliver* are brilliant," says literary critic Bruce Bickley, the strength of the book is "the depiction of the restlessness, uneasiness, and strange silence pervasive among the blacks who are trying to come to grips with their new freedom after the war. Gabriel sees their restlessness as natural, but many of his elders in the community interpret it as the harbinger of violent rebellion or revenge-taking."[34]

In a *Constitution* editorial in 1880, Harris, although still believing that most master-slave relationships were as caring as those on Turnwold, nevertheless had explained the atmosphere in Southern life after the Civil War:

> The disastrous and demoralizing mistake that the Southern people made after the surrender was in refusing to take their old slaves into their care and confidence instead of allowing them to be manipulated into a mechanical and false sympathy with an intolerable policy of the carpet-baggers. The Southern people have made other political mistakes since, but

this was altogether the most disastrous. In a manner, we held the poor blacks responsible for the shock that their emancipation gave to our social organism. This was human nature, perhaps, but it was the most deplorable blunder that Southern human nature ever made. Looking back over it all, the solution to the problem seems so simple that reflecting people are inclined to go off into some quiet place and beat their heads against the walls out of sheer vexation. We had only to hold out our hands to these poor, unfortunate people to renew the confidence and affection that had always existed between the white and colored races of the South; but instead of that we sulked in our tents and allowed them to be turned from their natural bent by means so monstrous and so vile that it is no wonder respectable republicans now join us in denouncing the agents through whose manipulations the ignorant negroes were made to rob themselves as well as the whites.[35]

In *Gabriel Tolliver*, Harris again attacked the radical Republicans who he said were aided by "ignorant negroes and criminals," and argued:

> The real leaders, the men in whose wisdom and conservatism the whites had confidence, were disqualified from holding office by terms of the reconstruction acts, and the convention emphasized and adopted the policy of the radical leaders in Washington—a policy that was deliberately conceived for the purpose of placing the governments of the Southern States in the hands of ignorant negroes controlled by men who had no interest whatever in the welfare of the people.[36]

Like most White Georgians, Harris always believed many of the problems of Reconstruction, exemplified by the members who united in 1877 to rewrite Georgia's

constitution, were caused by Northern carpetbaggers. Several years after the publication of *Gabriel Tolliver*, Sam W. Small, without referring to Harris or the beliefs of hundreds of thousands of Georgians during Reconstruction, corrected Harris's impressions: "The [Constitutional Convention] was composed of many of the most experienced, astute and conservative statesmen, old and new, that the commonwealth possessed."[37]

Once again, Harris received mixed reviews, with some critics suggesting that the novel failed because of the lack of an Uncle Remus figure. The *New York Times* puffed that Harris "has accomplished quite a feat…for he has written 448 pages (and not over large type either) about nothing…. [The book] plods along though its numberless chapters of tranquillity leading to the reader yawningly after it."[38] The *Nation* dismissed it as inferior literature: "It is very poor work, rambling, shuffling; indeed, without characterization, form, or style. From a passage in the 'prelude' we gather that the prelude was an afterthought, meant to declare that the author knows the book to be careless and tedious and unimpressive, and that he is proud of all that."[39]

Harris, the consummate journalist and editorialist whose power of story-telling and his journalistic style had upset many reviewers, brought forth innumerable social issues to help the people better understand a part of their history and of their lives. If the book failed as an "artistic" work, it certainly did not fail as a work of substance.

A few reviewers, however, did see a powerful story. *The Critic* called it "one of the sanest books on the South that has appeared in a long time, and one of the most charming as well."[40] *Outlook* claimed the book would be regarded as an important part of the history of Reconstruction. *Dial* and a number of major newspapers noted that *Gabriel Tolliver* was second only to Thomas Nelson Page's *Red Rock* as a work of historical journalism.

Many of the reviewers suggested the book was far superior to Thomas Dixon's political invective *The Leopard's Spots* or the racist literary history *The Clansman*, a national best-seller that would eventually become the basis for D. W. Griffith's epic film, *Birth of a Nation* (1915).

By the end of 1902, Harris and McClure, Phillips had begun questioning their exclusive contract. After two years, neither Harris nor his publisher had received as much income as they first believed possible. "I am not sure that our present form of contract is the best possible for the future," John S. Phillips wrote, asking Harris, "If you have any suggestion, I wish you would let me know."[41] Harris agreed that the contract was in need of revision, stating:

> The figures submitted by you indicate that I have received no substantial benefit from the contract. From your point of view, you could say the same, except that you have had the exclusive privilege of publishing my books, which, under the contract, will amount to four thus far... Accordingly, the agreement is not what it was meant to be—mutually beneficial. I am of the opinion, however, that I have the worst end of the bargain.

He acknowledged that his illness had "reduced the value of the contract," but because of the contract, "felt compelled to work at times when I could not do myself justice." He argued that the eighty dollar weekly payments "have been worth their face value to me," but also stated that he believed he could have earned that amount had he not been under exclusive contract because he "should have thought less about furnishing books for publication [and] could have gotten a better value for the...children's stories than you give me." He then proposed a revision of the contract, and stated, "I

think there will be no difficulty in regard to a less burdensome contract." [42]

Phillips—who well understood not only the business practices of publishing companies but also how to work with the peculiarities, frustrations, and complaints of authors—agreed a change was necessary if for no other reason than because "I can not bear to work under any arrangement with you which is unsatisfactory to you." He explained he was upset because the company did "not come up to your expectations" about the potential income, and told Harris, "I have felt as if we had a friend in you, and I cannot feel that I have been mistaken no matter what our business relationship may be." He emphasized that McClure, Phillips would continue to "do everything that we possibly can for you and your writings, for our interest in you and them is sincere and beyond business considerations." [43] He concluded his three-page typed letter: "I have not been very well myself during the past year, having been away for many months at a time. If this had been different and you had not been in ill health, probably we could have worked out our mutual problems much more satisfactorily." [44]

An exchange of letters in January, with both parties showing the friendship and respect they had for each other as well as the pain of separation, led to a contract-mandated six month notice of termination. During the next few months, as the two tried to work through a new contract, Phillips continued to emphasize how "very proud and very happy" he was to have been Harris's publisher, and again apologized for McClure's magazine not being able to use Harris's articles. [45] Harris had been upset that McClure's, then at the height of its popularity and one of the nation's leading magazines, was unable to use his articles, bringing in the additional income he once expected; but, as a journalist, he completely understood that his tales and articles were written for a different audience than what *McClure's* targeted.

In mid-March, Phillips directly addressed Harris's earlier concern that he believed under the previous contract he was almost compelled to produce a high volume literary output to assure that McClure, Phillips did not lose money on its eighty dollar a week payments. Phillips suggested a fifty dollar a week payment against royalties, the logic being that Harris, by now prone to illness and mental fatigue, would not feel as if he "had to work at one time or another but be reasonably sure that [the] average product over a considerable period would make the income which we would advance." Phillips explained several of the advantages to both Harris and the publisher, and truthfully concluded, "I hate to give up this relationship of ours, partly for business reasons and very much for personal reasons."[46] Both men admired and respected the other; both wanted something to work out; both knew it was not going to happen. Phillips explained several of the advantages to both Harris and the publisher, and truthfully concluded, "I hate to give up this relationship of ours, partly for business reasons and very much for personal reasons."[47] Both men admired and respected the other; both wanted something to work out; both knew it wasn't going to happen. His last check under the contract was dated 21 April 1903.

Harris would continue to work with McClure, Phillips, but on a non-exclusive basis. In 1907, with an income of $160 a week from eleven major newspapers for an Uncle Remus weekly comic strip, but with expenses of $167 a week—forty dollars for the artist, seventy-seven dollars for production costs, and fifty dollars for Harris's writing,[48] and with the syndicate absorbing editorial and promotion costs—T. C. McClure proposed cutting Harris's payment in half, in exchange for Harris having unlimited use of original engraving plates of the cartoons.

Their relationship would end sixteen years after Samuel S. McClure first bought the rights for *On the Plantation*, and less than seven years after the four-year exclusive contract to McClure, Phillips ended.

------

[1] Letter from Joel Chandler Harris to John Henderson Garnsey. Quoted in *The Life and Letters of Joel Chandler Harris*, by Julia Collier Harris, 345.

[2] Actually, for his professional writing he usually used a lead pencil, more appropriate to a newspaper journalist than would be a pen. In a letter to editor Richard Watson Gilder on 22 July 1886, Harris noted, "a pen cramps both my thoughts and hand." Near the turn of the century, he had begun using a typewriter. However, he composed many stories in the "backshop," writing and setting type at the same time. Interestingly, and yet another dichotomy in his life, he used a pen and ink for much of his correspondence, especially to his children.

[3] Letter from Joel Chandler Harris to Lillian and Mildred Harris, 19 March 1898.

[4] Ray Stannard Baker, "Joel Chandler Harris," 598.

[5] Letter of 28 September 1881. Quoted in *The Training of an American: The Early Life of Walter H. Page*, by Burton J. Hendrick, 149.

[6] Letter from Joel Chandler Harris to Richard Watson Gilder, 10 October 1886 [Virginia].

[7] Quoted in Julia Collier Harris, *The Life and Letters of Joel Chandler Harris*, 171.

[8] Letter from Joel Chandler Harris to Richard Watson Gilder, 22 July 1886.

[9] Letter from Joel Chandler Harris to Ambrose Bierce, 16 July 1896.

[10] Julia Collier Harris, *The Life and Letters of Joel Chandler Harris*, 214.

[11] See "The Best Novel," *Atlanta Constitution*, 21 April 1888, 4.

[12] Quoted in Julia Collier Harris, *The Life and Letters of Joel Chandler Harris*, 569.

[13] Letter from Joel Chandler Harris to Lillian Harris, 1 April 1896. Quoted in Julia Collier Harris, *The Life and Letters of Joel Chandler Harris*, 340.

[14] Letter from Joel Chandler Harris to Edward Burlingame, 31 October 1893.

[15] Letter from Walter Hines Page to Joel Chandler Harris, 23 March 1900.

[16] Letter from Walter Hines Page to Joel Chandler Harris, 2 June 1900.

[17] Letter from Walter Hines Page to Joel Chandler Harris, 2 August 1900.

[18] Letter from Walter Hines Page to Joel Chandler Harris, 7 September 1900.

[19] Letter from Henry Lanier to Joel Chandler Harris, 8 September 1900.

[20] Letter from Joel Chandler Harris to Walter Hines Page, 10 October 1900.

[21] Letter from Walter Hines Page to Joel Chandler Harris, 23 October 1900.

[22] Letter from Walter Hines Page to Joel Chandler Harris, 23 October 1900.

[23] R. Bruce Bickley, Jr., *Joel Chandler Harris*, 54.

[24] Letter from Henry Lanier to Joel Chandler Harris, 12 November 1900.

[25] Joel Chandler Harris, New York Times, December 28, 1901; p. 1016.

[26] Quoted by Francis Whiting Halsey in *Authors of Our Day in Their Homes*, 163.

[27] Julia Collier Harris, *The Life and Letters of Joel Chandler Harris*, 339.

[28] Julia Collier Harris, *The Life and Letters of Joel Chandler Harris*, p. 291.

[29] Letter from Joel Chandler Harris to George Lorimer, 22 July 1902.

[30] Although there was an actual village named Shady Dale near Eatonton, in Harris's writings, Shady Dale, like Hillsborough and Halleyton, was often the substitute for Eatonton.

[31] Joel Chandler Harris, *Gabriel Tolliver: A Story of Reconstruction*, 3-4. Interestingly, with a change of name to "Sophia" and place to "Upton, Quebec," Harris could easily have been talking about his wife who loved her own hometown. "I had heard mother speak of it so often in such glowing terms, her eyes sparkling with pleasant memories," wrote her son, Evelyn, in 1949.

[32] Letter from Joel Chandler Harris to Julian Harris, 1 September 1890.

[33] Quoted in Julia Collier Harris, *The Life and Letters of Joel Chandler Harris*, 454-55.

[34] R. Bruce Bickley, Jr., *Joel Chandler Harris*, 141.

[35] [Joel Chandler Harris], "Negro Suffrage in the South," *Atlanta Constitution*, 17 January 1880, 2.

[36] Joel Chandler Harris, *Gabriel Tolliver*, 243

[37] Sam W. Small, "Story of the Constitution's Half Century of Service to the City, State and Country," 24.

[38] "In the Quiet Village of Shady Dale," *New York Times*, 22 November 1902, 808.

[39] Review, *The Nation*, 11 December 1902, 467.

[40] Review, *The Critic* (December 1902): 581.

[41] Letter from John S. Phillips to Joel Chandler Harris, 29 October 1902.

[42] Letter from Joel Chandler Harris to John S. Phillips, 6 December 1902.

[43] Letter from John S. Phillips to Joel Chandler Harris, 15 December 1902.

[44] Letter from John S. Phillips to Joel Chandler Harris, 15 December 1902.

[45] Letter from John S. Phillips to Joel Chandler Harris, 4 March 1903.

[46] Letter from John S. Phillips to Joel Chandler Harris, 13 March 1903.

[47] Letter from John S. Phillips to Joel Chandler Harris, 13 March 1903.

[48] Memo from T. C. McClure to Joel Chandler Harris, 4 January 1907

Atlanta Constitution offices, about 1890

Joel Chandler Harris, with family at Wren's Nest

Chapter 10

'The Good Old Times We Used to Have'

L ike most persons in the antebellum era, Joel Chandler Harris had dropped out of formal schooling long before he would have graduated from high school. Four decades later, on 11 June 1902, Emory College awarded him the honorary degree of Litt.D., the first honorary degree it ever awarded. True to form, Harris was too shy, modest, nervous, or frightened to attend the ceremony on the campus of the college in nearby Oxford that made him Dr. Harris.[1] Three years later, the University of Pennsylvania withdrew an offer of an honorary doctorate because Harris would not go to Philadelphia to personally accept the university's offer.[2]

Still shy and hiding from his public, still believing in the anonymity of the writer—in 1899, he had written that he regretted having his name on the books because it "created for me a world of discomfort"[3]—Harris was elected to the Academy of Arts and Letters in 1905, its first year—fortunately, he did not have to attend a ceremony. Robert Underwood Johnson, secretary of the parent National Institute of Arts and Letters, had written to Harris to ask permission to nominate him for membership. Harris had always replied promptly to Johnson's letters when he was editor at *Century*, and a colleague; but now Harris just laid aside the letter from Johnson; Harris thought that respect from his peers and readers was important; however, honors just did not matter all that much. Knowing Harris's modesty, Johnson wrote back, "I took silence on your part...to be consent."[4] So, on 15

May 1905, Johnson was able to write to Harris that he had "the honor to inform you that at a Conference of the first twenty members of the Academy of Arts and Letters…you were duly chosen a member of that body, now in process of organization from the Institute."[5] He was the twenty-fourth member elected; among the others were Henry Adams, Samuel L. Clemens, William Dean Howells, Henry James, William James, Thomas Jefferson (posthumously), and Theodore Roosevelt.

Theodore Roosevelt—whose aunt was a Georgian, and who had read Uncle Remus stories while a youth—tried several times to meet the master story teller, mostly because he admired the journalist, partially because he believed Harris could help him better understand the American South. Writing to journalist and confidante Silas McBee in July 1904, Roosevelt suggested that if he were elected, "I am going to get him [Harris] and you and two or three others, like [Edwin] Alderman [president of the University of Virginia]…to come to see me at the White House, and see if I cannot arrive at some policy as regards the South which will, as far as possible *not* be susceptible of misconstruction."[6]

Nevertheless, Harris, a staunch Democrat who admired and praised the Progressive Republican Roosevelt, found ways to graciously decline the president's invitation. Perhaps it was because Harris was too modest to believe that a "cornfield journalist" should be dining at the White House; perhaps it was because he was terrified that he would stammer and embarrass himself and the president; perhaps it was because he did not like to travel outside of Georgia because he feared the crowds of authors, publishers, and the public who would try to entice him into various dinners in his honor, to become a part of the aura he believed he never had; perhaps it was because of his numerous small illnesses, many brought about by overwork, that he was terrified at leaving the comfort and security of the Wren's Nest and Atlanta. Whatever were the reasons, Harris stayed in Atlanta.

On 20 October 1905, Roosevelt visited Atlanta, having previously sent word that he wished to meet Harris. Still afraid of crowds, Harris had not planned to be at the train station to meet the president, but was "escorted" there by employees of the *Constitution*. Before several thousand Georgians—including Harris who had snuck away for about thirty minutes before being dragged back into the crowd by fellow journalists—the president pointed out:

> Georgia has done a great many things for the Union, but she has never done more than when she gave Mr. Joel Chandler Harris to American literature…. Where Mr. Harris seems to me to have done one of the greatest services is that he has written what exalts the South in the mind of every man who reads it, and yet what has not a flavor of bitterness toward any other part of the union… There is not another American anywhere who can read Mr. Harris's stories…who does not rise up with a better citizen for having read them.[7]

The next year, Roosevelt became one of the first subscribers to *Uncle Remus's Magazine*.

Accompanied by Julian Harris and Don Marquis—"I was afraid he would not go until Julian got him on the train," said Essie Harris[8]—the shy and reclusive writer finally visited Theodore Roosevelt at the White House, 18 November 1907. "I had the biggest time I ever had in my life,"[9] he later wrote. The president was equally complimentary. "I do not think there was an evening at the White House that we have all of us enjoyed more than the one that you were here."[10]

Personal

October 11, 1905.

Dear Mr. Howell:

    Mrs. Roosevelt will only be a couple of hours in Atlanta. She will arrive with me at eleven o'clock, and will be obliged to leave on the one o'clock train. I wonder if Mrs. Howell would care to come to the train and take her for a drive to see the interesting points in Atlanta, and if she could bring Joel Chandler Harris with her, or arrange in some way for Mrs. Roosevelt to meet him. As you know, our entire household is devoted to Joel Chandler Harris. Of course answer perfectly frankly if it will not be convenient for Mrs. Howell to do this.

    With regard,

        Sincerely yours,

        Theodore Roosevelt

Hon. Clark Howell,
    Atlanta, Georgia.

Although Joel Chandler Harris wanted anonymity, he still needed recognition as a novelist. During the last decade of life, he was having even more problems than acknowledging that his strength was not as a novelist, and that his contribution to literature would be more significant in the form of the column and shorter fiction.

There was yet another part of Harris's life that would dictate his stories. The brilliant recorder of the Old South, who with Henry Grady had given a vision to the people to create a New South, had trouble adjusting to the new industrialization and the end of a more rural-agrarian life. In *Wally Wanderoon and His Story-Telling Machine* (1903), a loosely structured allegorical novel of eight stories, Wally looks for the good times he once had.

Wally Wanderoon, however, was not only Harris' longing for what he had seen in his youth, a life long before he became famous, but it also shows him criticizing those who tried to claim that all written folklore must go beyond mere storytelling. Harris, who had been an active member of the American Folklore Society in the 1880s, had begun doubting the value of "scientific ethnology" by the 1890s. In the amusing satire, "The Late Mr. Watkins of Georgia," a story in *Tales of the Home Folks* (1899), Harris had set up the academic folklorists as incompetents whose lives appeared to revolve around tying together folktales, even if there was no relationship. Poking fun even at himself, Harris wrote about the introduction to his first book and how folklorists and other academics came to praise him as a scholar: "It is the habit of man, the world over, to stand in awe, secret or avowed, of that which he does not understand. When I say, therefore, that the introduction is wonderfully learned, I mean that I do not understand it."[11]

Underlying Harris's distrust of the academics was also his distrust of their integrity. By the 1890s, ethnologists had begun using their "scientific research" to try to prove that since civilizations go through a "primitive" stage, the American Black was, at least in the nineteenth century, culturally inferior to the White population.[12] Harris, who had carefully studied the lives and folktales of the former slaves, disagreed; the Blacks may have been more "primitive," but they were not culturally inferior. More important, Harris, unlike the "scientific folklorists," believed a good story should be just that—a good story, with no mixing of "science." His friends Mark Twain, one of the founders of the American Folklore Society, and George Washington Cable, founder of the Chicago Folklore Society, had both dropped their memberships, questioning the attempts by others to turn folklore into a science. In the introduction to *Uncle Remus and His Friends* (1892), Harris had declared:

> I have gone far enough into the subject [of folklore] (by the aid of those who are Fellows of This and Professors of That, to say nothing of Doctors of the Other) to discover that at the end of investigation and discussion Speculation stands grinning.
>
> The stories in this volume were written simply and solely because of my interest in the stories themselves, in the first place, and, in the second place, because of the unadulterated human nature that might be found in them.[13]

In *Wally Wanderoon*, the "academic" storyteller/folklorist says: "It was one of the principles taught at the university where I graduated that a story amounts to nothing and worse than nothing, if it is not of scientific value. I would like to tell the story first, and then give you my idea of its relation to oral literature, and its special relation to the unity of the human race."[14] Wally says he wants "no prefaces and no footnotes; we don't care where the story comes from."[15] However, the storyteller was

Grandfather's Reminiscences of the Mexican War.

Illustration from "Wally Wanderoon"

having trouble finding stories—not too unlike the situation Harris had found himself to be in—and Wally resorts
to a storytelling machine that fights with him. In a new
era with "new standards," the machine produces sanitized tales that are devoid of messages and folklore. A
tale told by Wally himself is not much better. But the tales
told by Drusilla in a form of American Black English
reflect the social struggle of people and their values, and
are enjoyed by the children. At the end of the eighth tale,
Wally leaves, telling Sweetest Susan and Buster John he
is leaving to find the "Good Old Times we used to have
if I am compelled to travel the wide world all over; and I
hope to find a better story-teller than the one you have
heard, or else find a remedy for this scientific foolishness,
which is a disease hard to cure."[16]

In "Brother Rabbit's Laughing-Place," published less
than two years after *Wally Wanderoon*, Harris had Uncle
Remus explain why he didn't tell the tales to adults:

> "It's mighty funny 'bout tales," he went on. "Tell
> um as you may an' whence you may, some'll say tain't
> no tale, an' den ag'in some'll say dat it's a fine tale.
> Dey ain't no tellin'. Dat de reason I don't like ter tell
> no tale ter grown folks, speshually ef dey er white
> folks. Dey'll take it an' put it by de side er some yuther
> tale what dey got in der min' an' dey'll take on dat
> slonchidickler grin what allers say, 'Go way, nigger
> man! You dunner what a tale is!' An' I don't—I'll say
> dat much fer ter keep some un else fum sayin' it.[17]

Even if Harris justifiably poked fun at the academics,
while doubting his own abilities at folkore and fiction, he
was still a respected and highly competent journalist who
continually hammered out his lifetime message—in fiction, essays, and editorials—of justice and respect for all
people. He always wove into his stories, whether for

adults or children, threads about mankind and its interactions within society, scolding those who believed themselves to be superior to anyone else. In a column that was syndicated to several dozen newspapers in 1900, Harris had argued:

> [R]ace prejudice is an affair that has nothing to do with color; it seems to be an instinct of the human mind. Men of widely divergent races will entertain prejudices, one against the other, in spite of the cruel injustice to which this instinct sometimes gives rise. It is but one of the equipments of our poor human nature and it rests with Christianity to eradicate and obliterate it.[18]

In *Wally Wanderoon* he spoke his beliefs through the words of the title character who talked to the former slave, Drusilla: "The Painter that painted you painted us all, I reckon—some one colour and some another, and some betwixt and between." Drusilla responds, "My mammy say dat it don't make no diffunce how black you is, ef yo' heart is in de right place."[19]

In a series of three *Saturday Evening Post* articles, published in January and February 1904, for which the magazine paid $250 per article, Harris explored what segregation was doing to American society, arguing in language more forceful than even the more liberal Northern press was accustomed to, that the American Black deserved no less equality than any White had earned by his birthright. However, like most Americans, Harris still had his prejudices, believing that it was the American White race which had civilized and educated the former slaves:

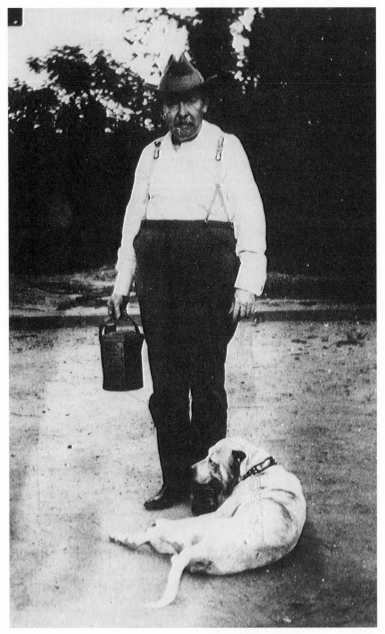

Joel Chandler Harris and Muldoon, 1902

I am bound to conclude from what I see all about me, and from what I know of the race elsewhere, that the negro, notwithstanding the late start he has made in civilization and enlightenment, is capable of making himself a useful member in the communities in which he lives and moves, and that he is becoming more and more desirous of conforming to all the laws that have been enacted for the protection of society.[20]

Shortly after the first article appeared, Booker T. Washington wrote to Harris:

It has been a long time since I have read anything from the pen of any man which has given me such encouragement as your article has. It has been read already by a large number of colored people, and it would surprise and delight you to hear the many pleasant things they are saying about it. In a speech on Lincoln's Birthday which I am to deliver in New York, I am going to take the liberty to quote liberally from what you have said.[21]

Historian Wayne Mixon points out that by 1907, the year of the publication of the final Remus book, "radical racism had reached the peak of its frenzy [and] Remus himself in the frame narratives wages all-out war on a white world characterized by materialism, scientism, and disdain for the imaginative sensibility."[22]

More than a decade after Harris had announced he was retiring Uncle Remus, and not long after he declared that the supply of folklore "has run out," that "the field seems to be exhausted," and that it was "useless to try to invent this sort of thing," Harris again began writing the tales. During the 1880s, Harris had advertised he was looking for sources for the tales, and unselfishly credited their origins, but had been briefly singed when he and journalist Harry Stilwell Edwards each came up with a similar episode. In response to a query from *Century* editor Richard Watson Gilder, an annoyed Harris wrote:

> I have heard that there was some such episode in real life. But isn't that what you want? Come! Are you going to confine us all to inventions of our own? Are we, who are working in a comparatively new field, to take no advantage of the legends, the traditions and the happenings with which we are familiar? Are you going to say to us, "If you have nothing to invent, pray send us nothing? If you are, you may put up the bars against one and against all the rest of us at once. As for me I have no new situation to invent, and if I should invent one it would probably be weak and ineffectual. Take *Azalia*. The Footprint business, as I have already said, was given to me by Mrs. Crawford.[23] That is beyond invention. It is real. It belongs to human nature. It is mine if I recreate characters that would be apt to employ it. So with the death scene which you extol. Do I make it natural—obvious? If so it is mine. I shall never hesitate to draw on the oral stories I know for incidents. The thing is, do I make my poor characters conform to the requirements of human nature? The most a writer can do now-a-days is to try to invest his characters with a certain nobility of purpose, a certain pathos, that shall relate them to human nature, or to a series of incidents that belong to human nature. Why should Edwards (for instance) claim to have invented the main coincidents of the "Two Runaways"? They might readily have happened and no doubt did. If they were possible, we may be sure they happened; if they were impossible why put them in literature at all?[24]

Gilder's response five days later, filled with praise for Harris, assured Harris that the editor had no objections to an author using real incidents in fiction, but editors always had to be concerned with issues of plagiarism and

Joel Chandler Harris, with Mulddon and a grandchild, Charles Collier Harris

Joel Chandler Harris and Joel Chandler Harris Jr., 1904

libel, something Gilder says he knew was not a problem with Harris.[25]

While searching to develop a reputation in a literary world outside of the Uncle Remus tales, Harris needed to believe the supply was exhausted—at least in his own recollections. But by the beginning of a new century, after a decade trying to be a "literary" author, Harris undoubtedly was now aware that editors and the public not only wanted those tales but were willing to pay better for them than his other work. Robert Underwood Johnson at *Century* had written Harris in 1900 that his magazine, which had a long and profitable association with Harris during the 1880s and early 1890s, would again like something from him—and suggested, "We want 'Uncle Remus' in it if at all possible, and the little boy—something very fetching."[26] J. Randolph Walker at *Cosmopolitan* was even more specific with his request, writing to Harris that the magazine "should be glad to see any fiction you may write, and our preference is toward the animal stories rather than the negro."[27] Entirely dependent upon income from freelance writing, without the cushion of a newspaper salary, Harris once again began producing the tales.

For *Collier's*, Harris contributed ten tales, at $250 each,[28] between June 1902 and November 1904. *Metropolitan*, which had been persistent in getting Harris's byline, reaped twelve tales and stories for $200 each, placing them in the issues between November 1904 and September 1906. Included was "Brother Rabbit's Laughing-Place," a place where Brer Rabbit "won't be pestered by de balance er creation," where he "kin go dar an' laugh his fill an' den go on 'bout his business, ef he got any business, an' ef he ain't got none, he kin go ter play."[29] Published in the January 1905 issue, and included in the collection, *Told by Uncle Remus*, published later that year, the story became one of the most popular

Uncle Remus tales, possibly because the readers realized each of them, like Brer Rabbit, needed a laughing-place to escape their own every-day problems.

For the *Saturday Evening Post*, Harris, who had written poetry at the beginning of his journalistic career, now told fifteen tales in iambic verse, leading with "Mr. Rabbit Run Fur—Mr. Rabbit Run Fas'" in the 19 September 1903, issue, and concluding with "Hog-Killin' Time" in the 6 January 1906, issue. As he did with most of his other newspaper and magazine tales, Harris collected nine verses from *The Saturday Evening Post*—including "Brer Rabbit and the Tar-Baby" from the 24 September 1904, issue—three more recent verses from *Century*, plus seventeen additional hymns and songs, into a book. *The Tar-Baby and Other Rhymes of Uncle Remus*—illustrated by A. B. Frost and E. W. Kemble, with some of the prints in color—was published in 1904 by the reorganized D. Appleton & Company, Harris's first book publisher with whom he now had a one-year exclusive contract.

Doubleday, Page & Company, which had published several of his works, but which in 1900 had not been able to sign him to an exclusive contract, had not given up, and asked D. Appleton for permission to use the tar-baby story in a collection of representative American humor. In two letters, Francis W. Halsey—former editor of the *New York Times Saturday Review* and current editor at D. Appleton—rejected the request. Halsey's letter to Harris two days later not only encapsulates the nature of book marketing, but also the reality of what the tar-baby story had done not only to give Harris a national reputation but also to trap him in that reputation:

> As you know, the "Tar Baby" is the story which has probably sold three-fourths of the "Uncle Remus" books. If we allow you to print the whole of that story elsewhere, we might as well let you print the whole

Esther LaRose Harris, with grandchild Charles Collier Harris, in Garden of the Wren's Nest, 1907

Joel Chandler Harris, Esther LaRose Harris, and grandchildren

book. For that reason, and in order to avoid endangering the Appleton copyright, I do not believe I have any right to consent to the use of the whole of the "Tar Baby" story.[30]

Our judgment has been distinctly against the use of this story [by another publisher]. We have had numerous requests for many years of a similar nature and have declined them all. Our experience is that nothing in your writings has become more widely known. When our salesmen go on the road, they frequently, when offering "Uncle Remus", are asked "does your book contain the Tar Baby story"; but now with your new book of verse [*The Tar-Baby and Other Rhymes of Uncle Remus*] the reasons for declining Doubleday, Page & Company's request are even greater. After your book gets out, and should Doubleday, Page & Company have the story also, there would be three books in which the public could buy it. This, in our judgment, would seriously impair the sale of your other two books.

The effect on the book of verses would probably be most serious. The introductory poem, in our judgment, is the one which would have most to do with selling the book, and we strongly advise against the proposed reprint.

Kindly let us hear from you on this matter. [31]

Always scrambling for a few dollars for his family, Harris understood the financial reasons to withhold publication, especially when he could make more money by not selling the rights.

During 1904-1905, Harris was one of six editors of the fifteen-volume set, *The World's Wit and Humor*, probably the best collection of reprinted newspaper and magazine humor to that time. In his introduction to the section on American humor, Harris reaffirmed his beliefs about humor, drawing from his knowledge of how slaves dealt with reality: "In the light of his own humor, the American stands forth as the conqueror of circumstances, who has created for himself the most appalling responsibilities, which he undertakes and carries out with a wink and a nod, whistling a hymn or a rag-time tune, to show that he is neither weary nor down-hearted."[32]

In the final year of his contract with McClure, Phillips, Harris completed *Told by Uncle Remus: New Stories of the Old Plantation* (1905) which targeted a second generation of readers, and would be the last Uncle Remus collection published during his lifetime. The collection of sixteen tales was held together by Harris's psychological study of an extended family. The book, says Bruce Bickley, "functions both sociologically and aesthetically as an epilogue to the Remus cycle of tales and to the old plantation era."[33] After enduring a decade of mixed reviews for his other books—the ones without Uncle Remus—Harris was again enjoying critical acclaim, even though American readers had become tired of the regional dialect stories that had proliferated during the three decades following the Civil War. Uncle Remus, stated a review in *The Dial*, "has presumably aged somewhat since his first appearance, but his story-telling faculty is unimpaired by time and disuse."[34] *The Critic* said the characters were "just as entertaining as ever,"[35] and the *New York Times* reported the new collection was "as full of the humor and charm of negro lore as ever."[36]

Harris opened the book by explaining why there had been a dearth of Uncle Remus stories, while slipping in yet another nostalgic look at the old plantation life:

> The main reason why Uncle Remus retired from business as a story-teller was because the little boy to whom he had told his tales grew to be a very big boy, and grew and grew till he couldn't grow any bigger. Meanwhile, his father and mother [John and Sally]

moved to Atlanta, and lived there for several years. Uncle Remus moved with them, but he soon grew tired of the dubious ways of city life, and one day he told his Miss Sally that if she didn't mind he was going back to the plantation where he could get a breath of fresh air.

He was overjoyed when the lady told him that they were all going back as soon as the son married. As this event was to occur in the course of a few weeks, Uncle Remus decided to wait for the rest of the family. The wedding came off, and then the father and mother returned to the plantation, and made their home there, much to the delight of the old negro.[37]

At the plantation, the Little Boy brings his own child to Uncle Remus for lessons about life. This "latest little boy":

...was frailer and quieter than his father had been; indeed, he was fragile and had hardly any color in his face...He was more like a girl in his refinement; all the boyishness had been taken out of him by that mysterious course of discipline that some mothers know how to apply. He seemed to belong to a different age—to a different time....[38]

Small as the lad was he was old-fashioned; he thought and spoke like a grown person; and this the old negro knew was not according to nature. The trouble with the boy was that he had no childhood; he had been subdued and weakened by the abnormal training he had received.[39] The problem, as Uncle Remus saw it, was that the Little Boy's wife was a harsh disciplinarian who had robbed her child of the adventures of life, even to the point of being a "great stickler for accuracy of speech [who] was very precise in the use of English, and could not abide the simple

dialect in which the stories had been related" to her husband, the original Little Boy.[40]

Now in his late fifties and a grandfather, Harris wove another theme through this book. It was a theme that helped unify all of Harris's previous works. According to Bruce Bickley:

> Allying themselves against the boy's mother in their efforts to introduce a little vigor into the lad's system helps bring Remus and Sally closer together, but primarily it is their mutual old age that seems to break down the barriers between black and white, and between lower and higher social station. Remus and Sally share a quiet sympathy; the two talk of feeling useless, and at times a gesture or glance is sufficient to express their sense of helplessness. In his mutually reflecting portraits of Sally and Uncle Remus, Harris is also suggesting that survivors of the Old South, those remaining patrons of former times, can only turn to each other for support and understanding; for the new postwar generation has a different system of values and a different cultural and social orientation.[41]

[1] On that same day, the University of Missouri conferred the degree of Doctor of Laws (LL.D.) upon Mark Twain.

[2] R. Bruce Bickley, Jr., *Joel Chandler Harris*, 58.

[3] Letter from Joel Chandler Harris to Houghton, Mifflin, 1 October 1889. Quoted in Paul M. Cousins, *Joel Chandler Harris*, 179.

[4] Letter from Robert Underwood Johnson to Joel Chandler Harris, 6 March 1905 [Virginia].

[5] Letter from Robert Underwood Johnson to Joel Chandler Harris, 15 May 1905 [Virginia].

[6] Elting E. Morison, ed., *The Letters of Theodore Roosevelt*, vol. 4, 857

[7] Quoted in "President Roosevelt an Official Character," *Atlanta Constitution*, 21 October 1905, and "Roosevelt's Tribute to Famous Georgian," *Atlanta News*, 21 October 1905.

[8] Esther LaRose Harris, quoted in Myrta Lockett Avary, *Joel Chandler Harris and His Home*, 12.

[9] See "'Uncle Remus' Breaks Bread With Roosevelt," *Atlanta Constitution*, 19 November 1907, 1, 5.

[10] Letter from Theodore Roosevelt to Joel Chandler Harris, 27 April 1908.

[11] Joel Chandler Harris, "The Late Mr. Watkins of Georgia," 98.

[12] See Kathleen Light, "Uncle Remus and the Folklorists," *Southern Literary Journal* (Spring 1975): 88-104.

[13] Joel Chandler Harris, *Uncle Remus and His Friends*, vii. Harris's distrust of the use of the scientific methodology to justify pre-conceived conclusions did not end with his attacks upon "scientific" folklore. For an article in the *Saturday Evening Post* of 13 October 1900, he attacked the education profession.

[14] Joel Chandler Harris, *Wally Wanderoon*, 179-80.

[15] Joel Chandler Harris, *Wally Wanderoon*, 32.

[16] Joel Chandler Harris, *Wally Wanderoon*, 292.

[17] Joel Chandler Harris, "Brother Rabbit's Laughing-Place," *Metropolitan Magazine* (January 1905): 451.

[18] Quoted in Julia Collier Harris, *Joel Chandler Harris, Editor and Essayist*, 111.

[19] Joel Chandler Harris, *Wally Wanderoon*, 19, 20.

[20] Joel Chandler Harris, "The Negro of To-Day," 5.

[21] Letter from Booker T. Washington to Joel Chandler Harris, 1 February 1904.

[22] Wayne Mixon, "The Ultimate Irrelevance of Race…," 473.

[23] The mother of a solider killed in war carefully preserves his footprint she had found in the clay of a cabin's floor.

[24] Letter from Joel Chandler Harris to Richard Watson Gilder, 24 December 1886.

[25] Letter from Richard Watson Gilder to Joel Chandler Harris, 29 December 1886.

[26] Letter from Robert U. Johnson to Joel Chandler Harris, 2 July 1900.

[27] Letter from J. Randolph Walker to Joel Chandler Harris, 30 March 1903.

28 Letter from Paul R. Reynolds to Joel Chandler Harris, 29 June 1903 [Virginia].

29 Joel Chandler Harris, "Brother Rabbit's Laughing-Place," 452-53.

30 Letter from Francis W. Halsey to Henry Lanier, 25 August 1904.

31 Letter from Francis W. Halsey to Joel Chandler Harris, 27 August 1904.

32 Joel Chandler Harris, *The World's Wit and Humor*, xxv.

33 R. Bruce Bickley, Jr., *Joel Chandler Harris*, 93.

34 Review, *The Dial*, 16 December 1905, 445.

35 Review, *The Critic* (December 1905): 576.

36 Review, *New York Times*, 2 December 1905.

37 Joel Chandler Harris, *Told by Uncle Remus*, 3-4.

38 Joel Chandler Harris, *Told by Uncle Remus*, 4-5.

39 Joel Chandler Harris, *Told by Uncle Remus*, 13.

40 Joel Chandler Harris, *Told by Uncle Remus*, 172.

41 R. Bruce Bickley, Jr., *Joel Chandler Harris*, 94

Joel Chandler Harris with daugher Midred on the steps
of The Wren's Nest.

Joel Chandler Harris, 1906

Chapter 11

'Neighbor Knowledge'

On Saturday evening, 22 September 1906, several hundred young men, their pockets full of money from their weekly paychecks, their brains clouded by alcohol, poured out of the city's bars, and began attacking Blacks. Their purpose, they claimed, was to avenge several assaults and rapes the previous year by Black men against White women. Joel Chandler Harris and his family, who had often spoken out against violence, now risked their own lives to open their home to shelter and protect Blacks fleeing from the mobs.

The city administration responded forcefully to the mob. The state mobilized 600 soldiers; the mayor spoke out against the mob; the fire department used heavy streams of water to sweep the crowd from block to block; the police chief found himself in hand-to-hand combat to save the lives of Blacks. But, more than three thousand persons—mostly young men—continued their attack. By the time the riot was brought under control, ten Blacks and two Whites were dead; sixty Blacks and ten Whites were seriously injured. None of the dead or wounded Blacks had ever been accused of assaulting or raping anyone.

The deaths of Evan, Mary Esther, and Linton in childhood had helped shape Harris's concern for all children, and for all life. But it may have been the deaths of two grandchildren and his need to influence a generation of Americans to live in peace among themselves that led to Harris's decision to re-enter journalism full-time during the last two years of his life.

In 1897, Julian, his oldest son, had married Julia Collier. She was the daughter of Charles Collier, former Atlanta mayor, a prominent Atlanta business executive, and, in 1895, president of the Cotton States and International Exposition, a precursor to world fairs. Julia was trained in art and design, having studied in Boston for three years following graduation from the prestigious Washington Seminary. Julia and Julian's only two children died within four months of each other—Charles Collier Harris from acute gastritis at the age of four, shortly after Christmas 1903, Pierre LaRose Harris from an intestinal indigestion at the age of three in April 1904. "Mother was like a consoling angel in the desolate household," wrote Evelyn Harris, but "her faith sustained her, and she brought hope and courage to them while she mingled her tears with theirs."[1] Nevertheless, the deaths had sent Julia into an extended depression. The recovery of the entire Harris family would begin with a new venture.

Upset with the "politics-ridden, milk-and-water policy" of the *Constitution*,[2] Julian Harris resigned as managing editor of the *Constitution* in 1904 to become part-owner and managing editor of the newly-created *Atlanta Daily News*, returning to the *Constitution* six months later when the management failed to meet Harris's expectations of what a newspaper should stand for. Two years later, however, Julian, a social liberal who would continually push his father into more liberal views, resigned in 1906 to create *Uncle Remus's Magazine* as a vehicle for social and political change.

Roby Robinson, the *Constitution*'s business manager, enthusiastically put together the package, first by forming a new corporate entity and business structure, then by arranging for a solid financial base.[3] The magazine was initially funded by $100,000 raised by several Atlanta residents[4] and $6,000 from Robinson's friend financier/

Julia Collier Harris

industrialist Andrew Carnegie.[5] Finally, Robinson killed the *Sunny South*, the *Constitution*'s weekly magazine, and directed its 100,000 circulation into the new monthly. As part of the new look, Robinson arranged for *Uncle Remus's Magazine* to be housed in a new four-story building near the *Constitution*. For printing, Robinson arranged for the manufacture of what would become the second-largest magazine press ever built.

Julian Harris became publisher and business manager. Don Marquis became associate editor;[6] Edwin Camp, another newspaper journalist, became managing editor.[7] Joel Chandler Harris, after much persuasion by his son and the investors, became editor with assurances that he would have complete editorial control.

The editorial philosophy of the magazine was similar to that which Harris had while chief editorial writer of the *Constitution*:

> [It] will preach a cheerful Philosophy and practice a seasonable toleration in all matters where opinions and beliefs are likely to clash. It will be a Southern Magazine by reason of its environment,... but all its purposes and intentions, its motives and its policies will be broader than any section and higher than partisanship of any sort. It is purposed to issue a magazine that will be broadly and patriotically American, and genuinely representative of the best thought of the whole country.
>
> The note of provinciality is one of the chief charms of all that is really great in English literature, but those who will be in charge of this Magazine will have nothing to do with the provinciality so prevalent in the North, the East, the South, and the West—the provinciality that stands for ignorance and blind prejudice, that represents narrow views and unhappy congestion of ideas.

Neighbor-knowledge is perhaps more important in some respects than most of the knowledge imparted in the school. There is a woeful lack of it in the North and East with respect to the South, and this lack the magazine will endeavor in all seemly ways to remove....

[T]he Magazine will hold itself high above partisan politics and prejudices, and will refuse to be blinded by the prolific and offensive suggestions of sectionalism. It shall be its purpose so faithfully to represent right and Justice that every man in the land from the humblest to the highest, will stand on a plane of perfect equality in its pages.[8]

In keeping with such a policy, Harris wanted to call the magazine *The Optimist*, but instead was persuaded to capitalize on the Uncle Remus name.

After a two-month delay because Harris refused to approve what he considered to be inferior typesetting and printing,[9] the first issue of *Uncle Remus's Magazine* was distributed in June 1907. That first issue included several works by Harris, including an obligatory Uncle Remus tale, "How Brer Rabbit Saved Brer B'ar's Life," and the first installment of *The Bishop, the Boogerman, and The Right of Way*, a five-part historic romance novel with a theme that underscored the problems of a changing nation and the conflict between the older and newer generations following the Civil War.[10] Revising a plot-line from his Daddy Jake story twenty-one years earlier, Harris told the story of Billy Sanders befriending a run-away slave who had hit a cruel overseer over the head. However, the main theme that Harris threaded through the novel was about an orphan and her imaginary playmate who live with, and eventually soften, a crabby uncle with whom they live. "Slight, uneventful and disconnected," declared *Booklist*, "but full of the author's characteristic charm and humor."[11] *The Nation* agreed,

Edited by JOEL CHANDLER HARRIS

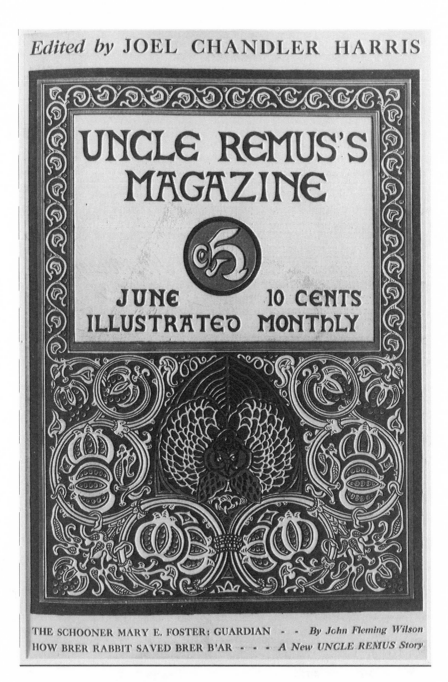

UNCLE REMUS'S MAGAZINE

JUNE   10 CENTS

ILLUSTRATED MONTHLY

THE SCHOONER MARY E. FOSTER: GUARDIAN   -   -   *By John Fleming Wilson*

HOW BRER RABBIT SAVED BRER B'AR   - - - -   *A New UNCLE REMUS Story*

noting that the structure of the book "exists only for the sake of its characters." However, the reviewer emphasized that the story was effective "because it revives in the reader the innocent emotions of childhood from which it springs."[12] The *New York Times* called it "charming, with its unexpected turns of thought and quaint forms of expression, its understanding of the child heart and the workings of the child brain, its kindliness, and its sweet bubbling humor."[13]

Circulation of *Uncle Remus's Magazine* for its first edition was 125,000, with about 100,000 of that being carry-over circulation from the *Sunny Side*. Within a year, *Uncle Remus's Magazine*, which included several tales in American Black English, bought out *The Home Magazine*, a general circulation magazine published by Bobbs-Merrill in Indianapolis, renamed itself *Uncle Remus's— The Home Magazine*, and reached a circulation of 240,000. To hold that circulation, one of the largest in the nation, Harris occasionally reprinted his tales from two decades earlier.

Because Harris was still concerned about social reform, including problems of race relations, yet unwilling to allow the magazine to be more than the optimist he had hoped for, he brought back Billy Sanders, his loquacious old-time White curmudgeon who had lived through the same eras as had Uncle Remus. The use of a foil allowed Harris to have Sanders castigate the editor in print for not bringing more social issues to the magazine, yet still talk about problems and their solutions. "Free Joe," his most famous short story, was reprinted in the January 1908 issue.

In response to a question from an unnamed reporter-interviewer, Billy Sanders—who had been visiting the *Constitution*—discussed the "negro business." Almost three decades after Harris first spoke out against mob vengeance, he was still writing about social justice for American Blacks:

"When some nigger tramp an' vagabond destroys a white 'oman, an' he's ketched an' lynched in the heat an' fury of the hour, I don't hide my face in a friendly pillow an' sob ontell my manly frame is shook wi' my feelin's, an' say, 'What a pity!' I don't say it bekaze I don't feel that way. But I'll tell you what I think when I git cool: I think the whole business is wrong, terribly wrong. We have come to a p'int whar we've got to grab ourselves by the seat of the britches, an' git lifted up ter whar we can take a sober an' civilized view of our troubles.

"The way things have been gwine lately, we ain't givin' the niggers a fa'r showin'; we ain't a-treatin' of 'em right. Time was, an' that not so mighty long ago, when our editors, big an' little, and all our public men, both great and small, was a-kickin' as high as my ol' speckled steer bekaze the papers an' the politicians of the North was a-callin' all on us barbarians ever' time anything happened down here. We show'd how onjest sech treatment was, an' we worried about it no little. Well, we oughter do as we'd be done by. Let a bow-legged nigger come along an' do his devilment, an' right straight we lay the responsibility of the crime on the whole nigger race; an' sometimes I'm afeard we want to do jest like you all up here in Atlanta done. We never stop for to consider that these debauched nigger criminals don't stand for the whole colored race; an' we constantly want to forget what never should be forgot—that what that's one of these sons of Satan, thar's ten thousand decent, industrious, well-behaved niggers....

I've hearn folks say that all niggers look alike to them, but they don't look alike to me, an' they never will, not whilst my eyesight's good. Thar's jest as much difference betwixt niggers as thar is betwixt white folks, an' a heap more ef you know the races right well. [14]

Nevertheless, as much as they fought for social equality, Harris and his son still believed that, with individual exceptions, Blacks were not yet ready to become a part of the American political and business communities.

For reviews, Harris created Anne Macfarland—a rural Georgian now living in London whose "style and views evoked the picture of a middle-aged woman of downright opinions and home-loving tendencies; of charitable disposition and unaffected manners; of wide information and shrewd vision."[15] Harris himself, reported Julia Collier Harris, "was averse to any critical analysis of a book or writer in conversation, and never had the occasion for the formal expression of his literary opinions in writing until 'Anne Macfarland' gave him an opportunity."[16] Just as Harris had once tried to hide the identity of "The Countryman's Devil" from Joseph Addison Turner, he now tried to hide Anne Macfarland's identity from the staff. And, just as Turner slyly knew the identity of the "bogus" author, the staff of *Uncle Remus's Magazine* figured out Anne Macfarland's identity, but they, like Turner, preserved Harris's "secret."

But the depth of Harris's concern for social justice was no secret. "I shall give my southern, as well as my northern, readers a few elemental truths that should be brought to the attention of both sections," Harris wrote to Wendell P. Garrison, editor of *The Nation*, four months after the magazine was first published.[17]

Even with a solid editorial philosophy and staff, the magazine could not bring Harris's message to the public if it did not survive financially. In a letter to Andrew Carnegie, to be hand-delivered by Julian, the ever-optimistic Joel Chandler Harris requested additional financial assistance and further explained his philosophy for the magazine:

The magazine has every prospect of success; subscribers are pouring in every day, and advertisers are beginning to wake up to the fact that its circulation is very much larger than that of any six months' old periodical ever issued in this country.... Six months more will place the concern on a paying basis—a basis that will enable me to carry out certain policies that I have in mind with respect to the negro question.... These policies cannot be successfully exploited in a daily newspaper, where they would fly in the face of the schemes of the politicians. I am sure that I shall be able to smooth over and soothe, and finally dissipate all ill feelings and prejudices that now exist between the races. At my time of life I have no higher ambition; in fact, it is the only ambition I have ever had, the only line of policy that I have ever deliberately mapped out in my own mind.... I think [the magazine's] success will mean more to the people of the whole south, white and black, than any work of purely local philanthropy. I have it in my mind to fit the magazine to such gentle and sure policies of persuasion with respect to the negro question, which is also the white man's question, that honest people cannot resist them—and, in the main, the people of the south are both honest and kindly. This, briefly, is the great work that I have set before me. I do not say that I am the only man who can carry it on, but no other man is in a better position to do it, provided the magazine weathers the financial crisis that seems to have struck the whole country. You see, I am not asking any financial aid for myself. If the magazine is doomed, I have other things to turn to. What I am anxious for you to do is to join hands with us, so that the policies and principles I have in mind—the obliteration of prejudice against the blacks, the demand for a square deal, and the uplifting of both races so that they can look justice in the face without blushing—may be definitely carried out....[18]

Although he wanted Carnegie's assistance, Harris never gave up his principles, as he continued to write against the robber-barons whose goal seemed to be to disregard the common courtesies of life as they exploited the masses in order to live an opulent lifestyle that included dozens of servants in their houses and million-dollar "summer cottages," and thousands of poorly-paid employees who were little more than slaves.

Burdened by knowing he had to write many of the stories for *Uncle Remus's Magazine*, and well aware that the readers expected to see more than essays, reviews, tales, and short stories from the creator of Uncle Remus, Harris continued to write for other magazines as well. To add to the perceptive voices of Billy Sanders and Anne Macfarland, and well aware of what the public wanted, Harris brought back Uncle Remus. Writing to Paul R. Reynolds, his literary agent, Harris inquired about possible sales: "The McClures write me that you have sold the Uncle Remus stuff to Collier's Weekly. Do you think you could sell them six or eight more? Now that I am on the Remus stuff, I want to work up all the material that I have gathered since the last book was published, which is more than ten years ago...."[19]

In 1904, McClure, Phillips had published *A Little Union Scout*, an episodic novel first serialized in the *Saturday Evening Post* earlier that year. Typical of his war stories, Harris structured plot twists with a layer of romance, this one ending with the Confederate soldier/narrator marrying the female Union scout. "There is certainly nothing startlingly novel in a plot of this kind," stated a review in the *New York Times*, but also pointed out that "in the working out of its details Mr. Harris has departed widely enough from the stereotyped order of things to give the old familiar happenings an air of decided freshness and reality."[20]

Although *A Little Union Scout* was one of Harris's more popular magazine stories, and had a successful book sale, Harris was not pleased with it,[21] and planned to write a powerful account of the horrors of war that he hoped would erase the defects he saw in *A Little Union Scout*, as well as several of his previous efforts to describe battles. "A Shadow Between His Shoulder-Blades" was published as a three-part novelette by the *Saturday Evening Post* in November 1907.[22] It was, suggests Bruce Bickley, "one of Harris's best war stories [made] even more appealing because it undercuts wartime heroics and shows the absurdity and confusion that often attended battle."[23] The *New York Times* said that the story "has the inimitable flavor of all Mr. Harris has written."[24] It was his last major work.

For several decades, Harris had been consumed by seemingly conflicting needs—to live simply and be a part of the people he wrote about, yet work harder than his friends and colleagues to earn as much income as possible, the money perhaps an acknowledgment of his worth as both a writer and as a capable provider for his family. Within the last few years of his life, his work ethic had changed, as he perhaps reflected upon the happiness of many on a plantation whose bodies were enslaved but their minds free:

*Brer Rabbit,
Uncle Remus,
and the 'Cornfield
Journalist'*

....

250

[The Farmer] was long ago convinced, though it is difficult to convince the multitude, that riches are a heartbreaking burden to those who are born in their shadow. Large prosperity stands for a whole swarm of secret troubles which its possessors refrain from imparting to the public through the medium of the genial reporters that haunt the doorsteps of the rich. These heartbreaking troubles, these fright-breeding worries, are never known to the multitude, who stand far off from the infection....

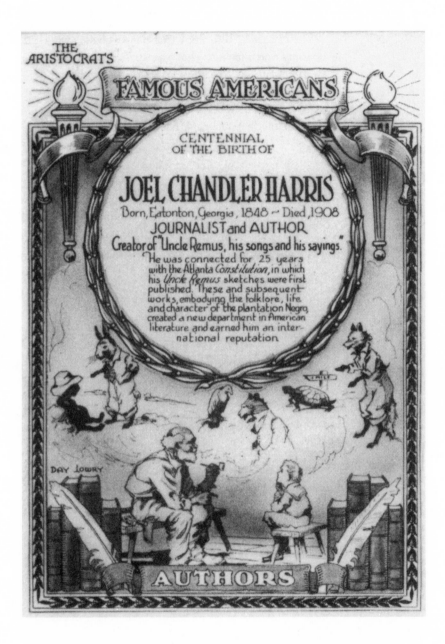

THE ARISTOCRATS

FAMOUS AMERICANS

CENTENNIAL OF THE BIRTH OF

JOEL CHANDLER HARRIS

Born, Eatonton, Georgia, 1848 ~ Died, 1908

JOURNALIST and AUTHOR

Creator of "Uncle Remus, his songs and his sayings."

He was connected for 25 years with the Atlanta *Constitution*, in which his *Uncle Remus* sketches were first published. These and subsequent works, embodying the folklore, life, and character of the plantation Negro, created a new department in American literature and earned him an international reputation.

DAY LOWRY

AUTHORS

The Farmer used to think that money could buy everything worth having. That was years ago, and he is heartily glad that the illusion has been dispelled. The best things of life are not on the market and never will be, and money has no power over them. It can buy neither happiness nor content, nor can it buy a home.[25]

At the end of his life, Joel Chandler Harris was doing exactly what he wanted to do—he was a journalist who, with a bit of cynicism and a lot of insight, underscored by a bed of humor, was writing about social issues and hoping to persuade a nation to live the simple life in peace.

---

[1] Evelyn Harris, A Little Story, 53.

[2] Letter from Julian Harris, quoted in Gregory Carroll Lisby, Someone Had to be Hated, 29.

[3] Julian LaRose Harris, quoted in Julia Collier Harris, The Life and Letters of Joel Chandler Harris, 519.

[4] Letter from Clark Howell, editor of the Constitution to Paul R. Reynolds, 24 October 1906. Some sources, however, place the figure at $200,000.

[5] It was an unusual friendship. Harris, a "commoner" who loved all people, accepted and returned the friendship with Carnegie, by most accounts one of the "robber barons" who had little respect for the working class, and who turned to philanthropy after earning millions in the steel industry.

[6] Marquis later became a featured columnist for the New York Sun. Influenced by the Uncle Remus stories and the use of foils, Marquis created Archy, a free-verse poetic cockroach.

[7] Camp and Mildred Harris would marry in 1909.

[8] "Principles and Scope of the Magazine," Uncle Remus's Magazine (June 1907): 6.

[9] See Julia Collier Harris, The Life and Letters of Joel Chandler Harris, 534, for Julian Harris's comments about his father's "outrage" at the artistic quality of the magazine.

[10] The novel was published in book form by Doubleday, Page in 1909 as *The Bishop and the Boogerman*.

[11] Review, *Booklist* (April 1908): 114.

[12] Review, *The Nation*, 18 February 1909, 171.

[13] "Mysterious Cally-Lou," *New York Times*, 20 February 1909, 103.

[14] Joel Chandler Harris, "Mr. Billy Sanders of Shady Dale: His Views of Problems and Remedies," 22.

[15] Julia Collier Harris, *The Life and Letters of Joel Chandler Harris*, 564.

[16] Julia Collier Harris, *The Life and Letters of Joel Chandler Harris*, 569. In the first decade of his professional career, Harris frequently reviewed books and magazines. Into the 1880s and 1890s, he praised, either in letters to the editor or commentary, the works of Mark Twain, Rudyard Kipling, Harriet Beecher Stowe, and Walt Whitman, among others.

[17] Letter from Joel Chandler Harris to Wendell Garrison, 22 October 1906. [Virginia.]

[18] Letter from Joel Chandler Harris to Andrew Carnegie, 2 November 1907. There is a question whether the letter was delivered.

[19] Letter from Joel Chandler Harris to Paul R. Reynolds, 8 May 1908.

[20] "A War Story," *New York Times*, 7 May 1904, 307.

[21] Letter from Joel Chandler Harris to Paul R. Reynolds, 2 June 1904 [Virginia].

[22] D. Appleton had planned to publish the book in spring 1908; however, Small, Maynard published the novel posthumously in 1909, changing the title to *The Shadow Between His Shoulder-Blades*.

[23] R. Bruce Bickley, Jr., *Joel Chandler Harris*, 143.

[24] "An Unmitigated Villain," *New York Times*, 6 November 1909, 689.

[25] Joel Chandler Harris, "Houses and Homes," 5

UNCLE REMUS'S HOME MAGAZINE

Founded By J...... ...NDLER HARRIS

Chapter 12

'An Excellent Thing to Die By'

For several years, Joel Chandler Harris had suffered from long-term illnesses, including the grippe (later named the flu), a massive head and throat infection caused from a diseased tooth, and several headaches each of which kept him out of work for a day or two, and which may have been migraines. Some of the illnesses may have been enhanced by extreme fatigue, others possibly from the effects of alcohol, although Harris often admonished his children not to begin to drink, and maintained that he had been sober for more than three decades.

The mental exhaustion Harris once experienced as both a newspaper editor and as a writer-journalist now became more apparent in his career as a magazine editor and writer-journalist. Harris was certainly accustomed to the stress of journalism, often working against deadlines and pressures while pushing aside his own exhaustion and personal problems until a time when he could relax. With the purchase of *The Home Magazine* in April 1908, and the probable financial success of *Uncle Remus's Magazine*, Harris finally relaxed. Julia Collier Harris recalled:

> [F]or the first time it became apparent that the unwonted responsibility had not been good for him. Of course, all the troublesome details of the business and the mechanical end of the affair had been kept from him as much as possible, for Julian was determined that his father's resistance should not be strained by any unnecessary demands upon it, but he had not calculated upon that intuitive and sensitive temperament

which was so delicately balanced that it responded almost instantly to whatever was in the air.[1]

For about a year, beginning perhaps in the late summer or early fall of 1907, Julia Collier Harris remembered that her father-in-law:

> ...had periods of depression when he fancied that his best days were over and that his power as a writer were on the wane. This was so unlike him, so out of keeping with his outlook and his lifelong habit of optimism, that it puzzled and distressed us. We could not know that these moods were the reflexes of a physical condition which was slow to give more obvious symptoms.[2]

Julia Collier Harris says that about May 1908, a month after *Uncle Remus's Magazine* purchased *The Home Magazine*, Essie Harris "began to notice that the 'Farmer' was not as energetic" as he once was, that he did not work as much on his rose garden and vegetable patch, and that he rested more than normal. Her husband, however, refused medical assistance, possibly believing he was just tired. In early June, Essie finally called a family friend, a physician, to "drop by the house in casual fashion and look father over."[3] The physician determined that Harris was suffering from cirrhosis of the liver and advised surgery. For two weeks, Harris refused until he was in pain. By then, it was obvious he was dying. His physician said that if everything was favorable, the creator of Uncle Remus might live at most another year. One morning, Julian had asked his father how he was; with characteristic humor, Harris responded he was "about the extent of a tenth of a gnat's eyebrow better."[4]

Knowing he had a terminal illness, Harris did something he had put off numerous times. For several years, he had accepted many of the beliefs of the Catholic church, the faith of his wife and children; two weeks from his death, he was baptized a Catholic. Essie knew "it was the culmination of a desire he had often expressed and an intention he had obviously postponed," according to Evelyn Harris.[5] Essie was one of the founders of the near-by St. Anthony's Catholic Church, and her husband had paid for the land upon which it was built. In a particularly enlightening letter to Lillian, who was then in her first year as a student at St. Joseph's Academy in Washington, Georgia, Harris wrote in 1896:

> My regards to Sister Bernard, and say to her that I am glad and grateful that she is praying for a special favor to me. I think I know what it is, and the idea is growing more and more pleasing to me every day. Say to her that if she had been raised a Protestant she would know how hard it is to root out of the mind the prejudices and doubts and fictions that have been educated into it. This is the task I am engaged in now. There are only small and insignificant weeds in my mind at this time, but I want to have them all cleared out and thrown over the fence in the trash-pile.[6]

Essie herself had few religious prejudices, having innumerable times reinforced in her children the importance of tolerance and acceptance of different views. As for her husband, whatever prejudices he may have had about organized religion certainly had not come from his mother. Although born into a Methodist family, Mary Harris was not a member of any church, but "was a student of the Bible all her life, and from childhood had instructed [her son] in its lessons, but had never attempted to instill creed or dogma," wrote Julia Collier Harris.[7] As a result of his mother's teachings and his own values, "Dogma in religion had no interest for [him] and he had

scant patience with church dissensions," said Julia Collier Harris, who also explained that he "respected every man's faith and had no wish to interfere with it."[8]

His religion, said the Reverend Dr. James W. Lee, a close friend "pervaded his whole life. It was more of an atmosphere you felt than a distinct entity you could describe.... His religion was expressed through every act and word of his life. As the quiet, silent sunlight manages to embody itself in all trees and flowers and animals in the world, so the religion of Mr. Harris found embodiment in all his writings and in all relations of his life."[9] During the last weeks of Harris's life, it was Essie who had to be the foundation for the family. "It was her faith that sustained her during the terrifying days when we were aware of the inevitable," said Evelyn Harris, "and she came through the ordeal with a bravery that could not entirely conceal the torture of her heart."[10]

Joel Chandler Harris had once written, "humor is an excellent thing to live by, and all things being equal, an excellent thing to die by." After more than five years of chronic illness and depression, the last year which had severely restricted his writing, Joel Chandler Harris died at the age of sixty-one, about 8:00 P.M. on 3 July 1908. The medical cause was acute nephritis and uremic poisoning, from complications of chronic cirrhosis of the liver.

Joel Chandler Harris did not leave a will, nor much of an estate except for his home and writings, having spent lavishly during his life for those less fortunate, and for the needs and wants of his family, including private schools, the annual summer vacations in Canada for his wife and children, and the house itself. At a memorial service the day after Harris died, the Reverend Dr. James W. Lee told about the soul of a man who was loved throughout the country:

The feelings of those brought up with Mr. Harris, and living all their lives in close proximity to his simple, beautiful life, may be defined as those of love and complete admiration. It has never occurred to them to engage in the critical business of forming dry and intellectual estimates of his mysterious mental powers. They have felt them and rejoiced in them, and with that they have been content. The people of Georgia feel very much toward Mr. Harris as the citizens of Venice feel toward their city—they love him too much to describe him. Outsiders may take intellectual interest in him; the interest we take in him is emotional and affectional. We have regarded him as the property of our hearts and not of our heads....

He never referred to himself, he never asserted himself, he never advertised himself. No man ever wore the honors that unbidden came to him with less self-gratulation....

We love Mr. Harris...not simply because he was genuinely true, and kindly and good, but because, in addition to all these traits of personal worth, he was a creator, and helped to give our state a place in the eternal realm of mind. By his work he enhanced us all by a process of artistic work by which he, at the same time, enriched himself. The wealth he created was of the high sort that...cannot be cabined, or cornered, or confined. It is of the sort that, when once produced, increases in proportion to the number of persons who share in it. It is of the kind that belongs to the universal spirit of man.[11]

But it was Joel Chandler Harris himself who had written the most appropriate eulogy. In 1890, for a memorial volume dedicated to Henry W. Grady who had died months earlier, Harris had written:

Four hundred children from West End, each with a bouquet of flowers, attended the funeral at Howell Pa

The effects of [Grady's death] were greater than sorrow could conceive or affection contemplate. Men who had only a passing acquaintance with him wept when they heard of his death. Laboring men spoke of him with trembling lips and tearful eyes, and working-women went to their tasks in the morning crying bitterly. Never again will there come to Atlanta a calamity that shall so profoundly touch the hearts of the people—that shall so encompass the town with the spirit of mourning.[12]

Less than two decades later, that same eulogy could have been said about Harris.

Thousands of telegrams of consolation poured into Atlanta to the family of the man who created the Uncle Remus legend. Harris's death "will be mourned wherever american [sic] literature is read," wrote Robert Underwood Johnson. James Whitcomb Riley, who several times had visited Harris at the Wren's Nest—and had once written Harris that a two-week stay at the Wren's Nest was "the highest honor and happiness of my life"— told Julian Harris, "Though his voice is stilled forever here, yet forever will it be heard gladdening alike the hearts of age and childhood."13 William M. Handt, Sunday editor of the *Chicago Tribune*, said that he, like the nation, "[mourns] the loss of the brilliant journalist, kindliest of critics and best of story tellers." Joseph M. Rogers, associate editor of the *Philadelphia Inquirer*, eulogized "no man since Abraham Lincoln got nearer to the hearts of the whole people. [His] monument is imperishable and his life a benison [blessing]."[14]

In the *Constitution* of 4 July, publisher Clark Howell, one of Harris's closest friends, and son of Evan P. Howell, wrote:

> From all his studied unobtrusiveness, the man wrought himself a broad and firm place in the spiritual history and traditions of his people; and it is from things spiritual that the things of substance take their color and substance....
>
> His reputation is worldwide because he was the articulate voice of that humble race, whose every mood and tense he knew with complete comprehension. His mission was—and is—broader [for] his folklore and his novels, his short stories and his poems breathe consistently a distinguished philosophy [of] optimism, of mutual trust, and of tolerance of all living things, [and] of common sense and of idealism....

Thomas H. English, literature professor at Emory University, later summarized Harris's literary life:

> [He] was the proponent of a living culture. He sought to preserve the memory of a gracious past, of all that possessed primary human values in the past of the South. He strove earnestly and intelligently for a solution to pressing problems of his own day. He sought to lay deep the foundations of the future. It is perhaps true that his heart yearned for the simplicities of the past, Uncle Remus's "old farming days," but his mind sprang to meet the challenge of the complexities of the future. He was not afraid of progress. He was

Tombstone and Plaque at Westview Cemetery

assured that all would be well with the world if only the human virtues of simplicity might be preserved even in the midst of complexity.[15]

On a rainy afternoon, Joel Chandler Harris was buried in Westview Cemetery, not far from the crypts of his friends and colleagues Henry W. Grady and Evan P. Howell. Shortly before he died, Harris had written Julian that he wanted no monument:

> If…they try to start any monument business, don't let them do it. A statue will stand out in the rain and the cold, or, dust-covered, useless and disfiguring, will soon be forgotten except by the sparrows in nesting-time. If what little I have done is found worthy of commendation, tell the people of the South to let the Magazine succeed. And if it is not too much trouble…run a little line somewhere—"Founded by Joel Chandler Harris."[16]

Julian Harris was determined to follow his father's wishes to keep the magazine from becoming "just a money-making machine."[17] It never did. Julian Harris, more socially aggressive and politically fiery than the father, would probably have moved the magazine more into muckraking had his father not emphasized the "optimist" editorial philosophy. Now in charge, against significant opposition, Julian led the magazine to increase its coverage of social and political issues, and called for racial equality, something his father had urged at his death-bed. Theodore Roosevelt had pleaded for the continuation of the magazine as a tribute to Harris, as a vehicle for public discussion of important social issues.[18] However, the muckraking era that highlighted an increased awareness of America's social conditions, led by writers who attacked crime, corruption, and social injustice, had begun to fade by 1909, after its peak in 1906, and the public wanted tales of rabbits and foxes, even if they were disguised allegories of the greater social issues.[19]

Although Julian Harris published several of his father's short stories and poems, several of which had first been published earlier in other magazines, the public knew the creator of Uncle Remus was no longer in charge. Soon, not even Julian Harris was in charge. As the magazine began a financial decline, Julian Harris insisted the magazine must survive to meet his father's last wishes. The corporate board eventually forced him to give up his stock to help pay for the magazine's survival, then brought in an outside general manager to save it. The "rescue," somewhat typical of when corporations scurry around to increase profits while forgetting the principles that established its product's reputation, turned Joel Chandler Harris's last journalistic enterprise into a weakened vehicle that tore away the respect it had earned. The magazine, which had once raised the public conscience, died in 1913 from an indifferent public.

[1] Julia Collier Harris, *The Life and Letters of Joel Chandler Harris*, 578.

[2] Julia Collier Harris, *The Life and Letters of Joel Chandler Harris*, 577.

[3] Julia Collier Harris, *The Life and Letters of Joel Chandler Harris*, 579.

[4] Quoted in Myrta Lockett Avary, *Joel Chandler Harris and His Home*, 24.

[5] Evelyn Harris, *A Little Story*, 59.

[6] Letter from Joel Chandler Harris to Lillian Harris, 25 April 1896.

[7] Julia Collier Harris, *The Life and Letters of Joel Chandler Harris*, 352.

[8] Julia Collier Harris, "Joel Chandler Harris—Fearless Editor," 10.

9 J. W. Lee, "The Character of Joel Chandler Harris," 112. [in Ivy L. Lee, "Uncle Remus"].

10 Evelyn Harris, A Little Story, 58.

11 James W. Lee, "The Character of Joel Chandler Harris," 87-88, 100, 91-92.

12 Joel Chandler Harris, Life of Henry W. Grady, 67.

13 Julia Collier Harris, The Life and Letters of Joel Chandler Harris, 426.

14 Telegram from Joseph M. Rogers to Julian Harris, 4 July 1908.

15 Thomas H. English, "In Memory of Uncle Remus," 77.

16 Letter from Joel Chandler Harris to Julian LaRose Harris, June 1906. Quoted in Julia Collier Harris, The Life and Letters of Joel Chandler Harris, 586-87.

17 Julia Collier Harris, The Life and Letters of Joel Chandler Harris, 587.

18 Letter from Theodore Roosevelt to Julian Harris, 6 July 1908, in Elting E. Morris, ed., The Letters of Theodore Roosevelt, vol. 6, 1109.

19 For more about the era of the muckrakers, including a demythologizing of what muckraking was, see Walter M. Brasch, Forerunners of Revolution: Muckrakers and the American Social Conscience (1990).

Julian Harris

Chapter 13

'A National Heritage'

The end of the Reconstruction Cycle shortly after the turn of the century,[1] had brought a relative quiet two-decade inter-cycle. But, World War I had shocked America into a "loss of innocence," an era that would be marked not only by the deaths of about 115,000 Americans, but by a further racial division that would lead to war on America's streets.

The "Great Migration" of American Blacks from the rural, agrarian South—the plantation economy Joel Chandler Harris so loved and understood—into the urban, industrialized North began during World War I as hundreds of thousands of Blacks moved North to seek what they believed were better jobs and better opportunities to raise their families. More than 400,000 Blacks had served in the war, about half of them overseas in segregated units. They returned to an America they believed would recognize their sacrifice and would welcome them home, perhaps even integrating them into the "melting pot" the White culture claimed was America. But, race riots in Houston, Philadelphia, and East St. Louis in 1917 near the end of the war, followed by the "Red Summer" of 1919, during which 120 persons were killed, and several thousands left homeless in riots in Chicago, Omaha, Charleston, Knoxville, and Washington, D.C.—punctuated by the lynchings of more than seventy Blacks in both North and South— proved that racism knew no geographical limits.

From fear, alienation, and betrayal there emerged a more militant literature that became the base of the Negro Renaissance

Cycle, an unprecedented burst of pandemic creativity, its spiritual capital set in Harlem, formerly a White upper-class suburb on Manhattan. In the decade following the beginning of World War I, Harlem grew from a community of about 14,000 Blacks to an urban city of about 175,000, home for Black artists, actors, singers, musicians, and writers whose works emphasized racial pride and an understanding of their cultural heritage.

Among the writer-journalists who emerged to lead "The New Negro," as the movement was first called, were Sterling A. Brown, Countee Cullen, Arthur Fauset, Jessie Redman Fauset, James Weldon Johnson, Charles Gilpin, Zora Neale Hurston, Nella Larsen, Alain Locke, Claude McKay, Jean Toomer, Carl Van Vechten, Ida B. Wells-Barnett, and Langston Hughes, who would be known as the "poet laureate" of the Renaissance. Their works would be published in *The Crisis*, official publication of the National Association for the Advancement of Colored People, and edited by W. E. B. DuBois from 1910-1934; *Opportunity*, the journal of the National Urban League, edited by Charles S. Johnson, who would become the first black president of Fisk University; by White-owned publications *The Nation*, *The New Republic*, and the *Saturday Review*; and by several New York book publishers who recognized what was emerging as not only some of the best Black literature ever written, but also some of the best American literature, a literature that would cross over and influence a White American audience.

"Black music," with a syncopated beat spread across a twelve-measure sequence in 2/4 or 4/4 time, now underscored American popular music and the hoped-for "good times" to usher the White nation past "The Lost Generation" and into the "Jazz Age," which would parallel the separate but equal Negro Renaissance.

It was during this era there emerged giants of litera-ture—Sherwood Anderson, Erskine Caldwell, Theodore Dreiser, T. S. Eliot, William Faulkner, F. Scott Fitzgerald, Robert Frost, Ben Hecht, Ernest Hemingway, Sinclair Lewis, Eugene O'Neil, John Steinbeck, and James Thurber, all of whom would complement the literature of the Negro Renaissance.

Almost every American writer-journalist in the twentieth century who used the narrative tale owed something to the creator and transcriber of the Uncle Remus stories, who readily acknowledged that it was the Black oral folklore that gave him his ideas and his popu-larity. Among the writers in this new era who drew upon Joel Chandler Harris were William Faulkner, whose Black characters in the fictional Yoknapatawpha County, Mississippi, spoke a mixture of Standard and Black English; DuBose Heyward, who created the story of *Porgy*, a Charleston beggar who spoke a variety of Gullah; and Margaret Mitchell who accurately used Black lan-guage of the 1930s Middle Georgia in the epic Civil War novel *Gone With the Wind*.

But, in counterpoint to the beauty and realism that Faulkner, Heyward, Mitchell, and dozens of others, including the Negro Renaissance writers, brought to the American people, racist stereotypes proliferated once again in the American media during the two decades fol-lowing World War I. Hundreds of products again bore images of Black mammies who—as White America knew "fo' sure"—were experts of which products to use for child-care, cooking, and gardening. Restaurants were again named Sambo's, Rastus's, and Uncle Remus's or Brer Rabbit's. Businesses, from realty companies to office supply houses, were named for characters in the tales.[2] In 1932, Coca-Cola, an Atlanta corporation, distributed more than three million cardboard cut-outs and almost 24,000 window display sets, all of them linking the soft

drink with Uncle Remus characters.[3] Magazines now published innumerable stories written by White writers using very bad representations of Black language. In response, many Black writers not only wrote in Standard English, but now called the use of American Black English in fiction racist, attacking not only the Uncle Remus tales, but the dialect verse of Black writers from the Reconstruction Cycle.

Nevertheless, during the post-war years several folklorists—among them Elsie Clews Parsons, Arthur Huff Fauset, J. Mason Brewer, Richard M. Dorson, and Zora Neale Hurston—continued the work that Joel Chandler Harris had established. But Parsons, who set the standard for folklore research in a newer era, although praising Harris for his accurate recording of the language and tales of the Civil War and Reconstruction Cycle Black, discounted African origins of the Remus tales. Eventually, linguists and folklorists would prove the tales were indeed African perspectives on life and their consequences.

During the four decades following Joel Chandler Harris's death, publishers brought out two unpublished novels and four additional compilations of tales first published in newspapers and magazines but never compiled into book form. The *Saturday Review of Literature*, soon to become the nation's leading book review magazine, argued in 1925 that Harris "remains one of our greatest truly American writers" who should rank along with Mark Twain and Walt Whitman, and that the Uncle Remus stories are "a national heritage."[4]

In 1926, a *Golden Book Magazine* survey of 400 high school and college literature teachers ranked the Uncle Remus tales fifth among all American works, behind Edgar Allan Poe's *Tales*, Nathaniel Hawthorne's *Scarlet Letter*, Mark Twain's *Huckleberry Finn*, and James Fenimore Cooper's *The Last of the Mohicans*.[5] Three

First Day of Issue, with original signatures of the six surviving Harris children. (from the collection of Keith A. Winsell)

decades after his death, Harris's popularity and legacy was still being honored—everything from radio shows to ships. On 24 June 1941, the DuPont Radio Network broadcast "Joel Chandler Harris," an original radio drama written by Arthur Miller, and starring Karl Swenson as Harris and Uncle Remus, with Agnes Moorhead as Essie.[6] On 12 August 1942, under contract to the J. H. Winchester Shipping Company, the Alabama Drydock and Ship Building Company launched the *Joel Chandler Harris*, one of 2,700 liberty ships designed for private companies to carry cargo during World War II.

In 1948, the accepted centennial of Harris's birth, Georgia, which in 1912 had declared 9 December as Uncle Remus Day, designated Highway 441, which runs through Eatonton, as Uncle Remus Highway. On 9 December, the U.S. Post Office honored Harris with a three-cent commemorative stamp in its Famous Americans Series. About 400,000 First Day of Issue covers were postmarked at the small Eatonton post office; another 100,000 stamps would be issued throughout the country. Overall, the U.S. Post Office issued about sixty million stamps.

But it was a film that was simultaneously praised for its animation and condemned for its depiction of Blacks in live-action sequences that brought the nation to recognize the Uncle Remus tales, even if by now the people did not necessarily know the name of their author. The film would distort the Uncle Remus legends and establish a new reality in the public's mind.

Walt Disney had optioned all rights to Harris's stories for $10,000 in 1939. "Ever since I have had anything to do with the making of motion pictures, I have wanted to bring the Uncle Remus tales to the screen," said Disney who had become familiar with the stories while a child. Joel Chandler Harris, Jr. explained why the Harris family had decided to allow Disney to secure film rights to the

Uncle Remus stories: "For many years the members of our family have been keenly desirous of having the stories of Uncle Remus given an impetus on the screen to be further immortalized for the older generation and brought more keenly into the minds of the younger generation who seem to get so many more of their ideas from the screen than from books."[7]

However, other major productions and World War II contracts had kept Disney from doing much with the investment. With the war almost over, Disney began to translate the Uncle Remus stories to film, setting the time frame as the late nineteenth century. In the role of Uncle Remus, and providing the voice of the animated Brer Fox, was James Baskett, a former vaudevillian and a nationally-known radio actor. Disney said for the central role he wanted someone who "never appeared on the screen. We want [the audience] to see 'Uncle Remus' and not some actor whose personality is already known to them through other screen roles."[8] The casting of Baskett also changed the look of Uncle Remus from a tall, thin man, envisioned by Harris and the illustrators of the late nineteenth century, to that of a large Black with a white beard that accented a round face. Hattie McDaniel, an Oscar-winning actress for her role as a maid in *Gone With the Wind*, played Tempy; Ruth Warwick was Miss Sally; Eric Rolf was the Little Boy who was now a crusading newspaper editor; newcomer Bobby Driscoll played their son, Johnny. The animation sequences starred Brer Rabbit, Brer Fox, and Brer Bear. In Disney style, the animated characters were more slapstick cartoons than what E. W. Kemble, Frederick S. Church, and A. B. Frost had envisioned several decades earlier. Disney would characterize the rabbit not as malevolent nor mischievous, and definitely not the trickster of the original tales, but as "the naive, happy-go-lucky little hero of the Tales—protagonist of the human race, actually—who stumbles into

one kind of trouble after another, always managing through belated thought, courage and a bit of 'fottswork' to squeak through." Brer Fox was the "sly, scheming leader of the forces of evil, who will stop at little or nothing—preferably nothing—to gain his sinister designs, and whose one burning ambition is to 'ketch dat biggity rabbit.'" Brer Bear, according to Disney, was "the great bumbling side of Brer Fox, whose strength is as the strength of twenty, but whose porridge-like brain is unequal to the task of becoming a true villain."[9] The "Brers," as the Disney publicity organization called them, "each resembles somebody everyone knows."[10]

On 12 November 1946—about seven years after Atlanta hosted the premiere of *Gone With the Wind*— *Song of the South*, after a two-year production cycle, premiered to a segregated audience of about 4,300 in Atlanta.[11] Filmed near Phoenix, the film was directed by Harve Foster (live action) and Wilfred Jackson (animation) from a story by Dalton Reymond. The final screenplay was credited to Reymond, Morton Grant, and Maurice Rapf; the story for the three animation sequences was credited to William Peed, Ralph Wright, and George Stallings. Thirty-six persons worked on the animation for two years; about 30 percent of the final cut was the three separate animated sequences and the "marriage" of live-action and animation.

"A living cast was absolutely necessary to get the full emotional impact and the entertainment values of the cartooned legends," said Walt Disney. Elaborating, he pointed out: "These players would be the immediate target of the Uncle Remus myths in the indirect approach to our audience. And the audience would be all the more entranced and stirred by watching the reactions of other living persons to the humorous homilies and sometimes biting satire."[12]

A front-page article in the next day's *Constitution* gushed, "'Song of the South' is unquestionably Walt Disney's greatest film."[13] It became one of the nation's more popular feature films, and the studio's second full-length film to combine live action and animation.[14] The film's music score, consisting of ten songs which covered all but five minutes of the film, was nominated for an Academy Award; and "Zip-a-Dee-Doo-Dah," a melody written by Allie Wrubel, with lyrics by Ray Gilbert, won that year's Academy Award for Best Song.

Based primarily upon Harris's book, *Told by Uncle Remus* (1905), the ninety-four minute film was a grossly romanticized and syrupy version of life on a Southern plantation. Unlike the book, the film emphasized the separation of Johnny's parents and the effects a divorce would have upon the child. To help Johnny understand more about life, Uncle Remus told three tales—"The Tar-Baby," "The Laughing Place," and "The Cornfield Story"—each of them animated.

A pre-release review in *Film Daily* said *Song of the South* was "a stirring gem that is going to prove important in box office competition, a delight to the young 'uns and a poignantly sentimental memento to grown-ups."[15] The Disney publicity operation called the film "an epochal event in screen history." Despite such billing, the *New York Herald-Tribune* called the film "a rather slipshod vehicle," and *Newsweek* called it "inconsequential."[16] The movie critics generally praised the acting, the bright animation, and the technology of the seamless marriage of live-action and animation, but believed the live-action sequences were not up to the cinematic excellence shown by other studios.

The depiction of American Blacks made the film one of the most criticized in history. Walt Disney himself, who seldom hired minorities, had declared it to be "a monument to the Negro race." Most disagreed, including the principal screenwriter. Clarence Muse, a Black writer whom Disney had hired to work on the story, abruptly resigned when his ideas of softening the Blacks' apparent stereotypes were rejected; he then condemned the depiction of Blacks in the film. Disney's insensitivity continued into the premiere in Atlanta. James Baskett and Hattie McDaniel were not allowed to stay at the "whites only" hotel that housed the cast, nor did they attend premiere functions sponsored by the Junior League of Atlanta and the Uncle Remus Memorial Association. Producer and syndicated columnist Billy Rose, in an open letter to Walt Disney, wrote: "Take it from an old admirer, this 'Uncle Tom' musical hasn't got it. Furthermore, we didn't like the way the picture was premiered in Atlanta. We felt embarrassed for you when we read that the colored actor who played 'Uncle Remus' wasn't permitted to attend the gala opening. In the world of fantasy, no one is good enough to carry your drawing pencil. When it comes to handling humans, I'm afraid you have plenty to learn."[17]

Time stated that the depiction of Blacks was "bound to enrage all educated Negroes, and a number of damnyankees." Bosley Crowther of the *New York Times* condemned the movie, calling it a "honeysuckle romance" and a "travesty on the antebellum South."[18] In a subsequent column, Crowther hit Disney hard for its unrealistic portrayal of the characters:

> [T]his "acted" story is the most meretricious sort of slush, not worthy of a second-grade producer, let alone your distinguished studio.... The boy (Bobby Driscoll) is a model of juvenile artifice—a completely contrived and confected little candy-box gentleman. He is just too elaborately gummy when he meets the lovely little po'-white girl (Luana Patten), who lives in a cabin but dresses in starched pinafores. And old Uncle Remus (James Baskett) is just the sweetest and

most wistful darky slave that ever stepped out of a
sublimely unreconstructed fancy of the Old South.[19]

Like many critics, Crowther erroneously believed the
movie depicted the antebellum South, and that Uncle
Remus was still a slave; even the Disney publicity organization stated that Uncle Remus was a slave.[20]

Pickets appeared before theaters in several northern
cities. The National Urban League called it "another rep-
etition of the perpetuation of the stereotype casting the
Negro in the servant role, depicting him as indolent, one
who handles truth lightly."[21] The National Association
for the Advancement of Colored People praised the animation, but condemned the movie:

> "[I]n an effort neither to offend audiences in the
> North or South, this production helps to perpetuate a
> dangerously glorified picture of slavery. Making use of
> the beautiful Uncle Remus folklore, "Song of the
> South" unfortunately gives the impression of an idyl-
> lic master-slave relationship which is a distortion of
> the facts."[22]

Equally angered, *Ebony* called the Uncle Remus portrayal "an Uncle Tom-Aunt Jemima caricature, complete
with all the fawning standard equipment thereof—the
toothy smile, battered hat, gray beard, and a profusion of
'dis' and 'dat' talk." It called for the creation of a Negro
Legion of Decency to monitor Hollywood films, declar-
ing, "No studio has clean hands when the indictment is
drawn up against the movie capital for gross distortion
and outright falsification in portraying the Negro on
screen."[23]

Disney's official response was that the film was "a sincere effort to depict American folklore, to put the Uncle
Remus stories into pictures." But, the man who portrayed

Uncle Remus, who could not stay with the rest of the cast in Atlanta, had almost no support among fellow actors and those in the industry for an Oscar. The Academy of Motion Picture Arts and Sciences maliciously refused to consider James Baskett for a Best Acting Oscar™ in Disney's "sincere effort"; only after actor and social activist Jean Hersholt spoke out against the racism of the academy did it award him an honorary Oscar™ in 1947 for his "able and heartwarming characterization of Uncle Remus, friend and story teller to the children of the world."[24] Baskett died four months later at the age of forty-four. He never acted in another film after *Song of the South*.

Even with the protests, *Song of the South* was one of the year's most popular films, earning $226,000 profit on a large–budget $2.125 million investment.[25] It would eventually gross about $13 million by 1977, and more than $20 million by its 1986 release, while simultaneously replacing in the public mind Harris's tales with Disney's portrayal. Within a year of the 1946 release, more tickets were sold for the movie than sales of all Uncle Remus books since 1880.

Song of the South was re-released in 1956, but withdrawn from distribution in 1958. During the late 1950s and 1960s, Disney continued to receive protests. The movie was permanently withdrawn in February 1970. "There is simply no editing out the built-in racial condescension of the day when it was created," wrote Ron Wise in *Variety*.[26] However, later that year, Disney reversed its position, announced a January 1972 release, and declared the movie was "a love story."[27] With a revenue of more than $7 million, the re-release made *Song of the South* "the highest grossing reissue in Disney history."[28]

The movie was re-released in 1980 and 1986. Protests were minimal, although *Newsweek* critic Barbara Kantrowitz discussed the controversy surrounding the

First Day of Issue, 1981, Turks and Caicos Islands

film, and pointed out the stereotyped caricatures; the headline asked if *Song of the South* was "A Film Unfit for the Kids?"[29] However, *San Diego Union* movie critic David Elliot stated that the film "is a remarkable entertainment; to enjoy it with an audience made up largely of happy, responding kids is like returning to childhood's innocent treasures."[30] *People* magazine's review of the 1986 re-release correctly noted: "No white character in the film is possessed of anything like this former slave's principles or sense of self-worth. Uncle Remus does more than just sing and tell tales; he listens and understands. There's a child in all of us who should not be deprived of the pleasure of his company."[31] Following the successful re-release in 1986, the Disney organization announced that the movie would now be included in the studio's classic reissue program for a re-release every seven years; however, the movie was never again distributed.

In typical Disney style, beginning with the 1946 release, the studio licensed innumerable subsidiary rights for everything from the songs and a record of dialect tales to children's picture books, a syndicated comic strip, and school kid lunch boxes. A few months after the film's premiere, Capitol Records produced an original-cast three-disk 78 r.p.m. album set, *Tales of Uncle Remus for Children*, with the Billy May orchestra and featuring Johnny Mercer, a Georgia native. The three main songs in the album were "Brer Rabbit and the Tar-Baby," "Running Away," and "The Laughing Place." Among dozens of picture books for children were *Uncle Remus and Brer Rabbit Stories*, *Brer Rabbit and the Pot o' Gold*, *Brer Rabbit Gets Tricked*, *Brer Rabbit Saves His Skin*, and *Brer Rabbit and His Friends*—all of them identified on the cover as "Walt Disney Productions Presents," none of which included the name Joel Chandler Harris on the cover. Walt Disney himself narrated a one-hour docudrama of Harris's life, complete with the tar-baby cartoon sequence from *Song of the South*, for the 14 September 1955, segment of the ABC-TV Sunday night series, "The Wonderful World of Disney."

In 1981, the Turks & Caicos Islands issued a series of nine stamps, designed by Disney artists, of scenes from the movie. Continuing to mine their original investment in the Uncle Remus stories, Disney created the animatronic Country Bear Jamboree at its amusement parks; in 1989, Disneyland premiered Splash Mountain, a flume/coaster ride that featured many of the Uncle Remus animals and situations, including a fibre glass Brier Patch. Splash Mountain rides later opened at Disney World and Tokyo Disneyland in 1992. The theme parks' Critter Corner features Brer Bar, a step-up-to-the-counter fast food restaurant.

'A National Heritage'

The year Splash Mountain opened, the Walt Disney Collectors Society released porcelain depictions of Brer Rabbit, Brer Fox, and Brer Bear, which were retired in 1997. Available only at the theme parks is a series of four plushes—Brer Rabbit, Brer Fox, Brer Bear, and Brer Frog. In May 1998, Disney introduced a series of four six-inch to seven-inch tall mini-bean bags—Brer Rabbit, Brer Fox, Brer Bear, and Brer Vulture—similar to Ty's Beanie Baby™ collection—available only at the theme parks. Among Uncle Remus collectibles not affiliated with Disney are a series of ten pewter sculptures first cast in 1990 by Michael Ricker of Estes Park, Colorado.[32]

Song of the South was satirized in both *Coonskin* (1975) and *Fletch Lives!* (1989). *Coonskin*, an ingenious film which combined live-action and animation, is Ralph Bakshi's vicious parody upon not only Disney's films, but also of American White values as well. Bakshi, who had earlier satirized American values in the X-rated, hilariously profound *Fritz the Cat* (1972) and *Heavy Traffic* (1973), opened *Coonskin* with scenes of two live-action convicts hiding out in a prison yard at night waiting for a moment to escape. While waiting, the older convict tells a story, set in animated sequences, about a militant rabbit, not-so-bright bear, and a fox who go to Harlem and eventually turn society's problems and many of its institutions into a giant tar-baby.

Fletch Lives was a much weaker two-star film starring Chevy Chase as a reporter who inherits an antebellum mansion in Louisiana. Believing it is everything portrayed in all the antebellum stories he had read, Fletch daydreams a "Zip-a-Dee-Doo-Dah" sequence, complete with animated animals and a blue bird on his shoulder. Naturally, since this was a comedy, the "mansion" probably looked better after Sherman's troops destroyed it than it did now.

Although Disney released a twenty-six minute sing-along videotape featuring "Zip-a-Dee-Doo-Dah," licensed five filmstrips for educational use, and has made millions off subsidiary licensing rights for images of the animated characters, it has never released *Song of the South* for a U.S. videotape release. The movie, on half-inch VHS videotape, was released in 1996 for purchase in Europe and Japan. The audio is in English, with Japanese subtitles appearing during parts of the musical score. Disneyy.com, an independent internet-based distributor from Minneapolis, not affiliated with the Walt Disney Co., sells original copies of the overseas edition for $300 each; in its advertising, the company warns purchasers, "[T]here are certain individuals & groups that have requested the Disney Co. not market this title within the U.S. The disclaimer, along with release form required for purchase found on our website…is required for all purchases."

---

[1] Although the Reconstruction era was primarily 1865-1877, the Reconstruction Cycle, which included media and the arts, was about forty years, beginning with the end of the Civil War.

[2] Dozens of businesses are still named the Briar Patch. In addition, there are an Uncle Remus Golf Course in South Eatonton, Georgia; Uncle Remus Restaurant chain in Chicago; Uncle Remus Sausage Company in Fayetteville, South Carolina; Uncle Remus Realty Company in Greensboro, Georgia; the Brer Rabbit Motel in Villa Park, Illinois; and Tar Baby's Pancakes restaurant in Cherry Grove Beach, South Carolina.

[3] Harris's widow filed suit for copyright infringement against the company, but lost when the 5th Circuit Court of Appeals, affirming a lower court decision, ruled that although the Harris estate had a copyright to the text, it had no copyright on the illustrations. For details, see 1 Fed. Supp. 713 and 73F(2) 370.

[4] "The Snap-Bean Sage," 741.

5 "Million Books and Best Books," *Golden Book Magazine* (4 September 1926): 382.

6 The show was produced by Batten, Barton, Durstine & Osborn, advertising agency for E. I. duPont de Nemours & Company. For decades, advertisers had significant influence upon radio and television content and programming.

7 Joel Chandler Harris, Jr., "Welcome," premiere program, *Song of the South*, 12 November 1946.

8 Quoted by Ernest Rogers, "World Premier of Disney's 'Uncle Remus' to be Here," 4.

9 *Walt Disney Presents "Song of the South,"* movie premiere souvenir edition, 1946, [13].

10 Disney press release, no. 21287, n.d.

11 The film was originally titled, "Uncle Remus." Disney himself told reporters that market research determined that the final title "possessed greater box office appeal."

12 Quoted by Ernest Rogers in "Uncle Remus...Movie Star," *Atlanta Journal Magazine*, 10 November 1946, 11.

13 Paul Jones, "Disney's Great 'Remus' Film Hailed For Abundance of Humor, Pathos," *Atlanta Constitution*, 13 November 1946, A-1.

14 The first film, *The Three Caballeros* (1945), was primarily an animated film, with occasional live-action sequences. *Song of the South* was primarily a live-action film with occasional animated sequences. During the 1920s, Walt Disney combined animation and live action, through a process known as rotoscoping, for the "Alice" cartoon shorts.

15 Review, *Film Daily*, 1 November 1946.

16 "Disney's Uncle Remus," *Newsweek* (2 December 1946): 109.

17 Billy Rose, "What Is Wrong, Walt?" *Atlanta Constitution*, 17 December 1946, 8.

18 Bosley Crowther, review, *New York Times*, 28 November 1946, 40.

19 Bosley Crowther, "Spanking Disney," *New York Times*, 8 December 1946, section 2, 5.

20 Disney press release, no. 27634, August 1980.

21 See Leonard Maltin, *The Disney Films* (1984), 78.

22 Telegram from Walter White, NAACP executive secretary, to American newspapers, 27 November 1946.

23 "Needed: A Negro Legion of Decency," *Ebony* (February 1947): 36.

24 Each year, the Academy of Motion Pictures Arts and Sciences gives an Oscar in Hersholt's name for humanitarian service.

[25] See Bob Thomas, *Walt Disney: An American Original* (1976). From gross rentals of $3,579,000, Disney press release, no. 20979 [n.d.].

[26] Ron Wise, "'Song of the South' Muted: Disney Shelves Big Coin Film," *Variety* (23 February 1970): 7.

[27] Disney press release, January 1972.

[28] Disney press release, no. 20979, n.d.

[29] Barbara Kantrowitz, "A Film Unfit for the Kids?" *Newsweek* (22 December 1986): 63.

[30] David Elliott, "Zip-A-Dee-Doo-Dah! 'Song of the South' is Back," *San Diego Union*, 25 November 1986, C-5.

[31] "Picks and Pans," *People* (8 December 1986): 17.

[32] The animals in the series are the rabbit, fox, bear, turtle, raccoon, and possum; other sculptures are the cabin, Uncle Remus and the Little Boy, Tar-Baby, and Brer Rabbit and the Tar-Baby

Town Square, Eatonton, Georgia

Chapter 14

'A Bad Odor Among
the Younger Generation'

James Weldon Johnson, Black civil rights leader and one of the nation's most respected writers to emerge from the Harlem Renaissance, stated in 1922 that "the Uncle Remus stories constitute the greatest body of folk lore that America has produced."[1] Two years later, W. E. B. DuBois, a founder of the NAACP and the editor of its journal, *Crisis*, pointed out that Harris was "the deft and singularly successful translator" of the Black folklore to a White audience.[2] Civil rights leader and author Alain Locke cited Harris for having "rendered as much poetic justice to the Negro as an orthodox Southerner could."[3] Sterling A. Brown disagreed. Brown—who would become one of the nation's most distinguished poets, folklorists, and interpreters of American Black life and culture—established seven classifications in 1933 for how White authors characterized Blacks in literature—(1) the contented slave, (2) the wretched freeman, (3) the comic negro, (4) the brute negro, (5) the tragic mulatto, (6) the local color negro, and (7) the exotic primitive.[4] Most of Harris's characters fall into the first two classes. Harris, said Brown, perpetuated the "plantation Negro" stereotype that had Harris believing slavery was "a kindly institution, and the Negro was contented."[5] Accepting Brown's classification system, two generations of critics not only attacked the Uncle Remus tales as racist, but had also begun a campaign to classify Joel Chandler Harris and his works as irrelevant.

The premiere of *Song of the South* had inadvertently ushered in a newer era. Harris and his works would now be attacked, often by persons who had not read his tales and knew almost nothing about their author but had seen the Disney film. Some of those academic critics often projected the Disney version onto the tales. Bernard Wolfe declared that not only were the Uncle Remus tales not of African origin, but that Harris provided the foundation for a racist society. In the July 1949 issue of *Commentary*, he argued that Harris's life:

> ...was built on a merciless, systematic plagiarizing of the folk-Negro. Small wonder, then, that the 'plantation darky' was such a provocative symbol for him. For, ironically, this lowly Negro was, when viewed through the blinders of stereotype, almost the walking image of Harris's ego-ideal—the un-selfconscious, 'natural,' free flowing, richly giving creator that Harris could never become."[6]

The article, filled with biases and errors, became the base of innumerable attacks by others against what they believed to be stereotypes and racial insensitivity in the Uncle Remus tales.

During the 1950s, with the rise of the Civil Rights Cycle, numerous social critics called Uncle Remus nothing more than a black-face minstrel[7] who stupidly defended his master against the Yankees. As for Harris, the critics said he wrote well but did not reflect the horrors of the antebellum era. However, they overlooked, or conveniently dismissed, the words of Samuel L. Clemens, who had attacked numerous Southern writers for "romanticizing" the antebellum era, but had praised Harris for his relatively accurate portrayal of the people—Black and White, slave and free—from that era.[8] Many critics even stated that because the Reconstruction era Uncle Remus longed for the Antebellum days, complained about the "uppity negroes," and believed that perhaps the ex-slaves really should not be educated, that Harris himself was racist. They took Harris's own words out of historical and literary context to express their shock that one of America's best writers was a segregationist.

Writers *may* put their own values and beliefs into their characters, and may immerse themselves into many personalities while creating stories, as Harris did on most of his stories. But the critics, possibly influenced by *Song of the South* and undoubtedly with their own biases, failed to realize that what a fictional character believes may not necessarily represent what the author believes but is expressed to give a broader perspective to other characters, the plot, or issues. In truth, although Harris himself continually longed for the rural South of his youth, he was a visionary of the "New South" and had set up Remus—a strong enough character who learned how to survive slavery and Reconstruction while presenting innumerable views about the nature of mankind—to show the social and geographical confrontations between the "old" and the "new" South. Paul M. Cousins argued in his 1968 biography of Harris:

> Harris projected [Uncle Remus] so completely as an individual character that he cannot be identified as merely a comic type nor simply as a loyal retainer. In fact, the reader of the folklore stories scarcely thinks of Uncle Remus as a slave, for his master and mistress appear only in the background. He is an independent and realistic figure, revealing his humor and his knowledge of human nature in his relationship with the little boy, expressing approval or disapproval of the little boy's conduct, putting the pert 'Tildy in her

place, and exercising his rightful authority over the household and yard servants.[9]

Literary critic Darwin T. Turner, although praising *Gabriel Tolliver*, nevertheless claimed that Harris "approved of Negroes only when they confined themselves to telling stories and serving their masters." He further charged:

> Even though he extended pity for the emotional abuses in slavery, he ignored the physical mistreatment. His slaves suffer only from unjust orders or food restrictions or separation from their families. Not once in Harris's works does a slave or freedman feel the sting of a whip.
>
> It is presumptuous to praise slavery for giving religion to the Africans, who observed a religious faith long before they became American slaves. Such praise seems especially reprehensible because the new religion, Christianity, was not used to help the slaves but to encourage them to submit to eternal bondage. It is irrational to praise slavery for graduating slaves into American citizens when slave holders, by every means in their power, attempted to deny citizenship to Negroes, both before and after emancipation.[10]

Jacqueline Shachter, an education professor at Temple University, shortly after publication of her book of stories, *Brer Rabbit in the Americas* (1977), told United Press International, "Uncle Remus was a servile, groveling old 'Uncle Tom'... As might be expected, [Harris] had a Confederate mentality which revealed itself when he told the Brer Rabbit tales through the mouth of Uncle Remus, destroying their appeal for blacks."[11]

Alice Walker—winner of the Pulitzer Prize for novels in 1983 for her novel *The Color Purple*—was born in Harris's birthplace of Eatonton and grew up hearing the

Brer Rabbit stories. But, unlike most Eatonton residents, she had no respect for Harris. In Eatonton, she remembered, was a mannequin of "an elderly, kindly, cotton-haired darkie" which was placed in a rocking chair at the front window of the town's segregated Uncle Remus Restaurant. Harris, said Walker, "stole a good part of my heritage [by making me] feel ashamed" of it.[12]

For a 1982 reprint of *Uncle Remus, His Songs and Sayings*, editor Robert Hemenway claimed that Brer Rabbit is "black from the tip of his ears to the fuzz of his tail," but stated that Uncle Remus is "a Victorian relic...whose plantation manners embarrass the modern reader. [He is] a cousin of those nineteenth-century minstrels who blackened their faces to entertain with jokes and songs. He is, in a way, [a] white [created] by a white Southerner [and] welcomed by an audience that wanted to believe Remus was a representative of his race."[13]

One of the most vicious attacks upon Harris came from Evelyn Nash, an English professor with a specialty in Afro-American literature. Nash accused Harris of writing "a collection of 'fakelore,' which degrades and stereotypes people about whom the original stories were written," and that the plots "are filled with degradations and stereotypes, folklore in disguise—all presented as humor and labeled Black Folklore." She further argued:

[B]y assuming his self-appointed role of compiler and preserver of Negro tales, [Harris] yielded an outcome much like a usurpation of folklore—legends, myths, proverbs, and folktales which should have remained a component of the African heritage as it paralleled the African global diaspora....

[The tales] are deviants in that they were handed down amidst the turmoil of a civil war, seized by the pen with which Harris so diligently wrote, seized by an opportunistic alien, observer, and transformed

into tales which degrade the original cast in a deliberate attempt to praise, to humor, and to appease his
[White] audience.[14]

Leigh Fenly, an editor with the *San Diego Union*,
recalled in 1994, "Like so many others growing up in the
South, I heard Uncle Remus tales slip like honey from my
mother's tongue. I loved the stories, and lived for the day
when crafty ol' Brer Rabbit would get his due." Although
she also believed that Uncle Remus "was an Uncle Tom
if ever there were one," she also knew that Harris "created a human figure in Uncle Remus who was complex and
contradictory, who loved language and tradition, who
spun yarns that still entrance."[15]

Responding to the profusion of criticism, author and
literary critic William B. Strickland, pointed out:

> Even as he sentimentally yearned for what he
> perceived as the lost grace and charm of the vanished
> Old South, Harris was a keen enough observer of
> human life to present realistic characters instead of
> stereotypes when the characters themselves engaged
> his attention and affection. That he did not do so at
> every turn is undeniable; but to say that all of his
> characters are stereotypes, or that none of them were
> subversive of the romanticized Old South way of life,
> is to exercise a blindness that lies in our own eyes, and
> not in those of Harris.[16]

Critic Robert Bone, acknowledging that "Harris is in
bad odor among the younger generation of literary men,"
also noted for a review of Black literature:

> The blacks, who tend to equate Uncle Remus
> with Uncle Tom—sometimes, one suspects, without
> having read either Harris or Stowe—reject the Uncle
> Remus books out of hand. And sympathetic whites,

who hope thereby to ingratiate themselves with the black militants, are fond of giving Harris a gratuitous kick in the shins. Both responses are regrettable, for they blind their victims to the archetypical figure of Brer Rabbit, who is not only a major triumph of the Afro-American imagination, but also the most subversive folk hero this side of Stagolee.

If the Uncle Remus books perpetuate the proslavery myths of the plantation tradition, they also contain one of the sharpest indictments of the institution in American literature.[17]

In an academic review of a book of critical essays about Joel Chandler Harris, Craig Werner argued:

...Harris seems doomed to share the fate of the stereotyped black he helped immortalize in Uncle Remus. Fixed in the popular mind as a cheerful and slightly sentimental storyteller, he hides an elusive awareness of a cruel, isolated and amoral world behind a smile. Like the much-discussed plantation uncle, Harris grins patiently while critic after curious critic 'discovers' the discrepancy between public image and private reality.[18]

Joel Chandler Harris had advised writers in *Nights With Uncle Remus* that the tales and language were so intertwined that to present them any other way would "rob them of everything that gives them vitality." In several personal letters to friends, fans, and editors, he discussed why the language of the American Black needed to be a part of the literature. To *Scribner's* editor Edward Burlingame, Harris pointed out, "I am very fond of writing the dialect. It gives a new coloring to statement and permits of a swift shading in narrative that can be reached in literary English only by the most painful and laborious methods."[19] Responding to a question about

Uncle Remus revisions by other authors who significantly modified or eliminated the dialect, Julia Collier Harris sharply responded that her father-in-law "would never have given permission for such an absurdity, no matter what compensation had been offered him. That the dialect is a vital part of the story, father always emphatically maintained."[20]

In 1926, George Philip Krapp, the nation's leading analyst of the American language, warned that the stories "have lived on, not because but in spite of their elaborate dialect. Yet so intimately is the relation between language and content in these tales, like that of twins brought up under the same vine and fig tree, that anyone who attempts to translate them into a simpler and more conversational idiom...soon finds in the process of translation a great deal of their charm is destroyed."[21]

Literary analyst John Goldthwaite six decades later reinforced George Philip Krapp's argument: "Harris's easy virtuosity with the dialect catches each tale in mid-leap, like Brer Rabbit himself. Rendered into standard English the stories can...only sit there in the rhetorical mud like Brer Fox with 'a spell er de dry grins.'"[22]

Two major collections, both published by Houghton, Mifflin, retained elements of American Black English. With sales of about 43,000 copies,[23] *Favorite Uncle Remus* (1948), compiled by George van Santvoord and Archibald Coolidge, published less than two years after *Song of the South*'s premiere, became the definitive children's version until Houghton, Mifflin published Richard Chase's *The Complete Tales of Uncle Remus* (1955) during the seventy-fifth year anniversary of Harris's first book. Augusta Baker, head of the children's library services section of the New York Public Library, forcefully gave the book credibility when she stated in the *Saturday Review*: "[T]his volume should be included in every storyteller's

collection and in every collection of folk source material. These stories are as American as the stars and stripes, even though they have some of their origins in Africa, and the story teller should make every effort to keep Brer Rabbit and his worthy cohorts alive."[24]

Some very well-meaning writers, editors, and publishers, however, believed that the Uncle Remus speech was a deterrent to readability. Others believed that the language was blatantly racist, spoken by "darkies," minstrels, and the ignorant, and reflective of a racist society—American Black English, they believed, was itself an "inferior" language. Almost anything written by Whites which included American Black English, especially nineteenth century folklore, was denigrated, the language now becoming an embarrassment. Whether the American Black English constructions were stripped because of readability issues or because of racial sensitivity issues, the result was that innumerable Brer Rabbit tales were now composed without any American Black English constructions.

Margaret Wise Brown says she had written her popular children's book, *Brer Rabbit: Stories From Uncle Remus* (1941), in Standard English in order to improve readability. The first Disney picture book of modified Uncle Remus tales, issued shortly after the premiere of *Song of the South*, modified the language, keeping a few American Black English syntactic constructions— "'Brer Rabbit,' say Brer Fox,"; and a simplified phonology— mostly, the letter "d" replaced "th," as in "de" and "den"; and "in'" replaced "ing." In a subsequent edition, Marion Palmer explained why the tales were recast into what was a mixture of Standard and Black English syntax and phonology:

To those few persons who are familiar with the dialect of the Georgia Negro at the time of the Civil War, it may seem an affront to change in any way the speech of Uncle Remus. Unquestionably the dialect is a living part of the legends themselves. But after much consideration, we have been forced to conclude that this dialect is much too difficult for the majority of modern, young readers. For this reason, we have greatly simplified it, although with regret that we had to alter it at all.

We do not expect that the stories in this book can take the place of the original Uncle Remus legends. Perhaps, however, they can help to introduce new readers to these legends. There, in the more archaic but picturesque language of the Old Negro himself, one may enjoy more fully the rhythm and the poetic fantasy that have made these stories classic.[25]

Although it is difficult in print to represent the spoken language phonology, and the construction of words to "sound" like the spoken language may make these words appear to be "foreign," the soul of American Black English is in its syntax, the construction of the sentences and thought patterns. By placing the tales into a Standard English phonology while retaining American Black English language constructions, it would have been possible to retain much of the "vitality" that Harris believed so important to understanding the tales.

In *The Days When Animals Talked* (1977), a compilation of twenty animal tales and ten different slave tales, William J. Faulkner, a Black writer unrelated to the Nobel Laureate, reflecting the views of a general population, explained that he deliberately wrote the book using Standard English because he objects "to allowing children, black or white, to use dialectal speech in school [and] would not want this book to encourage such language patterns."[26]

Dolores Draper, editor at Western, which had published the illustrated *Song of the South* children's book following the release of the Disney motion picture, said in 1980:

> We have not received any favorable comments about this title in the last few years.... We have received...unfavorable response these past few years criticizing the dialect and its improper use of the English language. We've explained to these readers that the correctness or incorrectness of the way a particular language is used depends on the customs of the area from which it comes.

Folklorist Roger D. Abrahams cut a fine line in *Afro-American Folktales* (1985), a collection of 107 tales from about the previous 150 years, including some of Harris's animal tales. Well aware of the legitimacy of American Black English and the need to preserve the language of the tales, yet sensitive to racial issues, Abrahams modified the Uncle Remus tales:

> [W]e simply cannot get beyond the racist resonances that the Uncle Remus-style tellings continue to carry, precisely because the stories are rendered in the dialects of slavery times. I have attempted to take some of this stigma away by using contemporary spellings, and by changing some of the vernacular turns of phrase that would have been familiar to the nineteenth-century reader but have been lost in their currency—and thus their pungency—today.[27]

However, Abrahams also pointed out that although many consider the tales "as predominantly the response of an enslaved and exploited people." and that such interpretation "must be dealt with seriously," that the "whole repertoire—Harris included—deserves to be looked at more closely and sympathetically."[28]

The American Library Association has a long and distinguished history of opposing censorship in its constant battles in defense of First Amendment rights. However, there have been exceptions by individual librarians—and by innumerable school administrators. For more than eight decades after its publication in 1885, schools had been banning Mark Twain's *Huckleberry Finn* because they believed the book advocated a disrespect for authority.

In 1885, Joel Chandler Harris had become one of the nation's strongest voices in support of *The Adventures of Huckleberry Finn*, a book which brought forth innumerable social issues, and also included Black English. Parents had refused to allow their children to read the book, citing its "irresponsible" anti-establishment tone of rebellion as their primary reason. They even had forbidden their children to visit Joel Chandler Harris's home where he encouraged children to read books, including those of Mark Twain, to each other.[29] Lashing out at innumerable critics, Harris had declared in a *Constitution* review:

> It is difficult to believe that the critics who have condemned the book as coarse, vulgar, and inartistic can have read it. Taken in connection with "The Prince and the Pauper," it marks a clear and distinct advance in Mr. Clemens's literary methods. It presents an almost artistically perfect picture of life and character in the southwest, and it will be equally valuable to historians and to the student of sociology. Its humor which is genuine and never-failing, is relieved by little pathetic touches here and there that vouch for its literary value.[30]

In a letter to the editor in the 18 November 1885, edition of the *Critic*, Harris continued his defense of Twain and of *Huckleberry Finn*:

> I know that some of the professional critics will not agree with me, but there is not in our fictive literature a more wholesome book than 'Huckleberry Finn.' It is history, it is romance, it is life. Here we behold human character stripped of all its tiresome details; we see people growing and living; we laugh at their humor, share their griefs; and, in the midst of it all, behold we are taught the lesson of honesty, justice and mercy.

In the February 1908 issue of *Uncle Remus's Magazine*, Harris declared Twain is "a man who is not only our greatest humorist, but our greatest writer of fiction." Harris, of course, was proven to be correct in his analysis; subsequent generations of literary scholars and the American public have agreed that *Huckleberry Finn* is unquestionably among the top five American novels.

However, now, during the Civil Rights Cycle, certain school districts, their parents, and affiliated organizations, began banning *Huckleberry Finn* and the Uncle Remus books from school libraries and curriculum. Disregarding that Twain's book was regarded by most literary critics as the greatest American novel, and that the various Uncle Remus tales were the greatest collections of Black folklore of the Antebellum and Reconstruction cycles, these individuals believed that banning books was justified because these two classics advocated racism, and mistakenly cited the American Black English passages as "proof." The impressions were fueled by innumerable articles in the mass media, most written by reporters who had no concept of linguistics, folklore, or even of Harris' role as one of the more forceful editorialists of the late nineteenth century.

A Black librarian in the Atlanta school district said in 1975 she hid Uncle Remus materials because they "recall bad times."[31] Other librarians, many of them employed by school districts, "hid" Uncle Remus books because of what they believed were racist images. In one of the greatest slaps to Harris's memory, the board of trustees of the Atlantic Public Library in 1982 ordered the name of the Uncle Remus Branch—which had been located at the Wren's Nest from 1913 to 1949 before moving into its own building—to be changed to the West End Branch, citing that the original name was "offensive." Michael Lomax, a member of the library's board and chairman of Georgia's Fulton County Commission, said that Uncle Remus was "a stereotyped character from the old plantation school of southern literature," and that "calling a library the 'Uncle Remus branch' in a black community is equivalent to calling a library the 'Shylock Branch' in the Jewish community."[32] However, the Uncle Remus Library System, consisting of eight libraries in six counties, including Putnam County, has not had any opposition to its name except "smirks from white Yankees," says its director.[33]

Three years after the Atlanta Public Library changed the name of the Uncle Remus branch, Michael Lomax declared he would not allow his daughter to read the Uncle Remus tales nor visit the Wren's Nest museum: "Harris presented a romantic, idealized vision of the Old South that was hopelessly narrowminded, if not reactionary. Uncle Remus was a stereotyped, contented shuffling slave. That certainly didn't assist in achieving racial equality for black people."[34] Thomas H. English, the ninety-year-old Emory professor emeritus who had been one of Harris's principal biographers, told the *Constitution*, "If Harris had lived in today's world, I think

he and Michael Lomax would think very much alike, and be friends."[35]

In 1986, at the same time *Song of the South* was playing in yet another national release, the Savannah-Chatham County School District banned a theatrical production of *Br'er Rabbit's Big Secret*. The acclaimed Savannah Theatre Company had scheduled the play, with Black actors in lead roles, for second graders; district administrators, objecting to the "inappropriate dialect," banned it after the first of its scheduled ten performances. The director said school officials told him the tar-baby scene "might be seen as a racial slur."[36] The next official explanation was that the theatre company had not provided adequate study guides for the play to explain its dialect and historical roots. According to a spokesman for the district, the "main concern was to prepare teachers and children for something that is very different," that they "needed to be coached on dialect and language not considered acceptable," and that the "children needed to be taught a historical perspective."[37] The theater company agreed to create "adequate" guides, but school administrators stated that the decision to ban the play was irrevocable.

However, the decisions to minimalize Harris's tales did have its opponents. In a strong editorial, the *Chicago Tribune* attacked the school board:

> The Uncle Remus stories…are a reflection of a rich African cultural heritage that ought to be a source of pride. Can they really disturb anyone but those who see "racism" in any reflection of black history and culture? And why should their sensitivities be the standard?
>
> The ban on "Uncle Remus" is an odd form of censorship, one based on a dread of criticism. The censor, far from imposing his will, hurries to let other

people impose theirs on him. Such censors are not exactly frightening, but they certainly don't do much for education.[38]

Stella Brewer Brookes, a Black activist and one of Harris's principal biographers, in response to attempts by librarians, teachers, and public officials to expunge Harris's creations, stated simply that Harris "will always have to be remembered in the realm of folklore and literature. His name will have to live."[39]

"[T]he only American children's book to exert a profound influence on storytellers at home and abroad has become a book without critical standing," wrote literary critic John Goldthwaite in *The Natural History of Make-Believe*, his analytical study of children's literature. "In its own day so famous as to make the unusual kinds of acknowledgment by the next generation of storytellers superfluous, it is, in the absence of overwhelming testimony, seen now as a work of no apparent importance whatsoever," said Goldthwaite, pointing out that the Uncle Remus collections' "influence on the major English fantasies from Kipling to Milne and on such popular Americans as Thornton Burgess and Howard Garis, from whom so much of our nursery reading derives, has gone unremarked...by any writer on children's literature."[40]

In addition to attacks for racism and the use of American Black English, there now came attacks from another direction. During the 1970s and 1980s, it became fashionable for some very good people to claim they were protecting children from a nation of violence. But they also self-righteously claimed that contributing to that state were all forms of media, including animated cartoons of the Roadrunner and Coyote, Bugs Bunny and Elmer Fudd, Tom and Jerry, and even Jay Ward's cold-war spoofs pitting Rocky and Bullwinkle against Boris and

Natasha. Caught in the shotgun tactics of the leaders for reducing violence in society by reducing depiction of violence in the media were the Uncle Remus tales. Overlooking the humanity and philosophical discussions about life in the Uncle Remus stories, these critics argued the animal characters usually engaged in violent acts. After all, not only is the tar-baby racist they mistakenly claimed, but the fox plans to eat the rabbit, and the rabbit maliciously kills other animals.

In 1980-1981, the centennial of the publication of the first Uncle Remus book, there was little critical recognition of Harris outside of Eatonton and Atlanta; no "outstanding book" lists included anything by Joel Chandler Harris. Even the children who attended Atlanta's Joel Chandler Harris elementary school had no idea who the school was named after.[41]

As the Civil Rights Cycle had begun dying out, a few writers and publishers had begun to reflect upon those tales not as racist but as a part of American culture. Even the more militant social activists, who rightly believed that nothing less than a social revolution would shake America from its righteous protection of segregation and discrimination, now realized that the stories Harris told were powerful indictments against racism.

Ennis Rees, with a Ph.D. from Harvard and years of experience teaching at Duke, Princeton, and the University of South Carolina, reworked Brer Rabbit tales into rhyming verse for his illustrated children's books, *Brer Rabbit and His Tricks* (1967) and *More of Brer Rabbit's Tricks* (1968), both illustrated by Edward Gorey. In the introductory note to the books, Rees discussed the folklore of the Brer Rabbit stories, stating they "are among the best folktales we have." But, like the editors for the Disney picture books, he failed to acknowledge Harris or others who first recorded them for an American audience. Most writers, however, readily acknowledge Harris.

On the title page of *Brer Rabbit and Brer Fox* (1973), the name of Joel Chandler Harris is larger than that of Jane Shaw, identified as the one who "retold" the tales. F. Roy Johnson and F. Mark Johnson, sharing their byline with Harris, teamed up for *In the Old South With Brer Rabbit and His Neighbors*, a 1977 book of forty-five tales, with pen-and-ink illustrations. However, sales were primarily in North Carolina, home of the Johnsons and their Johnson Publishing Company.

Virginia Hamilton, who had created the modern trickster Jahdu at the end of the 1960s, compiled an Afro-American folklore anthology, *The People Could Fly* (1985), for the 1980s. The book, which faithfully recorded the spirit of the original Brer Rabbit stories, includes seven animal tales written in a variation of American Black English syntax but without Black English phonology or orthography. Short discussions at the end of each tale explain its history and place within the greater folklore of American Blacks.

Van Dyke Parks and Julius Lester brought the spirit of Brer Rabbit and the Uncle Remus tales back into mainstream America during the 1980s and 1990s. In 1982, Parks—one of the nation's leading musicians, composers, arrangers, and producers—wrote and produced the song cycle *Jump!* an orchestral-pop album which combined musical influences of nineteenth century America, the Hollywood musicals of the 1930s, and a playfully signifying Brer Rabbit to expand upon the Uncle Remus tales. "I had read the Uncle Remus tales as a child," says Parks who was born in Mississippi, "and I now had a daughter who wanted me to read her the tales in English." The song cycle was originally destined to be a one-time performance with the North Carolina Symphony, with a regional PBS telecast, but when Warner Brothers asked him to do the cycle as an album, Parks says he realized "it would bring the tales to a much

larger audience." That album received both popular and critical acclaim. Soon after, Parks secured a grant from the National Endowment for the Arts to develop a treatment for a musical, and eventually secured a $3 million investment package to develop and produce the tales for the Broadway stage. But, when both of his co-authors died, he abandoned the project.

The *Jump!* cycle, nevertheless, was adapted for yet another medium. Harcourt Brace Jovanovich, with a large children's book division, asked Parks to adapt the tales for the print medium. *Jump! The Adventures of Brer Rabbit* (1986), by Parks and Malcolm Jones,[42] was a compilation of five revised Uncle Remus animal tales, but without the Tar-Baby story or Uncle Remus; the third-person narrator is unnamed, but is distinctly a modernized Uncle Remus who speaks a more standard English. "I made a creative decision that's one of the most important I ever made in my career," says Parks. At the time, schools were systematically pulling the works of both Joel Chandler Harris and Mark Twain from their shelves, "and I decided that to preserve these tales which I consider an immensely vital part of American history, and to make sure even the smallest children had a chance to read them, I would have to drop the character of Uncle Remus."

However, he also had to drop other things. "I loved Harris's phrase, 'a gaggle of gigglement,'" says Parks, "but my editor made me drop it in the first book." He says there were "several other words and phrases" that also were dropped because of editorial concerns. "I have serious reservations about the 'correction' of the original text," says Parks who says he "has a problem with text that has to be bowdlerized because of 'politically correct' concerns." The reviewers, however, appreciated Parks changing the language of the tales. "By eliminating the fictional Uncle Remus as well as the attempted phonetic transcription of the Gullah dialect," wrote the reviewer for *The Horn Book*, "the collaborators have also eliminated the stereotypic devices which have obscured the original vivacity and universality of these remarkable tales."[43]

In the introduction to *Jump!*, Parks and Jones pointed out that although Harris was "both applauded and deeply criticized for his portrayal of life in the Old South...the lessons in these stories are universal," and that readers will not find "a better example of pluck and cleverness triumphing over brute strength." To cut into some of the opposition to Uncle Remus, Parks and Jones concluded, "Tempered by hardship and nourished by hope, these tales are a testament to the belief that no one can be wholly owned who does not wish it."[44]

The book, said critic Peter Neumeyer in the *New York Times*, "is readable, joyous, racially irreproachable and—because of Barry Moser's illustrations—important."[45] The *Horn Book Magazine* reported that in Moser's watercolors "the strong characterization of the animals seems to leap out of the pictures, adding rich drama and playful humor to the endless struggle of Brer Rabbit's wits against the greater strength and size of Brer Fox, Brer Bear, and Brer Wolf."[46] The consensus of most reviewers was that Moser was matched only by the line art illustrations of A. B. Frost almost a century earlier. The next two books—*Jump Again! More Adventures of Brer Rabbit* (1987) and *Jump on Over* (1989)—were written solely by Parks, with Moser's watercolors. The *New York Times*, reflecting most critics' opinions, said the second book was "as accomplished and appealing as the first" book.[47]

"These tales," says Parks, "should be a source of Black pride; I believe my family in Mississippi would be happy I could help preserve the tales of Brer Rabbit."

In *Black Folktales* (1969), Julius Lester—author, folk-lorist, and educator—had retold several classic tales, including the story of Stagolee. However, the reviews were mixed, possibly because the reviewers, both Black and White, did not understand the nature of Black folklore. Many of the reviewers believed Lester was nothing more than a '60s Black militant using folklore to further the revolution. Two years later, for *The Knee-High Man and Other Tales* (1971), Lester included a few Brer Rabbit tales.

Then, almost fifteen years later, Augusta Baker, who in 1955 had praised the Richard Chase collection of Uncle Remus stories, suggested that Lester consider a larger reworking of the Brer Rabbit/Uncle Remus tales. "I knew immediately that it was a book I was born to do," says Lester. For an interview with United Press International, Lester stated: "The tales are fine in their authentic black expression. To have them fall into disre-pute was a tragedy. I wanted to bring the tales back and let people know, 'Hey, these are wonderful tales.' Once you separate them from the slave stereotype, people can enjoy them again."[48]

In the foreword to *The Tales of Uncle Remus* (1987), the first of the four-book series, and winner of the Coretta Scott King Award, Lester discussed numerous questions he had before undertaking the project. Among the most important of those questions was in which lan-guage (variations of American Black English, standard American English, Southern English, or a mixture of all) he should write the tales. He concluded: "The answers came once I decided that what is most important are the tales themselves. They are extraordinary and should be part of people's lives again. They are funny, touching, horrifying, and some partake of that quality of magic found in myth."[49] Lester notes in the introduction that he did not "duplicate black speech precisely," but wrote them in "a modified contemporary Southern Black English."[50] The critics, who had just seen the re-release of *Song of the South* a year earlier, praised Lester for bringing the Uncle Remus stories back to their origins.

Critic June Jordan disagreed. Reflecting a sociopolitical philosophy that Bernard Wolfe had argued four decades earlier, for a review in the *New York Times* she attacked Lester's book and sharply criticized the Uncle Remus tales:

> With lamentably few exceptions, the Uncle Remus stories center on a pathological hustler, a truly bad rabbit. Knavery of every sort defines this "cornerstone." Premeditated violence, compulsive cruelty, exploitation of children and regular opportunism abound. Add to these characteristics a fundamental laziness (why can't Brer Rabbit grow his own darn cabbages and carrots, for example?), plus a fulsome enthusiasm for lying all the time, and you have summarized the substance of Brer Rabbit and his not so merry misadventures.[51]

Disregarding Jordan's criticism, Lester continued writing Uncle Remus tales. Other books in the series are *More Tales of Uncle Remus* (1988), *Further Tales of Uncle Remus* (1990), and *The Last Tales of Uncle Remus* (1994).

In 1994, Lester retold the folk-story of John Henry. Jerry Pinkney, who had illustrated the four Uncle Remus books, also illustrated *John Henry*, which would win the prestigious *Boston Globe/Horn Book* award. In his acceptance speech, Pinkney told the audience that the three literary heroes of his childhood—Little Black Sambo, John Henry, and the Brer Rabbit tales—gave him "support and comfort in a world where almost all heroes in literature were white."[52]

Two years after the publication of *John Henry*, Lester and Pinkney reworked Helen Bannerman's 1899 story of "Little Black Sambo" into *Sam and the Tigers*, eliminating what became American racist interpretations while using the language of the Uncle Remus tales. *Publishers Weekly* called it "a hip and hilarious retelling that marries the essence of the original with an innovative vision of its own."

By the end of the 1990s, several other illustrated Uncle Remus children's books—almost all written in Standard English, most of which were rewritten tales without the Uncle Remus character—were published. In the introduction of *Giant Treasury of Brer Rabbit* (1991), an illustrated children's book, editor Anne Hessey, perhaps explaining the absence of Uncle Remus in most 1990s Tar-Baby books, said she rewrote only the Brer Rabbit tales and left out Uncle Remus who introduced the tales because "racial stereotypes of the nineteenth century are inappropriate today and may be offensive to many contemporary readers."[53]

Among other children's books published during the last two decades of the twentieth century were *The Adventures of Brer Rabbit* (1980) by Ruth Spriggs, illustrated by Frank Baber; *Brer Rabbit* (1984) by Barbara Hayes, illustrated by Virginio Livraghi; *Hello Brer Rabbit* (1985) by Rene Cloke; *Young Brer Rabbit* (1985) by Jacqueline Shachter Weiss, illustrated by Clinton Arrowood, with audio cassette in 1991 narrated by Eartha Kitt; *Brer Rabbit* (1988) by Mark Davies, illustrated by Arthur Suydam; *Brer Rabbit Again* (1989) by Rene Cloke; *Brer Rabbit and the Peanut Patch* (1990) by Susan Dickinson, illustrated by David Frankland; *The Story of Brer Rabbit and the Wonderful Tar Baby* (1990) by Eric Metaxas, illustrated by Henrik Drescher; *Giant Treasury of Brer Rabbit, Retold from the Stories of Joel Chandler Harris* (1991), *Brer Rabbit: From the Collected Stories of*

Joel Chandler Harris (1995) by David Borgenicht, illustrated by Don Daily; *The Return of Brer Rabbit* (1995) by G. A. Clay; *Brer Rabbit's Adventures* (1995) by Rene Cloke; *Brer Rabbit and the Tar Baby; An African-American Legend* (1997) by Janet P. Johnson, illustrated by Charles Reasoner; *Brer Rabbit and the Great Tug-o-War* (1998) by John Agard, illustrated by Korky Paul; and *Uncle Remus and Brer Rabbit* (1999), a reproduction of the full-color 1907 edition, and *Tar-Baby: Tales of Brer Rabbit* (2000), illustrated by Thomas Deryk.

During the past three decades, a few writers adapted the philosophy of the Brer Rabbit tales for theatrical performances. One of the most successful Brer Rabbit plays is *Livin' de Life*, a one-act children's play written by Ed Graczyk in 1970. Graczyk, who would later write the Broadway hit, *Come Back to the 5 and Dime, Jimmy Dean, Jimmy Dean*, says while in his childhood, he "had loved" the tales of Uncle Remus, and wrote the play, consisting of ten Brer Rabbit stories and three of his own, while director of a children's theatre company in Midland, Texas. He was aware of the controversy over the Uncle Remus/Brer Rabbit stories but says he and his publisher believed the "play will last longer than the controversy." In the three decades since it was first performed, there have been more than a hundred productions, including a bluegrass version, in all regions of the country. Graczyk says he is unaware of any protests.

The Adventures of Brer Rabbit, by Gayle Cornelison, a one-act play of four vignettes—"The Laughing Place," "The Rabbit Trap," "Wahoo," and "The Wonderful Tar-Baby"—opened during the 1976-1977 season of the California Theatre Center in Sunnyvale, California, and has been produced regularly for more than two decades.

Brer Rabbit, a two-hour multi-media musical with American Black English dialogue in rhyme couplets, produced by the Visual and Performing Arts department of

California State University at San Marcos, opened in December 1998 at the California Center for the Arts in Escondido. Written and directed by Loni Berry, professor and professional actor-director, *Brer Rabbit* is based upon *Brer Rabbit Whole*, by George Houston Bass. The play had began as a workshop production at Fisk University, then went into full production as a musical the following year at Brown University where Bass was professor and artistic director, and Berry was a part of the production. The play was later produced at Philadelphia's Freedom Theater, with Berry as musical director. Berry inherited the rights to further develop the production after Bass's death in 1995. Unlike the original musical, which emphasized how the rabbit through introspection becomes a whole individual, the newer multi-media version, still set in Ol' Black Hollow, shows the rabbit as a contributor to the entire community rather than just to himself. The newer story focuses upon the rabbit's quest to find the golden mean and how he escapes the three parts of Miss Fortune—envy, sloth, and greed.

Among other plays have been *The Adventures of Brer Rabbit*, by Pat Hale, written in 1962, and produced several times by regional theatre companies, the most successful being the Ranger Summer Theater production in Hamburg, New Jersey, in 1994;[54] the musical *Brer Rabbit*, by Richard Smithies and Maura Cavanagh; "Mr. Fox, Mr. Rabbit and Mr. Terrapin," a puppet show that opened in 1990 in London's Puppet Theatre Barge; and *Brer Rabbit*, by Mabel Dearmer, which opened at London's Everyman Theatre in 1997.

Several of the Brer Rabbit tales have been recorded. Rabbit Ears Productions, under the direction of Mike Pogue and Mark Sottnick, produced two audio and video productions of the tales in 1991. "Br'er Rabbit and Boss Lion," narrated by Robert Townsend, and "Brer Rabbit and the Wonderful Tar Baby"—a twenty-two-minute animated film adapted by Eric Metaxas, directed by Tim Raglin, and narrated by Danny Glover—were seen over a 240-station public/educational television network, then made available in a "mini-book/cassette" package and video cassette.

References to the Uncle Remus tales, especially the symbolism of the tar-baby, appear as tangential references in the mass media, including greeting cards, political cartoons, and books.[55] Ralph Ellison had used Brer Rabbit/Tar-Baby themes in *Invisible Man* (1952), his powerful autobiographical indictment of White attitudes toward American Blacks, and discussed Black folklore in *Shadow and Act* (1964), a collection of autobiographical essays, most of which were first published in magazines. In "Hidden Name and Complex Fate," Ellison encapsulates the Tar-Baby metaphor:

> Let Tar Baby, that enigmatic figure from Negro folklore, stand for the world. He leans, black and gleaming, against the wall of life utterly noncommittal under our scrutiny, our questioning, starkly unmoving before our naive attempts at intimidation. Then we touch him playfully and before we can say *Sonny Liston!* we find ourselves stuck. Our playful investigations become a labor, a fearful struggle, an agony. Slowly we perceive that our task is to learn the proper way of freeing ourselves to develop, in other words, technique.
>
> Sensing this, we give him our sharpest attention, we question him carefully, we struggle with more subtlety; while he, in his silent way, holds on, demanding that we perceive the necessity of calling him by his true name as the price of freedom.[56]

Toni Morrison uses the tar-baby symbolism in *Tar Baby* (1981), her contemporary narrative that explores innu-

Sesquicentennial postmark.

merable Black-White, master-servant, affluent- impoverished, parent-child conflicts, and how life entraps all
persons.

Robert Ludlum's 1990 spy-thriller *The Bourne
Ultimatum* includes the character Uncle Remus, the
code-name for a retired Black forger who gives advice
and consolation to the spy Jason Bourne whom he code-
names "Brer Rabbit." Both characters, however, spoke
standard American English.

Brer Rabbit was proposed as the mascot for the 1996
Summer Olympics in Atlanta. The campaign—complete
with posters, T-shirts, and bumper stickers—was developed under the direction of the Joel Chandler Harris
Association, and completely supported by civil rights
leader and former mayor Andrew Young. However, the
Olympic organizers—possibly unable to find a way to use
the rabbit for myriad promotions, possibly afraid that any
reference to Harris, Uncle Remus, and Brer Rabbit would
be an embarrassment upon a city they believed was urban

and more liberal than most of the South—chose a non-descript computer-generated mascot named Whatizit. Possibly embarrassed by its choice, the Olympics organizing committee itself deleted Whatizit from opening and closing ceremonies. But there was still a murmur from some who believed the mascot should have been Brer Rabbit. The year before the Olympics, and after Whatizit became the mascot, G. A. Clay and Mark Ledford teamed up to produce *The Return of Brer Rabbit*, a picture book with a theme of how the Olympics overlooked the South's most famous rabbit. *Constitution* columnist Colin Campbell, who has written several articles about Joel Chandler Harris and the Wren's Nest museum, spoke out against the city's snub of one of its most famous residents: "What a pity—in light of his genius, his sweetness, his merging of black and white, old South and new—that some Atlantans seem to find him minor and troublesome. Avoiding Harris is a waste of art and meaning. This is especially true in a city that some find bland, crass and forgetful."[57]

In December 1998, both the Wren's Nest and the town of Eatonton celebrated the sesquicentennial of Harris's accepted birth. The Joel Chandler Harris Association created "A Victorian Christmas at the Wren's Nest," with storytelling sessions, Victorian decorations, and carolers.

The Eatonton/Putnam County Chamber of Commerce created "Christmas in the Briar Patch," a month-long celebration of Harris's life. A 9 December celebration at the courthouse square featured an arts and crafts fair, storytelling sessions, and a parade. The Rosewood Bed and Breakfast, which includes a Joel Chandler Harris Room, invited the town to "Br'er Rabbit Tea Parties" and a special one-day art show, "A Celebration of Christmas and Critters." During that

month, 125 students in the Putnam County Elementary School created special birthday cards for Harris, and twenty students in the Putnam County Middle School wrote essays about Harris and the Br'er Rabbit folktales. In addition, the U.S. Post Office issued a special cancellation/stamper. In August 1999, the Eatonton Literary Festival—with storytellers, tours, a book fair, and special lectures—for one day celebrated the works of Harris and Alice Walker, as well as Flannery O'Connor, born in nearby Milledgeville. The one-day success began a yearly tradition.

Three days after Joel Chandler Harris died, Theodore Roosevelt wrote to Julian Harris, "I very firmly believe that his writings will last; that they will be read as long as anything written in our language during his time is read."[58] Biographer Paul M. Cousins, who as a boy had met Joel Chandler Harris, wrote:

> He will be remembered by those who, like him, place loyalty to their common country above a blind emotional loyalty to any one section of it, by those who in private and public take their stand for simple justice to all men irrespective of their race or creed, by those who respect the dignity of the individual without regard to his social, economic, political, or color status, and by those, who out of their generosity of mind, spirit, and wholesome humor, help to soften the blows that afflict erring humanity.[59]

Sadly, Roosevelt and Cousins were wrong. Even with recently-published children's books and plays, occasional references in the mass media to the tar-baby, and a few academic articles and celebrations during the Sesquicentennial, Americans know few, if any, of the

tales; and, certainly, most Americans do not connect the
name of Joel Chandler Harris to them. Those who do

Wren's Nest exhibit

probably get their impressions of the Uncle Remus tales from *Song of the South.*[60] "It is very difficult to make a complete collection of the negro tales," wrote Alcée Fortier, "as the younger generation knows nothing about them, and most of the old people pretend to have forgotten them."[61] Fortier, a nationally-respected folklorist who had collected and translated Louisiana creole tales, wrote those words in 1895. The tales are not being told in the schools; the major bookstore chains don't regularly stock the titles; the primary journalism histories barely mention Harris in any connection.

At the Wren's Nest, storytellers continue to recreate the oral folklore of the late nineteenth century, telling the tales to hundreds of school children a year; among lower-income Black families, the mother or grandmother may tell Br'er Rabbit stories "to pass on group-affirming morals to children," according to sociologist Ruth Leslie.[62] But, these tales are told only to specific audiences in specific economic regions. Literary critics have relegated Harris to the role of a minor author who may have influenced major authors; and the public is spending its reading time and money with genre books, self-help books, and celebrity tell-alls.

By refusing to look at and understand the life of Joel Chandler Harris and the stories he and dozens of others told during the nineteenth century, three generations of Americans have failed to better understand the language, folklore, and social conditions of America's Blacks during the Reconstruction era, and the nature of human emotion and life. Their failure led a new generation of Americans to be denied not only a part of America's social and literary history, but also a key to insight into human nature and the problems of society.

In 1924, Stanley Walker, legendary city editor of the *New York Herald Tribune*, outlined what makes a journalist great, then caustically concluded, "When he dies, a lot of people are sorry, and some of them remember him for several days." The vaporous nature of fame—whether because later generations mistakenly believed that Harris was racist and deliberately decided to bury his writings or because Americans do not have a sense of historical importance—may, ironically, be what Harris himself had wished.

A prophetic grave marker of Georgia granite in Atlanta's Westview Cemetery, with a plaque engraved with the dedication to A. B. Frost in the fifteenth anniversary republication of his first Uncle Remus book, best explains Harris's life and philosophy of how he had wished to live it:

> I seem to see before me the smiling faces of thousands of children—some young and fresh—and some wearing the friendly marks of age, but all children at

heart. And while I am trying hard to speak the right word, I seem to hear a voice, lifted above the rest, saying, "You made some of us happy." And so I feel my heart fluttering and my lips trembling and I have to bow silently and turn away and hurry into the obscurity that fits me best.

Joel Chandler Harris wrote thousands of articles, essays, and editorials; thirty-three books; and about 200 Uncle Remus tales that explored human emotions, actions, and the nature of society, and which by the time of his death had been translated into twenty-seven languages. American culture, with less respect for understanding its history than in living for the present while promoting its future, essentially relegated the works of Joel Chandler Harris, as it does to almost all persons, to the catacombs of history, to be dug out every now and then by a curious visitor. Nevertheless, the legacy that Joel Chandler Harris left the nation helped make it better understand its history, its culture, and its people. No author could ask for more.

And many a moon will wax and wane
Before we see his like again.
The rabbit will hide as he always hid
And the fox will do as he always did
But who can tell us what they say
Since Uncle Remus has passed away?

—anonymous

(Popular poem circulated after Harris's death)

---

[1] James Weldon Johnson, *The Book of American Negro Poetry,* 10.

2 W. E. B. DuBois, *The Gift of Black Folks*, 296.

3 Alain Locke, "The Negro in American Literature," 26.

4 Sterling A. Brown, "Negro Character as Seen by White Authors," 180.

5 Sterling A. Brown, "Negro Character as Seen by White Authors," 185.

6 Bernard Wolfe, "Uncle Remus and the Malevolent Rabbit," 40.

7 See, for example, Daniel G. Hoffman's review-essay in *Midwest Folklore* (Summer 1951): 133-38, and a brief summation in *Form and Fable in American Fiction* (Oxford University Press, 1961).

8 One of the most powerful indictments against racial intolerance is "A True Story," Twain's story of a sixty-year-old former slave, published in the November 1874 issue of the *Atlantic Monthly*.

9 Paul M. Cousins, *Joel Chandler Harris*, 132-33.

10 Darwin T. Turner, "Southern Fiction, 1900-1910," 284.

11 Interview with Jacqueline Shachter, United Press International, distributed to newspapers during September 1977.

12 Alice Walker, "Uncle Remus, No Friend of Mine," 31. The manikin was a quarter-sized straw-and-cloth doll, with painted face, which sat in a children's rocking chair. The restaurant itself closed in the early 1980s. Off-and-on for two decades, the building either remained unoccupied or housed antique stores.

13 Robert Hemenway, *Uncle Remus: His Songs and Sayings*, reprint edition, 1982, 8, 9.

14 Evelyn Nash, "Beyond Humor in Joel Chandler Harris's Nights With Uncle Remus," 223, 217, 218.

15 Leigh Fenley, "Uncle Remus Still a Teacher," *San Diego Union*, 3 April 1994; Book Section, 6.

16 William Bradley Strickland, "Stereotypes and Subversion in the Chronicles of Aunt Minervy Ann," 138.

17 Robert Bone, *Down Home*, 19.

18 Craig Werner, review, *Mississippi Quarterly* (1982): 74.

19 Letter from Joel Chandler Harris to Edward Burlingame, 4 November 1898.

20 Interview, WATL-AM Radio, Atlanta, n.d. The script is in the Special Collections archives at Emory University.

21 George Philip Krapp, "The Psychology of Dialect Writing," 523.

22 John Goldthwaite, "The Black Rabbit: Part One," 94.

23 Letter from Houghton Mifflin Company to biographer Paul Cousins, 2 February 1966.

24 Augusta Baker, "Books for Young People," *Saturday Review*, 18 February 1956, 54.

25 [Marion Palmer], *Uncle Remus Stories*, 7. As with most things associated with Disney, the signature of the introduction was that of Walt Disney.

26 William J. Faulkner, *The Day When Animals Talked*, 7.

27 Roger D. Abrahams, *Afro-American Folktales*, xvi.

28 Roger D. Abrahams, *Afro-American Folklore*, 3.

29 Thomas H. English, *Mark Twain to Uncle Remus: 1881-1885*, 6.

30 Joel Chandler Harris, review, *Atlanta Constitution*, 26 May 1885, 4.

31 Quoted in Ron Taylor, "Uncle Remus Lives," 12-B.

32 Quoted in Sharon Bailey, "Name Change Lands in Brier Patch," Metro-1.

33 Steve Schaefer, library director, Uncle Remus Library System.

34 Quoted in Alan Patureau, "Most Authorities Think Harris Was Just a Man of His Times," 1.

35 Quoted in Alan Patureau, "Most Authorities Think Harris Was Just a Man of His Times," 2H.

36 Michael Hirsley, "Thrown Into the Briar Patch," 4.

37 Barry Ostrow, spokesman for Savannah-Chatham County School District, quoted by Associated Press, 12 December 1986.

38 "Uncle Remus vs. the Censors," *Chicago Tribune*, 2 January 1987, 20.

39 Quoted in Ron Taylor, "Uncle Remus Lives," 12-B.

40 John Goldthwaite, "The Black Rabbit: Part One," 92.

41 Ron Taylor, "Uncle Remus Lives," 12-B.

42 Jones, a newspaper reporter at the time, later became general culture editor for *Newsweek*.

43 Review, *The Horn Book Magazine* (March-April 1987): 228.

44 Van Dyke Parks and Malcolm Jones, *Jump! The Adventures of Brer Rabbit*, vii.

45 Peter Neumeyer, "Children's Books," *New York Times*, 1 February 1987, section 7, 29.

46 Review, *The Horn Book Magazine* (March-April 1990): 213.

47 "Bookshelf," *New York Times*, 1 November 1987, section 7, 36.

48 Ken Franckling, "Bringing Brer Rabbit Into the '80s," syndicated news-feature, distributed 12 October 1987.

49 Julius Lester, *The Tales of Uncle Remus*, xvii.

50 Julius Lester, *The Tales of Uncle Remus*, xviii.

51 June Jordan, "A Truly Bad Rabbit," section 7, 32:1.

52 Transcript of speech, October 1995, Boston.

53 Anne Hessey, ed., *Giant Treasury of Brer Rabbit*, 6.

[54] The professional theatre company, under the direction of Paul and Patricia Meacham, later changed its name to the Tri-State Actors Theater, serving northeast Pennsylvania, northwest New Jersey, and south central New York.

[55] See R. Bruce Bickley, Jr. and Hugh Keenan, *Joel Chandler Harris*.

[56] Ralph Ellison, "Hidden Name and Complex Fate," 147.

[57] Colin Campbell, "City Should Embrace Harris, Not Shun Him," *Altanta Constitution*, 25 June 1996, C-1.

[58] *The Letters of Theodore Roosevelt* (1952), edited by Elting E. Morison, VI:1110-11.

[59] Paul M. Cousins, *Joel Chandler Harris: A Study in the Culture of the South*, 1848-1908, 224.

[60] While doing research for this book, the author asked an official at Disney for specific information about *Song of the South*. The official of Disney's distribution company asked the reason, and the author stated he was writing a book about Joel Chandler Harris. The official was unfamiliar with the name and asked, "Is he one of the actors in the film?"

[61] Alcée Fortier, *Louisiana Folk-Tales in French Dialect and English Translation*, ix.

[62] See Annie Ruth Leslie, "Using the Moral Vision of African American Stories to Empower Low-Income African American Women," *Affilia Journal of Women and Social Work*, Fall 1998

Addendum

Following the death of her husband, Esther (Essie) Harris, who had been the force that had protected Joel Chandler Harris from the public, and who gave him a love that carried though thirty-five years of marriage, moved from the Wren's Nest, and into the home of Mildred Harris and Edwin Camp. "The prospect of moving from the Wren's Nest filled her with a child-like dread," according to Evelyn Harris "but father's absence caused the home, which she loved so dearly, to seem desolate and lonely. She could not endure the thought of living there without his jovial companionship."[1]

A devoted mother, she continued to take care of her extended family, worrying like all mothers about her two sons and two grandchildren who were in France during World War I. Like the rest of her family, she spoke out against racial intolerance and the resurgence of the Ku Klux Klan after the war. In a different age, Essie Harris might have been attacked by others for not having "reached her potential." She would probably have encouraged and supported those who chose their own careers, and expected them to also respect her choices. But, says Evelyn Harris, "Her life was busy and happy and she seemed to enjoy the early obscurity as wholeheartedly as she did the later fame. Her faith, her love and her cheerful disposition enabled her to surmount successfully the difficulties of her personal and family life. The affection of husband and children was ample reward for her."[2]

In March 1925, she suffered a stroke which confined her to her bed and abruptly ended her talent for embroidery. Although physically restricted, she did not lose the keen mind and unqualified love that had been so important in raising her children and grandchildren, and protecting her husband. Essie died in October 1938 at the age of eighty-four, about fourteen years after her stroke.

The Harrises' daughters each married and became housewives. Lillian Harris (1882-1956) married Fritz Wagener (1882-1964); Mildred Harris (1885-1966) married Edwin Camp (1882-1955), a columnist for the *Atlanta Journal*. Mary Esther "Rosebud" Harris (1879-1882) died during childhood.

The Harrises' sons went into journalism. Lucien Harris (1875-1960), who married Aileen Zachary (1876-1958), was an editor with the *Constitution* before becoming an insurance executive. Evelyn Harris (1878-1961), who married Annie Hawkins (1879-1954), began his career at the *Constitution* before becoming public relations director for Southern Bell. Joel Chandler Harris, Jr. (1888-1954), known as J. C. and Jake, also began his career at the *Constitution* before becoming an advertising executive; he married Hazelle White (1888-1919), then three years after her death married Dorothy Dean (1898-1996). Joel Chandler Harris had been reluctant to name any child after him, but Clark Howell had insisted that the name be continued. Most thought Harris's reluctance stemmed from modesty; however, J. C. knew differently. In an enlightening interview with the *Atlanta Journal*, he recalled what his father once told him about naming a son, "Junior":

Evelyn Harris, 1950s

Julian and Julia Harris, 1950s

About the only thing a man can earn in this world that has permanent value is a good name. It's something you have to earn yourself, and you can't will it to anyone. A man who bestows his name on his son is a gambler. There's no telling what's going to happen to that name in a couple of generations. A young fellow ought to get ahead on his own ability and not because he is [someone's son.] If you'll just be respectful to your mother and sisters, stay out of jail and out of debt, that's all I ask.

Harris's other two sons, Evan Harris (1876-1878) and Linton Harris (1883-1890), both died during childhood.

Julian LaRose Harris (1874-1963), with his wife Julia Collier Harris (1875-1967), continued his father's journalistic legacy of social justice. Julian had spent fourteen years on the *Constitution*, including six years as managing editor, before launching *Uncle Remus's Magazine*. Following the magazine's failure in 1913, Harris became Sunday editor of James Gordon Bennett's *New York Herald*; his wife became a correspondent for the Herald Syndicate. Within two years, Harris was editor of the *Paris Herald*, Bennett's International edition. In 1917, shortly before the U.S. entered World War I, Harris was commissioned an Army first lieutenant, rising to captain in Military Intelligence. After the war, he returned to the *Paris Herald* as editor-in-chief, leaving in 1920 when the *Herald* and *New York Tribune* merged.

Julia, trained in the fine arts, was a prolific author of almost inexhaustible energy whose works crossed all genre and almost every conceivable topic. She was one of two women who reported the signing of the Treaty of Versailles, ending World War I. At a time when society believed a woman's role was best as a mother and wife, Julia became active in community affairs and spoke out on behalf of women's rights, birth control, and sex education in public schools.

In 1920, Harris bought a part-interest in the *Columbus* (Georgia) *Enquirer-Sun*, a small morning daily. He and Julia borrowed $7,500[3] and became sole owners in November 1922, and redesigned the newspaper as a regional voice that became one of the nation's better newspapers. Against massive opposition, the Harrises supported the teaching of evolution in public schools, and spoke out against corruption, the suppression of civil liberties, and racial intolerance.[4] Their crusade against the Ku Klux Klan and lynching, during which they endured threats against their lives, led to a drop in circulation—and the Pulitzer Prize in 1926 for meritorious public service. That citation stated that the Pulitzer was issued to the Harrises and the newspaper: "For its fight against the Klan...against dishonest and incompetent public officials and for justice to the Negro and against lynching."[5]

Although the work that Julia and Julian Harris did in Columbus was "journalistically outstanding," according to journalist-biographer Gregory Carroll Lisby, Harris's "brand of journalism was not widely appreciated in Columbus, but he kept pushing, attempting to reflect the best thought of Columbus citizens and urging them forward instead of the status quo as did the [competing] Ledger."[6]

By 1929, the Enquirer-Sun was failing, and the Harrises, faced by almost a decade of financial loss from readers who cancelled their subscriptions to protest the Enquirer-Sun's liberal crusades, sold their stock to two businessmen in exchange for them assuming all debts. As was the case at the end of Uncle Remus's Magazine, these new owners began to decimate the newspaper editorially and forbid Harris from writing against the pending Prohibition Amendment (Volstead Act), about religion, or evolution.[7] Following more financial and editorial interference by the new owners, as well as several broken promises, Harris resigned as editor by the end of the year. The newspaper was sold a few months later to the R. W. Page Corporation, parent company of the Ledger; William Eyer Page, the corporation's president, was a relative of Thomas Nelson Page.[8] Julian returned to the Constitution, serving five years in a variety of editorial positions, including news editor, then became executive editor of the Chattanooga Times for seven years. He was laid off in 1942 when the parent company cut back its newspaper operation in Chattanooga and reduced its staff; he then became the Southern correspondent for the New York Times. Three years later, at seventy, he retired.

Julia, after the sale of the Enquirer-Sun, continued both her multi-faceted writing career which included two biographies of her father-in-law, and her active participation in civic organizations. Both Julia and Julian Harris lived to see the emergence of the Civil Rights era during the 1960s.

In 1996, Julian and Julia Harris were posthumously elected by the Georgia Press Association into the Georgia Journalism Hall of Fame at the Henry Grady School of Journalism, University of Georgia. In 1998, Julia was named a "Georgia Woman of Achievement" (The program, initiated by Rosalyn Carter while she was Georgia's "first lady," recognizes women who have been overlooked by historians and the people.).

The grandchildren also achieved distinction in their own chosen fields. Lucien Harris, Jr. became a naturalist and wrote the definitive *Butterflies of Georgia*, among other books. Lucien Harris III, a great-grandson, retired from a successful banking career to devote his life to nature painting, becoming one of the South's more eminent painters of birds and butterflies.

Mary Harris Rowsey (1908-1979), daughter of Lucien and Aileen Harris, was society editor of the *Constitution*. Her youngest brother was named Remus A. Harris (1916-1979). He was one of the nation's leading public relations executives, and also wrote several popular songs, including "So Long," the theme song for TV host and entertainer Arthur Godfrey; "A Rose and a Prayer" for the Jimmy Dorsey band; and "The Georgian Waltz."

Robin Harris, a great-grandson, was president and chief executive officer of a major savings and loan association in the Atlanta area, and a member of the Georgia House of Representatives during 1963-1970 and 1973-1974. He chaired the committee to rewrite the Georgia constitution.

LaRose Grant, daughter of Lillian and Fritz Wagener and as of 2000 the only living grandchild, was born in Joel Chandler Harris's bed in 1908.

The *Atlanta Constitution* would continue into the twentieth century as one of the nation's better newspapers, basing a part of its reputation upon attacks against political corruption and racism. Led by Clark Howell, Sr., its editor/owner from 1889 to 1936, the newspaper won the Pulitzer Prize in public service for 1931. Howell was succeeded as owner by his son, Clark Howell, Jr. Ralph McGill, who became editor in 1938, won the Pulitzer Prize for editorial writing in 1959 for his campaigns against the Ku Klux Klan and racism. Eugene Patterson, who became editor in 1960 after McGill became publisher and a nationally-syndicated columnist, also won the Pulitzer Prize for editorial writing in 1967 for campaigns against racism.

In 1939, the Cox chain bought the *Atlanta Journal*; shortly after, it bought the *Georgian* and merged it into the *Journal* to strengthen competition against the *Constitution*. In 1950, Cox also bought the *Constitution*. The two newspapers kept separate editorial identities, with a combined Sunday edition, until they merged the news staffs in 1982; however, the morning *Constitution* retained the liberal editorial page; the afternoon *Journal* retained the conservative editorial page.

[1] Evelyn Harris, *A Little Story*, 59.

[2] Evelyn Harris, *A Little Story*, 3-4.

[3] Gregory Carroll Lisby, *Someone Had to be Hated*, 36-37.

[4] For an excellent account of the decade that Julia and Julian Harris owned the *Enquirer-Sun*, with emphasis upon their crusades for social justice, see Gregory Carroll Lisby, *Someone Had to be Hated*, 1977.

[5] The *Commercial Appeal* (Memphis Tenn.) and the *Montgomery* (Ala.) *Advertiser* also won Pulitzers that year for campaigns against the Klan and racial intolerance.

[6] Gregory Carroll Lisby, *Someone Had to be Hated*, 159.

[7] Gregory Carroll Lisby, *Someone Had to be Hated*, 144.

[8] The *Ledger-Enquirer*, the result of a subsequent merger of the *Ledger* and *Enquirer-Sun*, won a Pulitzer Prize in 1955 for a series of articles about corruption in neighboring Phenix City, Alabama. The newspaper was later sold to the Knight-Ridder chain.

Appendixes

The Harris Family, early 1920s. Esther LaRose Harris (center) is surrounded by her children. From the front center, clockwise, are Joel Jr., Julian, Lillian, Evelyn, Mildred, and Lucien.

A Mother's Wisdom:
Essie Harris and Respect

by Evelyn Harris

"The construction activities at Fort McPherson gave us our first intimate contact with boys and girls from the North. Their parents were members of the civilian staff and some of them lived near us. When these strangers came into our midst they were accepted without question, and in our neighborhood they were always referred to in respectful terms. Of course, there were others who had a deep-rooted prejudice, perhaps a hatred, for all northerners. That our hearts and minds were free of this was due to mother's sympathetic and understanding attitude, which we no doubt absorbed and reflected in our youthful relations.

"Mother had observed the Civil War from a vantage point in neutral Canada. Her sympathies were with the South, but she often told us that both sides fought for what they believed to be right. The boys and girls from the North, she said, had not personally engaged in the combat and should be accorded the privilege of loyalty to the cause of their fathers, just as we enjoyed the same privilege....

"I recall how patiently and sympathetically mother explained the situation [of slavery] when one of our guests made a remark that astonished and shocked us. She told him that the South had not been responsible for the tragedy of slavery, but that it had been a national responsibility. Certainly, she said, the negroes should not be blamed for it, nor for the distress and misery which followed their freedom. She said it was a complex and disturbing problem and she cautioned them to remember that negroes are human beings with souls like our own; that they were our friends and neighbors and justly entitled to our consideration so long as they were worthy of it.

"Mother was sincere in her concern for the welfare and comfort of her servants, and this interest included others who were afflicted with poverty or distress.... By nature, understanding and sympathetic, she soon won the loyalty and respect of everyone. She was greatly aided by father who thoroughly understood the negro character and was a firm friend of the face from boyhood until his death. Even so, mother's success with a people who were complete strangers to her was a tribute to her tact and intelligence....

"Whenever we were exposed to incidents involving prejudice and intolerance, we were made aware of the warmth of mother's heart and her love of her fellow man. She encouraged us to consider such matters in a spirit of charity and justice.

"There was a Jewish family who were our friends. We admired their loyal, devoted family life and the deference and obedience of their children. One day a companion made a vicious remark about Jews in general and our Jewish friends in particular. We had always regarded them as we did other people and gave no thought to their race or creed. When I repeated the incident to mother, she said she was glad I had come to her, and had not allowed a thoughtless remark to influence my estimate of others. She reminded me that Christ was a Jew, and that the Blessed Virgin, whom mother reverenced with sincere devotion, was [also a Jew]... It was those who disliked Jews, she thought, who persisted in blaming the [crucifixion] on people now living who are so remotely removed from the actual scene. And she cautioned us to strive always to be as true to our faith and as loyal to our parents as our Jewish friends were to theirs."

—*A Little Story* (unpublished)

341

Appendix

Uncle Remus Museum, exterior

Uncle Remus Museum, interior

The Uncle Remus Museum

Almost every Southern city has a Civil War monument, a landmark usually in the center of town at or near a court house square. Eatonton also has such a statue, but the people of Joel Chandler Harris's hometown mark their location by a cast iron three-foot high rabbit on top of a three-foot high stone pedestal. The statue of Brer Rabbit, erected in 1955, is the landmark for a town that has never lost its love of its most famous resident.

Three blocks from the Brer Rabbit statue, in Turner Park, named for Joseph Addison Turner, is the Uncle Remus Museum, a one-room cabin built in 1963 from three slave cabins that were once located in the Northwestern part of the county. Inside are a fireplace and antebellum era cooking utensils and furniture; first editions of Harris's books, plus several boxes of correspondence and articles about Harris; twelve shadow boxes, each with several wooden "critters" carved by Frank Schnell of Columbus, Georgia; and three large murals of the cotton fields, a slave cabin, and the Big House, painted by Wyndel Taylor, also of Columbus.

About 12,000-14,000 persons a year visit the cabin and, for a brief moment in their lives, get the tiniest piece of understanding about slavery and the tales that the slaves told to each other—and to the man who would preserve them.

The Deed Presentation Ceremony. Esther LaRose Harris presents the deed to the Sign of the Wren's Nest to the newly-formed Uncle Remus Memorial Association; January 18, 1913.

Appendix 3

The Wren's Nest

For $25,000 the Uncle Remus Memorial Association pur-chased Joel Chandler Harris's gabled twelve-room house and land in 1913, and turned it into a museum and library repository. The Association itself was originally a Ladies Auxiliary to an all-male association that had floundered trying to raise funds for a memo-rial to Harris.

A fund-raising dinner in 1910, with former president Theodore Roosevelt as guest speaker, had given the association its credibility and raised $4,927, matched by a gift from Andrew Carnegie. Among the donations during a four-year campaign were almost $3,000 from school children and the general public, and $5,000 from Esther LaRose Harris. At the time of the trans-fer, Essie told the guests:

> This has been my home for a long time, and I hate to give it up, but I feel that this is for the best. If it passed into private hands, it might suffer change. Now, I know that you will cher-ish every tree, flower, and shrub that he spoke of and loved, as I have cherished them. You will let the wild things feel at home here as he did and I have done. It would please him, if he could know, that the little children will always play about the place.[1]

Ironically, in what must have been the ultimate insult to the man who believed in racial equality and whose house the non-profit organization took over and tried to preserve, for six decades Blacks were not allowed into the house unless accompanied by

Whites or in an integrated tour group. There were a few protests, but the association—a closed society limited to 100 White women—kept its "standards" and its racism.

In 1966, at the height of the civil rights era, Dr. Rufus Clement, president of Atlanta University, declared that the racist policies of the museum and association "besmirched the memory" of Joel Chandler Harris; the Atlanta school board refused to permit class tours of the Wren's Nest as long as individual Blacks were not permitted into the house; and the city of Atlanta withheld its annual $1,000 grant from the house.

The association's attorney, in a letter to the city's Community Relations Commission, stated that his client "has no intention of changing its present admissions policies." Association members claimed that the policy was set by Harris himself who put a "whites-only" clause into his will; it was a claim that local media often accepted without verification. However, Harris left no will. Mildred Harris Camp Wright, in a strongly-worded letter to the editor, published in the 7 December 1967, issue of the *Constitution*, said that her grandfather "had no idea that there would be a memorial to him—and if he had, he would not have required such a policy. His stories were written with affection, sympathy, and understanding."

At the end of 1967, the Reverend Clyde Williams, a Black minister who was denied admission, filed suit in U.S. District Court. In September 1968, the court determined that the association policies violated the 1964 Civil Rights Act, and ordered that the museum must be integrated. The order applied only to house visitors, not to membership in the association itself.

Once, the neighborhood was composed only of Whites. By the mid-1970s, because of "White flight" to the suburbs, beginning as soon as Blacks began to move

Akbar Imhotep is one of a dozen storytellers at the Wren's Nest who helps keep alive the memory and wisdom of Joel Chandler Harris

Brer Rabbit, Uncle Remus, and the 'Cornfield Journalist'

into the neighborhood, the West End became primarily a Black community.

The U.S. Department of the Interior in 1976 designated the museum as a National Historic Landmark, but by the end of the 1970s, the Wren's Nest had deteriorated and was in need of significant repairs, not only to the house but to the association as well. By now composed mostly of aging White ladies, the association elected Gloria Baker, a school psychologist, as president in 1981. She would lead the association into a new era as it began a capital restoration campaign, while finally absorbing the ideals of Joel Chandler Harris, bringing people of all beliefs, cultures, values, and races together as visitors, volunteers, and staff. In 1984, the association finally dropped its "whites-only" membership policy. So integrated has the Wren's Nest become that it hosted the wedding reception for civil rights leader Ralph David Abernathy's youngest daughter; the street the Wren's Nest now faces is no longer the Gordon Street of Joel Chandler Harris's time, but Ralph David Abernathy Boulevard.

The first two professional executive directors, Laura Waller and Madelyn Ramey, each served about a year. With the hiring of Carole Mumford in 1987, and the addition of several part-time professional and volunteer staff, the museum began to make significant advances in preserving Harris's legacy. Mumford had been a social worker for about fifteen years with the National Urban League and the Atlanta Urban League before becoming cultural affairs officer for Atlanta.

Under Mumford's direction, the Association began a major four-year, $535,000 capital restoration project for the house which was becoming more of a slum than a museum. The project, with significant assistance from a Jack Daniel's advertising campaign and numerous pledges and grants, was completed in 1990. National Public Radio has named the Wren's Nest one of the "top five things to [visit] in Atlanta."

In March 1997, the board of directors elected Lyn May, a Black, as board president. May had been press secretary to Mayor Maynard Jackson, worked several years in the Olympics press office, and at the time of her election was vice-president of the Georgia Foundation for Independent Colleges. In November 1999, Sharon Crutchfield, a Black who had worked several years in non-profit organizations, became executive director. Joel Chandler Harris would not only have approved of May's election and Crutchfield's appointment, but would have encouraged them. The association had, indeed, come a long way in more than eight decades in preserving Harris's ideals.

Appendix 4

The Wonderful Tar-Baby Story

II.

THE WONDERFUL TAR-BABY STORY.

"DIDN'T the fox *never* catch the rabbit, Uncle Remus?" asked the little boy the next evening.

"He come mighty nigh it, honey, sho's you bawn— Brer Fox did. One day atter Brer Rabbit fool 'im wid dat calamus root, Brer Fox went ter wuk en got 'im some

tar, en mix it wid some turkentime, en fix up a contrapshun wat he call a Tar-Baby, en he tuck dish yer Tar-Baby en he sot 'er in de big road, en den he lay off in de bushes fer ter see wat de news wuz gwineter be. En he didn't hatter wait long, nudder, kaze bimeby here come Brer Rabbit

3

pacin' down de road—lippity-clippity, clippity-lippity—dez ez sassy ez a jay-bird. Brer Fox, he lay low. Brer Rabbit come prancin' 'long twel he spy de Tar-Baby, en den he fotch up on his behime legs like he wuz 'stonished. De Tar-Baby, she sot dar, she did, en Brer Fox, he lay low.

" ' Mawnin' !' sez Brer Rabbit, sezee—' nice wedder dis mawnin',' sezee.

" Tar-Baby ain't sayin' nuthin', en Brer Fox, he lay low.

" ' How duz yo' sym'tums seem ter segashuate ? ' sez Brer Rabbit, sezee.

" Brer Fox, he wink his eye slow, en lay low, en de Tar-Baby, she ain't sayin' nuthin'.

" ' How you come on, den ? Is you deaf ? ' sez Brer Rabbit, sezee. ' Kaze if you is, I kin holler louder,' sezee.

" Tar-Baby stay still, en Brer Fox, he lay low.

' · Youer stuck up, dat's w'at you is,' says Brer Rabbit, sezee, ' en I'm gwineter kyore you, dat's w'at I'm a gwineter do,' sezee.

" Brer Fox, he sorter chuckle in his stummuck, he did, but Tar-Baby ain't sayin' nuthin'.

" ' I'm gwineter larn you howter talk ter 'specttubble fokes ef hit's de las' ack,' sez Brer Rabbit, sezee. ' Ef you don't take off dat hat en tell me howdy, I'm gwineter bus' you wide open,' sezee.

" Tar-Baby stay still, en Brer Fox, he lay low.

" Brer Rabbit keep on axin' 'im, en de Tar-Baby, she keep on sayin' nuthin', twel present'y Brer Rabbit draw back wid his fis', he did, en blip he tuck 'er side er de

head. Right dar's whar he broke his merlasses jug. His
fis' stuck, en he can't pull loose. De tar hilt 'im. But
Tar-Baby, she stay still, en Brer Fox, he lay low.

" 'Ef you don't lemme loose, I'll knock you agin,' sez
Brer Rabbit, sezee, en wid dat he fotch 'er a wipe wid de
u lder han', en dat stuck. Tar-Baby, she ain't sayin' nuthin', en Brer Fox, he lay low.

" 'Tu'n me loose, fo' I kick de natal stuffin' outen you,'
sez Brer Rabbit, sezee, but de Tar-Baby, she ain't sayin'
nuthin'. She des hilt on, en den Brer Rabbit lose de use
er his feet in de same way. Brer Fox, he lay low. Den
Brer Rabbit squall out dat ef de Tar-Baby don't tu'n 'im
loose he butt 'er cranksided. En den he butted, en his
head got stuck. Den Brer Fox, he sa'ntered fort', lookin'
des ez innercent ez wunner yo' mammy's mockin'-birds.

" 'Howdy, Brer Rabbit,' sez Brer Fox, sezee. ' You
look sorter stuck up dis mawnin',' sezee, en den he rolled
on de groun', en laft en laft twel he couldn't laff no mo'.
' I speck you'll take dinner wid me dis time, Brer Rabbit.
I done laid in some calamus root, en I ain't gwincter take
no skuse,' sez Brer Fox, sezee."

Here Uncle Remus paused, and drew a two-pound yam
out of the ashes.

"Did the fox eat the rabbit ?" asked the little boy to
whom the story had been told.

"Dat's all de fur de tale goes," replied the old man.
" He mout, en den agin he moutent. Some say Jedge B'ar
come 'long en loosed 'im—some say he didn't. I hear Miss
Sally callin'. You better run 'long."

wid dem w'at lies down on de groun' en plays dead w'en dar's a free fight gwine on,' sezee.

"Den Brer Possum grin en laff fit to kill hisse'f.

"'Lor', Brer Coon, you don't speck I done dat kaze I wuz 'feared, duz you?' sezee. 'W'y I want no mo' 'feared dan you is dis minnit. W'at wuz dey fer ter be skeered un?' sezee. 'I know'd you'd git away wid Mr. Dog ef I didn't, en I des lay dar watchin' you shake him, waitin' fer ter put in w'en de time come,' sezee.

"Brer Coon tu'n up his nose.

"'Dat's a mighty likely tale,' sezee, 'w'en Mr. Dog ain't mo'n tech you 'fo' you keel over, en lay dar stiff,' sezee.

"'Dat's des w'at I wuz gwineter tell you 'bout,' sez Brer Possum, sezee. 'I want no mo' skeer'd dan you is right now, en' I wuz fixin' fer ter give Mr. Dog a sample er my jaw,' sezee, 'but I'm de most ticklish chap w'at you ever laid eyes on, en no sooner did Mr. Dog put his nose down yer 'mong my ribs dan I got ter laffin, en I laft twel I ain't had no use er my lim's,' sezee, 'en it's a mussy unto Mr. Dog dat I wuz ticklish, kaze a little mo' en I'd e't 'im up,' sezee. 'I don't mine fightin', Brer Coon, no mo' dan you duz,' sezee, 'but I declar' ter grashus ef I kin stan' ticklin'. Git me in a row whar dey ain't no ticklin' 'lowed, en I'm your man,' sezee.

"En down ter dis day"—continued Uncle Remus, watching the smoke from his pipe curl upward over the little boy's head—"down ter dis day, Brer Possum's bound ter s'render w'en you tech him in de short ribs, en he'll laff ef he knows he's gwineter be smashed for it."

IV.

HOW MR. RABBIT WAS TOO SHARP FOR MR. FOX.

"Uncle Remus," said the little boy one evening, when he had found the old man with little or nothing to do, "did the fox kill and eat the rabbit when he caught him with the Tar-Baby?"

"Law, honey, ain't I tell you 'bout dat?" replied the old darkey, chuckling slyly. "I 'clar ter grashus I ought er tole you dat, but ole man Nod wuz ridin' on my eyeleds 'twel a leetle mo'n I'd a dis'member'd my own name, en den on to dat here come yo' mammy hollerin' atter you.

"W'at I tell you w'en I fus' begin? I tole you Brer Rabbit wuz a monstus soon beas'; leas'ways dat's w'at I laid out fer ter tell you. Well, den, honey, don't you go en make no udder kalkalashuns, kaze in dem days Brer Rabbit en his fambly wuz at de head er de gang w'en enny racket wuz on han', en dar dey stayed. 'Fo' you begins fer ter wipe yo' eyes 'bout Brer Rabbit, you wait en see whar'bouts Brer Rabbit gwineter fetch up at. But dat's needer yer ner dar.

"W'en Brer Fox fine Brer Rabbit mixt up wid de Tar-Baby, he feel mighty good, en he roll on de groun' en laff. Bimeby he up'n say, sezee:

"'Well, I speck I got you dis time, Brer Rabbit,' sezee; 'maybe I ain't, but I speck I is. You been runnin' roun' here sassin' atter me a mighty long time, but I speck you done come ter de een' er de row. You bin cuttin' up yo'

capers en bouncin' 'roun' in dis naberhood ontwel you
come ter b'leeve yo'se'f de boss er de whole gang. En den
youer allers some'rs whar you got no bizness,' sez Brer Fox,
sezee. 'Who ax you fer ter come en strike up a 'quaint-
ence wid dish yer Tar-Baby ? En who stuck you up dar
whar you iz ? Nobody in de roun' worril. You des tuck
en jam yo'se'f on dat Tar-Baby widout waitin' fer enny invite,' sez Brer Fox, sezee, 'en dar you is, en dar you'll stay
twel I fixes up a bresh-pile and fires her up, kaze I'm gwineter bobbycue you dis day, sho,' sez Brer Fox, sezee.

"Den Brer Rabbit talk mighty 'umble.

"'I don't keer w'at you do wid me, Brer Fox,' sezee,
'so you don't fling me in dat brier-patch. Roas' me, Brer
Fox,' sezee, 'but don't fling me in dat brier-patch,'
sezee.

"'Hit's so much trouble fer ter kindle a fier,' sez Brer
Fox, sezee, 'dat I speck I'll hatter hang you,' sezee.

"'Hang me des ez high as you please, Brer Fox,' sez
Brer Rabbit, sezee, 'but do fer de Lord's sake don't fling
me in dat brier-patch,' sezee.

"'I ain't got no string,' sez Brer Fox, sezee, 'en now
I speck I'll hatter drown you,' sezee.

"'Drown me des ez deep ez you please, Brer Fox,' sez
Brer Rabbit, sezee, 'but do don't fling me in dat brier-
patch,' sezee.

"'Dey ain't no water nigh,' sez Brer Fox, sezee, 'en
now I speck I'll hatter skin you,' sezee.

"'Skin me, Brer Fox,' sez Brer Rabbit, sezee, 'snatch
out my eyeballs, t'ar out my years by de roots, en cut off

my legs,' sezee, ' but do please, Brer Fox, don't fling me in dat brier-patch,' sezee.

"Co'se Brer Fox wanter hurt Brer Rabbit bad ez he kin, so he cotch 'im by de behime legs en slung 'im right in de middle er de brier-patch. Dar wuz a considerbul flutter whar Brer Rabbit struck de bushes, en Brer Fox sorter hang 'roun' fer ter see w'at wuz gwineter happen. Bimeby he hear somebody call 'im, en way up de hill he see Brer Rabbit settin' cross-legged on a chinkapin log koamin' de pitch outen his har wid a chip. Den Brer Fox know dat he bin swop off mighty bad. Brer Rabbit wuz bleedzed fer ter fling back some er his sass, en he holler out:

"'Bred en bawn in a brier-patch, Brer Fox—bred en bawn in a brier-patch!' en wid dat he skip out des ez lively ez a cricket in de embers."

Appendix 5

A Brief Overview of the Basic Theories of American Black English[2]

There are three major theories about the origins of American Black English (ABE).

The Deficit Theory

The Deficit Theory, occasionally known as the Theory of Verbal (or Language) Deprivation, claims that not only is American Black English a "deficient" language, but that because it is not a "complete" language, Blacks have cognitive deficiencies as well. They argue there is only one "proper" language for Americans. American Black English, as well as any nonstandard language, is "poor," "sloppy," or "substandard" English.

A major branch of the Deficit Theory, now discredited, argues that the American Black is genetically and anatomically unable to achieve the same level of speech as the American White. They argue that because the nose, lips, teeth, gums, and larynx are articulators of speech, all anatomical differences would change sound.

Although Joel Chandler Harris was a master at recording the speech of Blacks of the Middle Georgia region, identified by dialectologists as Piedmont Southern English, and adept at recording Gullah from the Georgian sea islands, like most Americans he believed that Gullah was "the negro dialect in its most primitive state...being merely a confused and untranslatable mixture of English and African words."[3]

Reflecting an ignorance of the language and what would be a base of the Deficit Theory, the prevailing theory for several decades, journalist-author Ambrose Gonzales, whose "Kinlaw tales" and "Silhouettes" paralleled the Uncle Remus stories, believed:

> Slovenly and careless of speech, these Gullahs seized upon the peasant English used by some of the early settlers and by the White servants of the Wealthier Colonies, wrapped their clumsy tongues about it as well as they could, and, enriched with certain expressive African words, it issued through their flat noses and thick lips as so workable a form of speech that it was gradually adopted by the other slaves and became in time the accepted Negro speech of the lower districts of South Carolina and Georgia. With characteristic laziness, these Gullah Negroes took short cuts to the ears of their auditors, using as few words as possible, sometimes making one gender serve for three, one tense for several, and totally disregarding singular and plural numbers....
>
> [They] retained only a few words of [their] jungle-tongue, and even these few are by no means authenticated... As the small vocabulary of the jungle atrophied through disuse and was soon forgotten, the contributions to language made by the Gullah Negro is insignificant, except through the transformation wrought upon a large body of borrowed English words...[4]

Although deficit theorists believe that American Black English is a "deficient" language, dialectologists and linguists/creolists point out that nonstandard English and dialects are not inferior languages, and are valuable for a better understanding of a people's life and culture.

The Dialect Geographer Theory

Most dialectologists believe that the language of the Southern Black was closer to American Southern English, itself similar to Elizabethan British English, than to the West African languages. They believe the English migration to the American colonies brought about a divergence of dialects, that as sociocultural groups were separated by geography, dialects were formed. For that reason, they claim that what is now identified as American Black English is in reality a reflection not of race, but of the geographical territory in which the Blacks lived. Thus, it is not surprising that dialectologists and some literary critics believe the Uncle Remus tales are not African in origin. With the publication of the first volume of the definitive *Linguistic Atlas of the United States* (1936), edited by Hans Kurath, the dialect geographer theory of language became America's primary theory about dialect origins and distribution.

J. P. Fruit, in an article for the 1896 volume of *Dialect Notes*, stated: "[Black English] represents the negro dialect that has most influenced the speech of the South. It is the language of the negroes when they were part and parcel of our households. Then the negro was a great factor in forming our spoken language."[5]

George Philip Krapp, one of the nation's leading authorities on American language, argued there were almost no African roots in American Black English. In the June 1924 issue of the influential *American Mercury*, Krapp concluded:

> The Gullah dialect is a very much simplified form of English, with cases, numbers, genders, tenses reduced to the vanishing point.... Very little of the dialect, perhaps none of it, is derived from sources other than English. In vocabulary, in syntax, and pronunciation, practically all forms of Gullah [and, thus,

Black English] can be explained on the basis of English, and probably only a deeper delving would be necessary to account for those characteristics that seem deep and mysterious.... [I]t is reasonably safe to conclude that not a single detail of Negro pronunciation or Negro syntax can be proved to have other than an English origin.[6]

In his subsequent seminal work *The English Language in America* (1925), Krapp praised Joel Chandler Harris, noting, "No more skillful literary transcriptions of Southern speech, both the speech of whites and of negroes, have been made than those of Joel Chandler Harris."[7] However, Krapp reinforced his earlier article, again claiming, "The speech of Uncle Remus and the speech of rustic whites as Harris records it are so much alike that if one did not know which character was speaking, one might often be unable to tell whether the words were those of a white man or of a negro.[8]

The words of Cleanth Brooks, influenced by Krapp, would dominate the language discussions of the first half of the twentieth century: "In almost every case the specifically negro forms turn out to be older English forms which the negro must have taken originally from the white man, and which he has retained after the white man has begun to lose them."[9] Guy B. Johnson, after lengthy research on St. Helena Island off the coast of Georgia and South Carolina, likewise concluded that Gullah, the most creolized of all varieties of American Black English:

...can be traced back in practically every detail to English dialect speech.... [B]oth the Negro and the white man in the South speak English as they learned it from the latter's ancestors....

[T]his strange dialect turns out to be little more than the peasant English of two centuries ago... From this peasant speech and from the "baby talk" used by masters in addressing them, the Negroes developed the dialect.[10]

The most complete phonological analysis of the Uncle Remus language was by Sumner Ives as a 1952 doctoral dissertation at the University of Texas. Ives concluded that the dialect of Uncle Remus was accurate and reflective of the language of the people of mid-Georgia in the post-Civil War period. In an article based upon his dissertation, Ives stated:

> Actually the field records of the *Linguistic Atlas*, aside from a very few Gullah records, show hardly any usages in Negro speech which cannot also be found in rustic white speech. And there are many similarities in usage as Harris wrote the dialects. However, the peculiarity of his Negro speech...consists in the greater density of nonstandard forms, and in the fact that the nonstandard items include, in greater number, features which are associated with Southern plantation speech rather than with Southern mountain speech. Since the same features can actually be found in the speech of both Negro and rustic white, Harris could more justly be accused of exaggerating the actual difference than of failing to indicate it. One additional point should, however, be mentioned. Some of the Atlas field records of rustic white speech show much closer agreement with the Uncle Remus dialect than do others. These other records show features which are neither in the records of cultured informants of the region nor in the records of Negro speech. Instead, they show characteristics of South Midland or Southern mountain speech, and in this respect, their usage agrees substantially with that of the "poor white" as Harris wrote it.[11]

The Creolist Theory

Since the 1950s, sociologists and linguists had been aware of Melville Herskovits' seminal work, *The Myth of the Negro Past* (1941), and had begun to recognize that the languages, philosophies, and even religions of the Blacks of the Revolutionary, Antebellum, and Reconstruction cycles were probably not so much bastardization of White America as they were of West African origin. Herskovits argued that the slaves created a pidgin language while in America that was significantly Niger-Congo in its syntax and phonology, but European in lexicon.

Prominent in the Gullah of Daddy Jack are numerous syntactical constructions that reflect a West African language base, such as serial phrasing ("'e bu'n bu'n—bu'n, bu'n; 'e do bu'n smaht") the frequent use of a pronominal cross-reference marker ("B'er Rabbit, 'e do hab 'e y-eye 'pon B'er Gator") and West African language tense construction ("you bin hab," "hab bin," "I bin git," "no bin see," "is bin run") Phonologically, there is a consistent shift between the voiced labiodental fricative [v] to the unvoiced labiodental fricative [f], as in *dife* and *lif*. Daddy Jack also uses the enclitic vowel, as in *shekky* and *mekky*. The lexical item *bumbye* is the Gullah for *baimbai* which eventually became the English "by and by." The words *w'en* and *w'at*, which may seem to be merely eye dialect, a grotesque mispelling meant to reflect dialect, actually reflect that American Black English, Gullah, and many West African languages do not have the aspirated [h] following the [w]. Thus, *when* and *w'en* are pronounced differently.

Lorenzo Dow Turner's *Africanisms in the Gullah Dialect* (1949) proved that Gullah was a creole that had a definable linguistic structure, with syntax, lexicon, and phonology based upon West African languages. In studying more than twenty-five African languages, Turner concluded that phonology, which the dialect geographers used as the basis for their arguments, was only a part of the complex patterns; analysis of syntax, intonation patterns, and paralinguistic features helped distinguish American Black English, including Gullah, as African-based languages.

Gilbert D. Schneider, who spent fourteen years in Nigeria and Cameroon researching and studying West African languages, wrote the definitive study of West African Pidgin English, which he named Wes-Kos. Schneider argued that most slaves spoke languages from Western Africa, with many speaking Wes-Kos, the trade language of large numbers of slaves before they were chained and brought to the United States:

> There is little doubt that the language of Uncle Remus is uniquely West African—everything from the obvious phonological constructions to the less obvious syntactical, ideophonic, and ideolectal constructions. The phrasing and use of African language structures reflect a strong West African, not an American, language base.[12]

Like the dialectologists, the creolists agree that the dialects presented by Harris were accurate representations of the speech during the post-Civil War era. However, with the research into African languages by Herskovits, Turner, and Schneider, and the Transformational Theory developed by Noam Chomsky, they disagree with the dialectologists on possible origins, pointing to both linguistic rules and historical development in West African languages to support their theory. While conceding that elements of Black speech may be present in the speech of the "rustic white," they argue that the antebellum variations of American Black English are distinctly West African in origin, especially in

the syntactic deep structure, which dialectologists had not studied. They argue that West African slaves did not lose their languages when they came to America, and that the deep structure of most of the varieties of American Black English is that of the African language families.[13]

Among the major folklorists who helped substantiate African origins of the Uncle Remus tales were Aurelio M. Espinosa, in the early 1940s, who collected 267 variations of the tar-baby stories, mostly from Africa, India, and the Caribbean islands;[14] and Florence Baer, whose excellent analysis, *Sources and Analogues of the Uncle Remus Tales* (1980), essentially put an end to claims of non-African origins, by revealing that 122 of the 184 tales she analyzed are traced to Africa.[15]

The Eradicationist Theory

The Eradicationist Theory, largely advanced by psychologists and educators during the 1960s, and promoted by the mass media, is a major variation of the Deficit Theory. Even if there is an African base in American Black English, argue these believers, the language retards the development of American Blacks, in both language and social development. The mission of the Eradicationists, quite simply, is to eradicate nonstandard English dialects, including American Black English which they believe is a deficient language. By eliminating nonstandard English, the eradicationists believe Blacks can better achieve linguistic, cultural, and social parity with Whites.

The National Association for the Advancement of Colored People, through its official magazine, *The Crisis*, argued in 1971 that "the so-called 'Black English' is basically the same slovenly English as spoken by the South's uneducated poor White population," called an educational program in Black English at Brooklyn College "a cruel hoax," and urged "Black parents throughout the nation to rise up in unanimous condemnation of this insidious conspiracy to cripple their children permanently.... Let the Black voice of protest resound thunderously throughout the land."[16]

Dialectologists and linguists, who disagree on American Black English origins, agree on the validity of the language variations. In response to the eradicationists, Raven I. McDavid, Jr., one of the nation's leading dialectologists, delivered "Sense and Nonsense About American Dialects," a scathing indictment of Deficit Theory and of the National Council of Teachers of English. "[W]e must conclude that our educators, however well intentioned, are talking nonsense," said McDavid about eradicationist beliefs and their "glib generalities" in his speech at the annual meeting of the Modern Language Association in December 1965.[17] His speech was reprinted dozens of times in professional journals—and attacked innumerable times. The only "nonsense," countered the teachers, was McDavid's speech. Other major attacks came from both creolists and dialect geographers, while the educational eradicationists, both Black and White, continue to hammer their theme that there is little African influence upon Afro-American culture ad folklore, that Joel Chandler Harris was a racist, that all forms of American Black English are deficient language variations, and that Blacks must be stripped of whatever traces of American Black English that they hold.

Because of the volumes of evidence presented by the dialectologists and creolists, both the Deficit Theory and its eradicationist off-shoot are now largely discredited. However, educators, psychologists, and the general public, influenced by innumerable articles in the mass media, still believe American Black English is a deficient language.

¹ Esther LaRose Harris, quoted in Myrta Lockett Avary, *Joel Chandler Harris and His Home*, 36.

² For more linguistic analysis of the language of the Uncle Remus tales, see the works of Florence Baer, Michele Birnbaum, Walter M. Brasch, Cleanth Brooks, Sumner Ives, Richard L. Long, Lee Pederson, and Gilbert D. Schneider.

³ Joel Chandler Harris, *Nights With Uncle Remus*, xxxii-xxxiii.

⁴ Ambrose Gonzales, *The Black Border*, 10, 17-18.

⁵ J. Fruit, "Uncle Remus in Phonetic Spelling," 349.

⁶ George Philip Krapp, "The English of the Negro," 192.

⁷ George Philip Krapp, *The English Language in America*, 240.

⁸ George Philip Krapp, *The English Language in America*, 250.

⁹ Cleanth Brooks, *The Relation of the Alabama-Georgia Dialect to the Provincial Dialects of Great Britain*, 64.

¹⁰ Guy B. Johnson, *Folk Culture on St. Helena Island, South Carolina*, 6, 53.

¹¹ Sumner Ives, "Dialect Differentiation in the Stories of Joel Chandler Harris," 91.

¹² Gilbert D. Schneider, *The Uncle Remus Dialect and Its Value to the Serious Scholar*, 4.

¹³ The Transformational Grammar Theory, formally proposed by Noam Chomsky in 1957, essentially argues that the surface structure similarities and differences are superficial and not conclusive. The same sentence, spoken by two different persons, could have different deep structures. The structuralists argued that you can not empirically measure what is in a person's mind or cultural background. The Transformational Grammar Theory would establish the paradigm to analyze deep structure arguments for the existence of an African language base in American Black English as a continuation of the Hamito-Bantu and Niger-Congo language families.

¹⁴ See A. M. Espinosa, "A New Classification of the Fundamental Elements of the Tar-Baby Story," *Journal of American Folklore* (January-March 1943): 31-37.

¹⁵ Other pioneering work during the 1960s and 1970s that helped solidify the Creolist Theory was done by Paul Christophersen, David Dalby, David DeCamp, Ralph Fasold, Robert A. Hall, Ian Hancock, William Labov, Richard A. Long, Edna O'Hern, Lee Pederson, George N. Putnam, Gilbert D. Schneider, Roger Shuy, William Stewart, and Walt Wolfram.

¹⁶ "Black Nonsense," *The Crisis* (April-May 1971): 78.

¹⁷ Raven I. McDavid, "Sense and Nonsense About American Dialects," 9

Bibliography

Joel Chandler Harris's articles, editorials, essays, and folktales appeared in the *Atlanta Constitution*, 1876-1908, and *Century Illustrated Monthly Magazine*, *The Critic*, *Scribner's Monthly*, *Metropolitan*, *Youth's Companion*, and *The Saturday Evening Post*, among other magazines, 1880-1910. His articles and tales were reprinted by hundreds of newspapers.

Most of the available manuscripts, photographs, letters, contracts, royalty statements, checks, and miscellaneous items by or about Joel Chandler Harris are preserved in the Joel Chandler Harris collection in the Special Collections department of Emory University's Woodruff Library; other primary documents are preserved in collections of the Joel Chandler Harris Association at the Wren's Nest museum, Atlanta, the Uncle Remus Museum, Eatonton; the Atlanta Historical Center; and the special collections department of the University of Virginia.

Abrahams, Roger D. *African Folktales, Traditional Stories of the Black World*. New York City: Pantheon Books, 1983.

———. *Afro-American Folktales, Stories from Black Traditions in the New World*. New York City: Pantheon, 1985.

Adair, Forrest. "Joel Chandler Harris—Master Builder." *City Builder*, September 1924, 5-8, 47-51.

———. "Stories and Incidents in the Life of Georgia's Best Known Author." *Atlanta Constitution*, 7 October 1906, 1 [Originally published in *The Methodist Messenger*].

Avary, Myrta Lockett. *Joel Chandler Harris and His Home: A Sketch*. Atlanta: Uncle Remus Memorial Association and Appeal Publishing , 1913.

Baer, Florence E. *Sources and Analogues of the Uncle Remus Tales*. Helsinki, Finland: Suomalainen Tiedeakatemia Academia Scientiarium Fennica, 1980.

Bailey, Sharon. "Name Change Lands in Brier Patch." *Atlanta Journal*, 19 February 1982. Metro-1 section.

Baker, Ray Stannard. "Joel Chandler Harris." *Outlook*, 5 November 1905, 594-603.

Baskervill, William Malone. "Joel Chandler Harris." *Chautaquan* (October 1896): 62-67.

————. "Joel Chandler Harris." In *Southern Writers: Biographical and Critical Studies*, 41-88. South Memphis TN: Methodist Episcopal Church of the South, 1897.

Bickley, R. Bruce, Jr., editor. *Critical Essays on Joel Chandler Harris*. Boston: G. K. Hall, 1981.

————. "Joel Chandler Harris." *Dictionary of Literary Biography*, edited by Stanley Trachtenberg, 11: 189-201. Detroit: Gale Research, 1982.

————. *Joel Chandler Harris*. Boston: Twayne, 1978 (revised: 1987, Athens: University of Georgia Press).

————, compiler. *Joel Chandler Harris: A Reference Guide*. Boston: G. K. Hall, 1978.

———— and Hugh T. Keenan. *Joel Chandler Harris, An Annotated Bibliography of Criticism, 1977-1996: With Supplement, 1892-1976*. Westport CT: Greenwood, 1997.

Birbaum, Michele. "Dark Dialects and Literary Realism in Joel Chandler Harris's Uncle Remus Series." *New Orleans Review* (Spring 1991): 36-45.

Bone, Robert A. *Down Home: A History of Afro-American Short Fiction From Its Beginnings to the End of the Harlem Renaissance*. New York City: Putnam's Sons, 1975.

Brainerd, Erastus. "Joel Chandler Harris at Home." *Critic* (16 May 1885): 229-41.

Brasch, Walter M. and Ila Wales Brasch. *A Comprehensive Annotated Bibliography of American Black English*. Baton Rouge LA: Louisiana State University Press, 1976.

Brasch, Walter M. *Black English and the Mass Media*. Amherst MA: University of Massachusetts Press, 1981.

————. *A ZIM Self-Portrait*. Cranbury NJ: Associated University Presses, 1990.

————. "Joel Chandler Harris." In *The Eye of the Reporter*, edited by Bill Knight and Deckle McLean, 131-55. Essays in Literature series. Western Illinois University: Macomb IL, 1996.

Brestensky, Dennis F. "Uncle Remus: Mere Buffoon or Admirable Man of Stature?" *Philological Papers* (December 1975): 51-58.

Brewer, J. Mason, editor. *American Negro Folklore*. Chicago: Quadrangle Books, 1968.

Brookes, Stella Brewer. *Joel Chandler Harris, Folklorist*. Athens: University of Georgia Press, 1950.

Brooks, Cleanth. *The Relationship of the Alabama-Georgia Dialect to the Provincial Dialects of Great Britain*. Baton Rouge: Louisiana State University Press, 1935.

———. *The Language of the American South*. Athens: University of Georgia Press, 1985.

Brown, Sterling A. "Negro Character as Seen by White Authors." *Journal of Negro Education* (April 1933): 179-203.

Caldwell, Erskine. "Foreword." *On the Plantation*. Athens: University of Georgia Press, 1980.

Campbell, Colin. "A Joel Chandler Harris Mystery for Then and Now." *Atlanta Journal and Constitution*, 9 June 1998, B-2.

———. "Brer Rabbit Returns to Tackle Thorny Issue." *Atlanta Journal and Constitution*, 21 November 1995, B-1.

———. "City Should Embrace Harris, Not Shun Him." *Atlanta Journal and Constitution*, 25 June 1996, C-1.

———. "Diversity Finds Roots in Wren's Nest." *Atlanta Journal and Constitution*, 11 March 1997, B-1.

———. "Games a Worry for Wren's Nest." *Atlanta Journal and Constitution*, 23 June 1996, D-1.

———. "More Evidence Harris Told Tall Tale About His Age." *Atlanta Journal and Constitution*, 2 July 1998, C-2.

Chase, Richard, compiler. *The Complete Tales of Uncle Remus*. Boston: Houghton, Mifflin, 1955.

Christensen, A. M. H. *Afro-American Folk Lore, Told Round Cabin Fires on the Sea Island of South Carolina*, Boston: J. G. Cupples, 1892.

Christensen, Mike. "Uncle Remus Author Remains Ambiguous Figure in Folklore." *Atlanta Journal and Constitution*, 23 November 1986, D-1.

Cousins, Paul Mercer. "Joel Chandler Harris: A Study in the Culture of the South, 1848-1908." Ph.D. dissertation, Columbia University, New York City, 1966.

Crane, T. F. "Plantation Folk-Lore." *Popular Science Monthly* (18 April 1881): 824-33.

Currell, W. S. Book review of *On the Plantation*. *North Carolina Journal of Education* (3 November 1981): 125-27.

Derby, James C. *Fifty Years Among Authors, Books and Publishers*. New York City: G. W. Carleton, 1885.

Dorson, Richard M. *American Negro Folktales*. Greenwich CT: Fawcett, 1967.

———. *Negro Folktales in Michigan*. Cambridge: Harvard University Press, 1956

Downs, Robert B. *Books that Changed the South*. Chapel Hill: University of North Carolina Press, 1977.

DuBois, *The Gift of Black Folks*. Boston: Stratford, 1924.

English, Thomas H. "In Memory of Uncle Remus." *Southern Literary Messenger* (February 1940): 77-83.

———. "Joel Chandler Harris's Earliest Literary Project." *Emory University Quarterly* (October 1946): 176-85.

———. *Mark Twain to Uncle Remus: 1991-1885*. Atlanta GA: Emory University Library, 1953.

———. "Memorializing Pride in an Adopted Son." *The Emory Alumnus* (March 1929): 7-8.

———. Book review of *On the Plantation*. *South Atlantic Review* (January 1981):125-27.

———. "The Twice-Told Tale and Uncle Remus." *Georgia Review* (Winter 1948): 447-60.

Fay, Donald J. Book review of Hugh T. Keenan's *Dearest Chums and Partners*. *Atlanta History* (Fall 1994): 44-46.

"Former 'Devil' Recounts Early Days in Forsyth." *Atlanta Journal*, 10 November 1946, 17-C.

Fortier, Alcée. *Louisiana Folk-Tales, in French Dialect and English Translation*. Boston: Houghton, Mifflin, 1895.

Franckling, Ken. "Bringing Brer Rabbit Into the '80s." United Press International, wire service release for the New England states, 12 October 1987.

Fruit, J. P. "Uncle Remus in Phonetic Spelling." *Dialect Notes* (1896): 196-98.

Garnsey, John Henderson. "Joel Chandler Harris: A Character Sketch." *The Book Buyer* (March 1896): 65-68.

Gerber, A. "Uncle Remus Traced to the Old World." *The Journal of American Folk-Lore* (October-December 1893): 245-57.

Goldthwaite, John. "The Black Rabbit: Part One." *Signal* (May 1985): 86-111.

———. "The Black Rabbit: Part Two." *Signal* (September 1985): 148-67.

Gonzales, Ambrose. *The Black Border*. Columbia SC: The State Co., 1922.

Graczyk, Ed. "Livin' de Life." Anchorage KY: Anchorage Press, 1970.

Griska, Joseph M., Jr. "Joel Chandler Harris: 'Accidental Author' or 'Aggressive Businessman'?" *Atlanta Historical Journal* (Fall-Winter 1986-1987): 71-78.

——. "Selected Letters of Joel Chandler Harris." Ph.D. dissertation, Texas A&M University, 1976.

Hale, Mrs. Arthur. *My Souvenir of "The Wren's Nest"* Atlanta: Donaldson-Woods, 1929.

Halsey, Francis Whiting. "Joel Chandler Harris." In *Authors of Our Day in Their Homes*, 159-71. New York City: James Post, 1902.

Ham, Tom. "Mr. Harris Never Did Tell His Younguns of Uncle Remus." *Atlanta Journal*, 10 November 1946, 17-C.

Hamilton, Virginia. *The People Could Fly*. New York City: Knopf, 1985.

Harlow, Alvin F. *Joel Chandler Harris: Plantation Storyteller*. New York City: Julian Messner, 1941.

Harris, Evelyn. *A Little Story*, manuscript/unpublished, Atlanta, 1949.

Harris, Joel Chandler. *A Little Union Scout*. New York City: McClure, Phillips, 1904.

——. "An Accidental Author." *Lippincott's Monthly* (April 1886): 417-20.

——. *Aaron in the Wildwoods*. Boston: Houghton, Mifflin, 1897.

——. *Balaam and His Master, and Other Sketches and Stories*. Boston: Houghton, Mifflin, 1891.

——. "Brother Rabbit's Laughing-Place." *Metropolitan Magazine* (January 1905): 452-53.

——. *Daddy Jake the Runaway, and Short Stories Told After Dark*. New York City: Century, 1889.

——. *Free Joe, and Other Georgian Sketches*. New York City: Charles Scribner's Sons, 1887.

——. *Gabriel Tolliver: A Story of Reconstruction*. New York City: McClure, Phillips, 1902.

——. "Houses and Homes." *Uncle Remus's Magazine*. (October 1907): 5, 6.

——. Introduction to *A Book of Drawings*, by A.B. Frost, New York City: F. Colllier & Son, 1904.

——. Introduction to *Christmas-Night in the Quarters and Other Poems*, by Irwin Russell, New York City: Century, 1888.

——, editor. *Life of Henry W. Grady*. New York City: Casell, 1890.

——. "Little Children on the Snap-Bean Farm." *Uncle Remus's Magazine* (September 1907): 5.

————. *Little Mr. Thimblefinger and His Queer Country: What the Children Saw and Heard There*. Boston: Houghton, Mifflin, 1894.

————. *Mingo, and Other Sketches in Black and White*. Boston: J. Osgood, 1884.

————. "Mr. Billy Sanders of Shady Dale: His Views of Problems and Remedies." *Uncle Remus's Magazine* (September 1907): 22.

————. *Mr. Rabbit at Home: A Sequel to Mr. Thimblefinger and His Queer Country* Boston: Houghton, Mifflin, 1895.

————. *Nights With Uncle Remus*. Boston: J. R. Osgood & Co., 1883.

————. *On the Plantation: A Story of a Georgia Boy's Adventures During the War*. New York City: D. Appleton, 1892. published in London by Osgood as *A Plantation Printer: The Adventures of a Georgia Boy During the War*.)

————. *On the Wing of Occasions: Being the Authorized Version of Certain Curious Episodes of the Late Civil War*. New York City: Doubleday, Page, 1900.

————. *Plantation Pageants*. Houghton, Boston: Mifflin, 1899.

————. *Qua, A Romance of the Revolution*. Atlanta GA: Emory University Library, 1946.

————. *Sister Jane: Her Friends and Acquaintances*. Boston: Houghton, Mifflin, 1896.

————. *Stories of Georgia*. New York City: D. Appleton, 1896, revised edition, American Book Co., 1896.

————. *Tales of the Home Folks in Peace and War*. Boston: Houghton, Mifflin, 1898.

————. *The Bishop and the Boogerman*. New York City: Doubleday, Page, 1909.

————. *The Chronicles of Aunt Minervy Ann*. New York City: Charles Scribner's Sons, 1899.

————. *The Making of a Statesman*. New York City: McClure, Phillips, 1902.

————. *The Story of Aaron (So Named) the Son of Ben Ali*. Boston: Houghton, Mifflin, 1896.

————. *The Shadow Between His Shoulder-Blades*. Boston: Small, Maynard, 1909.

————. "The Negro as the South Sees Him." *Saturday Evening Post* (2 January 1904): 1-2, 23.

————. "The Negro of To-day." *Saturday Evening Post* (30 January 1904): 2-5.

————. "The Negro Problem." *Saturday Evening Post* (27 February 1904): 6-7.

———. *The Tar-Baby and Other Rhymes of Uncle Remus.* New York City: D. Appleton, 1904.

———. *Told by Uncle Remus: New Stories of the Old Plantation.* New York City: McClure, Phillips, 1905.

———. *Uncle Remus and Brer Rabbit.* New York City: Frederick A. Stokes, 1907.

———. *Uncle Remus and the Little Boy.* Boston: Small, Maynard, 1910.

———. *Uncle Remus, His Songs and Sayings, The Folklore of the Plantation.* New York City: D. Appleton, 1881.

———. *Uncle Remus Returns.* Boston: Houghton, Mifflin, 1918.

———. *Uncle Remus and His Friends: Old Plantation Stories, Songs, and Ballads, with Sketches of Negro Character.* Boston: Houghton, Mifflin, 1892.

———. *Uncle Remus Stories.* Adaptation by Marion Palmer. Racine WI: Western, 1946.

———. *Wally Wanderoon and His Story-Telling Machine.* New York City: McClure, Phillips, 1904.

———, editor. *World's Wit and Humor.* New York City: Review of Reviews Co., 1905.

Harris, Julia Collier. "Joel Chandler Harris: Constructive Realist." In *Southern Pioneers in Social Interpretation*, edited by Howard W. Odum, 141-64. Durham: University of North Carolina Press, 1925.

———, editor. *Joel Chandler Harris: Editor and Essayist.* Chapel Hill: University of North Carolina Press, 1931.

———. "Joel Chandler Harris—Fearless Editor." *The Emory Alumnus* (March 1929): 9-10.

———. "Remus Tales Charmed World for 65 Years." *Atlanta Journal*, 10 November 1946, 17-C.

———. *The Life and Letters of Joel Chandler Harris.* Boston: Houghton, Mifflin, 1918.

Harris, Mrs. L. H. "The Passing of Uncle Remus." *The Independent* (July 1908): 190-92.

Hemenway, Robert. "Introduction: Author, Teller, and Hero." *Uncle Remus: His Songs and Sayings*, by Joel Chandler Harris, reprint edition, New York City: Penguin Books, 1982.

Hendrick, Burton J. *The Training of an American: The Earlier Life and Letters of Walter H. Page.* Boston: Houghton, Mifflin, 1928.

Hill, Hamlin L. "Archy and Uncle Remus: Don Marquis's Debt to Joel Chandler Harris." *Georgia Review* (Spring 1961): 78-87.

Hirsley, Michael. "Thrown Into the Briar patch." *Chicago Tribune*, 28 December 1986, 4.

Horton, Mrs. Thaddeus. "The Most Modest Author in America." *Ladies Homes Journal* (May 1907): 17-18, 75.

Hubbell, Jay B. "Letters of Uncle Remus." *Southwest Review* (January 1938): xxiii, 216-23.

———. *The South in American Fiction*. Durham: Duke University Press, 1934.

Inscoe, John C. "The Confederate Home Front Sanitized: Joel Chandler Harris's *On the Plantation* and Sectional Reconciliation." *Georgia Historical Quarterly* (Fall 1992): 652-74.

Ives, Sumner. "Dialect Differentiation in the Stories of Joel Chandler Harris." *American Literature* (March 1955): 88-96.

———. "The Negro Dialect of the Uncle Remus Stories." Ph.D. dissertation, University of Texas, Austin, 1950.

———. "A Theory of Literary Dialect." In *Tulane Studies in English* (1950), 137-82.

Jacobs, Hal. "Remembering Joel Chandler Harris: Southern Folk Tales He Collected Live On." *Atlanta Journal and Constitution*, 6 December 1998, M-4.

Johnson, James Weldon. *The Book of American Negro Poetry*. New York City: Harcourt, Brace, 1922.

Jones, Charles C. *The Religious Instruction of the Negroes in the United States*. Savannah GA: Thomas Purse, 1842.

Jones, Lynda. "Georgia's Aesop." *Southern Telephone News* (March 1963):[n.p.].

Jordan, June. "A Truly Bad Rabbit." *The New York Times*, 17 May 1987, section 7, 32: 1.

Kelly, Karen M. "The Early Days of the Uncle Remus Memorial Association." *Atlanta Historical Journal* 30/3-4 (1986/1987): 113-27.

Keenan, Hugh T., editor. *Dearest Chums and Partners: Joel Chandler Harris's Letters to His Children: A Domestic Biography*. Athens: University of Georgia Press, 1993.

———. "Joel Chandler Harris." *Dictionary of Literary Biography*, edited by Stanley Trachtenberg, 42: 227-28. Detroit: Gale Research, 1982. Vol.

———. "Rediscovering the Uncle Remus Tales." *Teaching and Learning Literature* (March/April 1996): 30-36.

Krapp, George Philip. "The Psychology of Dialect Writing." *Bookman* (July 1926): 522-27.

Lanier, Doris. "Uncle Remus and the Hoosier Poet." *Atlanta History* (Fall-Winter 1988-1989): 19-37.

Lanier, Sidney. "The New South." *Scribner's Monthly* (October 1880): 847.

Lee, Ivy L. *"Uncle Remus": Joel Chandler Harris as Seen and Remembered by a Few of His Friends.* New York City: privately printed, 1908.

Lee, James W. "The Character of Joel Chandler Harris." In *"Uncle Remus": Joel Chandler Harris as Seen and Remembered by a Few of His Friends,* 83-113. New York City: privately printed, 1908.

————. "Joel Chandler Harris." *Century* (April 1909): 891-97.

Lester, Julius. *Further Tales of Uncle Remus.* New York City: Dial, 1990.

————. *More Tales of Uncle Remus.* New York City: Dial, 1988.

————. *The Last Tales of Uncle Remus.* New York City: Dial, 1994.

————. *The Tales of Uncle Remus.* New York City: Dial, 1987.

Leverette, F. L. "Odds and Ends About Joel Chandler Harris." *Eatonton Messenger,* 9 December 1948, 2.

Lisby, Gregory Carroll. "Someone Had to be Hated, The Pulitzer Prize-Winning Campaigns of Julian Harris and the Columbus (Georgia) Enquirer-Sun." Master's thesis, University of Mississippi, 1977.

Locke, Alain. "The Negro in American Literature." In *New World Writing,* 26. New York City: New American Library, 1952.

Long, Richard A. "The Uncle Remus Dialect: A Preliminary View." Professional paper delivered before the Southeastern Conference on Linguistics, 28-30 March 1969.

Lowery, John Henry, Jr. "Joel Chandler Harris: His Journalistic Rise to Literary Fame." Master's thesis, Athens: University of Georgia, 1965.

Marquis, Don. "The Farmer of Snap-Bean Farm." *Uncle Remus's The Home Magazine* (September 1908): 7.

May, Lee. "Gains from the Pain of Images Past." *Los Angeles Times,* 26 February 1990, A-1.

McCreery, Charles William. "An Annotated Checklist of Joel Chandler Harris Manuscripts in the Memorial Collection of the Emory University Library." Master's thesis. Atlanta GA: Emory University, 1934.

McDavid, Raven I. "Sense and Nonsense About American Dialects." *PMLA* (May 1966): 7-17.

Miller, H. Prentice. "Bibliography of Joel Chandler Harris." *The Emory Alumnus* (March 1929): 13-14.

"'Million' Books and 'Best' Books." *Golden Book Magazine* (September 1926): 382.

Mixon, Wayne. "The Ultimate Irrelevance of Race: Joel Chandler Harris and Uncle Remus in Their Time." *The Journal of Southern History* (August 1990): 457-71.

Montenyohl, Eric L. "Joel Chandler Harris and American Folklore." *Atlanta Historical Journal* 30/3-4 (1986/1987): 79-88.

Moore, Opal J. "Joel Chandler Harris." In *Writers for Children*, edited by Jane M. Bingham, 269-75. New York City: Scribner's, 1968.

Morrison, Elting, editor. *The Letters of Theodore Roosevelt.* (Cambridge MA: Harvard University Press, Volume 4: 1951; Volume 6: 1952; Volume 7: 1954.).

Morrow, James. B. "Joel Chandler Harris Talks of Himself and Uncle Remus." *Boston Daily Globe*, 3 November 1907, 5-6.

Mugleston, William F. "An Attempt to Break the 'Solid South.'" *Alabama Historical Quarterly* (Summer 1976): 126-36.

Nash, Evelyn. "Beyond Humor in Joel Chandler Harris's *Nights With Uncle Remus*." *The Western Journal of Black Studies* 14/4 (1990): 217-23.

Nash, J. V. "Joel Chandler Harris, Interpreter of the Negro Soul." *The Open Court* (February 1927): 103-110.

Nixon, Raymond B. "Henry W. Grady, Reporter." *Journalism Quarterly* (December 1935): 341-56.

Norris, Thaddeus. "Negro Superstitions." *Lippincott's* (July 1870): 90-95.

O'Shea, Brian P. "Joel Chandler Harris: Journalist and Storyteller." Manuscript handout of the Joel Chandler Harris Association (Atlanta), 1986.

Osinski, Bill. "Main Street: A Rare Volume of Georgia History Was Written by Joel Chandler Harris..." *Atlanta Journal and Constitution*, 11 May 1997, G-3.

————. "Main Street: 'Color Purple,' 'Uncle Remus' authors focus of Unique Event." *Atlanta Journal and Constitution*, 21 March 1999, D-3.

————. "Main Street: 441 Detour to Discovery: Literary Giants Hail From Small Slice of Georgia." *Atlanta Journal and Constitution*, 22 March 1998, D-9.

Page, Thomas Nelson. "Immortal Uncle Remus." *Book Buyer* (December 1895): 642-45.

————. "Introduction" to 40th year anniversary edition of Joel Chandler Harris's, *Uncle Remus: His Songs and Sayings*. D. Appleton, 1920.

Parks, Van Dyke and Malcolm Jones. *Jump! The Adventures of Brer Rabbit*. San Diego: Harcourt Brace Jovanovich, 1986.

Parks, Van Dyke. *Jump Again! More Adventures of Brer Rabbit*. San Diego: Harcourt Brace Jovanovich, 1987.

Parks, Van Dyke. *Jump on Over!* San Diego: Harcourt Brace Jovanovich, 1989.

Parsons, Elsie Clews. "Joel Chandler Harris and Negro Folklore." *The Dial* (May 1919): 491-93.

Patureau, Alan. "Most Authorities Think Harris Was Just a Man of His Times." *Atlanta Constitution*, 18 August 1985, H-1, 2.

————. "Wren's Nest: Altering an Image, Inside and Out." *Atlanta Constitution*, 8 October 1990, C-1, 4.

Pederson, Lee A. "Language in the Uncle Remus Tales." *Modern Phonology* (February 1985): 292-98.

————. "Rewriting Dialect Literature: The Wonderful Tar-Baby Story." *Atlanta Historical Journal* (Fall-Winter 1986-1987): 57-70.

Puckett, Newell Niles. *Folk Beliefs of the Southern Negro*. London: Oxford University Press, 1926.

Ray, C. A., compiler. "Joel Chandler Harris." In *Bibliographical Guide to the Study of Southern Literature*, edited by Louis D. Rubin. Baton Rouge: Louisiana State University Press, 1969.

Reed, Wallace P. "The Real 'Uncle Remus.'" *Chicago Times-Herald*, 2 June 1901, 6.

Ringel, Eleanor and Steve Murray. "Coloring Disney's World." *Atlanta Journal and Constitution*, 31 July 1994, N-1.

Rogers, Ernest. "World Premiere of Disney's 'Uncle Remus' to Be Here." *Atlanta Journal*, 8 July 1946, [section/page numbers].

Rose, Billy. "What Is Wrong, Walt?" *Atlanta Constitution*, 17 December 1946.

Rubin, Louis D., Jr. *The Writer in the South: Studies in a Literary Community*. Athens: University of Georgia Press, 1972.

————. "Uncle Remus and the Ubiquitous Rabbit." *Southern Review* (October 1974): 784-804.

Schneider, Gilbert D. "The Uncle Remus Tales and Their Value to the Serious Scholar." Paper presented at the Linguistics Colloquium on Black English, Ohio University (Athens, Ohio), 20 February 1973.

Sibley, Celestine. "This Old Desk." *Atlanta Journal and Constitution*, 27 November 1995, C-1.

Small, Sam W. "Story of the Constitution's First Half-Century of Service to the City, State and Country." *Atlanta Constitution*, 26 September 1917, 24.

————. "Uncle Remus in Brief: A Sketch of the Greatest Humorist in the South." *Atlanta Daily Constitution*, 20 April 1879, 5 [reprint from *New Haven Register*].

Smith, C. Alphonso. "Dialect Writers." In *Cambridge History of American Literature*, William Peterfield Trent, et. al, editors, 2:347-66. New York City: Putnam's Sons, 1918.

————. "Joel Chandler Harris: A Discussion of the Negro as Literary Material." In *Southern Literary Studies*, edited by Howard W. Odum, 128-57. Durham: University of North Carolina Press, 1927.

Smith, Herbert F. "Joel Chandler Harris's Contributions to Scribner's Monthly and Century Magazine, 1880-1887." *Georgia Historical Quarterly* (June 1963): 169-79.

Stephenson, Frank. "Remembering Remus." *Research in Review* (Spring/Summer 1998): 16-27, 40-45.

Strickland, William Bradley. "A Checklist of the Periodical Contributions of Joel Chandler Harris." *American Literary Realism* (Summer 1976): 207-222.

————. "Joel Chandler Harris: A Bibliographical Study." Ph.D. dissertation, University of Georgia, Athens, 1976.

————. "Stereotypes and Subversion in the *Chronicles of Aunt Minervy Ann*." *Atlanta Historical Journal* (Winter 1987): 129-39.

Sundquist, Eric J. *To Wake the Nations: Race in the Making of American Literature*. Cambridge MA: Harvard University Press, 1993.

Taylor, Ron. "Uncle Remus Lives." *Atlanta Journal and Constitution*, 9 November 1975, B-12, 13.

"The Snap-Bean Sage." *Saturday Review of Literature* (2 May 1925): 741.

Thomas, Kenneth H., Jr. "Roots and Environment: The Family Background [of Joel Chandler Harris]." *Atlanta Historical Journal* (Fall-Winter 1986-1987): 37-56.

Ticknor, Caroline. "The Man Harris: A Study in Personality." *Book News Monthly* (January 1909): 317-20.

Tourgee, Albion W. "The South as a Field for Fiction." *Forum* 16/12 (1888): 404-413.

Turner, Darwin T. "Daddy Joel Harris and His Old Time Darkies." *Southern Literary Journal* (Fall 1968): 20-41.

———. "Southern Fiction, 1900-1910." *Mississippi Quarterly* (Fall 1968): 281-82, 284.

Turner, Joseph Addison. *Autobiography of "The Countryman."* Edited by Thomas H. English. Atlanta GA: Emory University Library, 1943.

———. *The Autobiography of Joseph Addison Turner.* Atlanta GA: Emory University Library, 1943 reprint.

Twain, Mark. *Life on the Mississippi.* New York City: Osgood, 1883.

Walker, Alice. "Uncle Remus, No Friend of Mine." *Southern Exposure* (Summer 1981): 29-31.

Walker, W. W. "The Story of Joel Chandler Harris...His Boyhood in Eatonton." *Eatonton Messenger*, 6 June 1963, 1.

Walt Disney Presents "Song of the South." Movie premiere souvenir edition, 1946.

Watterson, Henry. *Oddities in Southern Life and Character.* Boston: Houghton, Mifflin, 1883.

Wiggins, Robert Lemuel. *The Life of Joel Chandler Harris: From Obscurity in Boyhood to Fame in Early Manhood.* Nashville TN: Publishing House of the Methodist Episcopal Church, 1918.

Winsell, Keith A. "A Look at Harris' Life and Writings." *Eatonton Messenger*, December 1998, 3.

Wolfe, Bernard. "Uncle Remus and the Malevolent Rabbit." *Commentary* (July 1949): 31-41.

Woods, George A. "In Uncle Remus Land." *New York Times Book Review*, 17 December 1967, 18.

Wooten, Katherine. "Uncle Remus Wrote 41 Books, Complete List of Author's Works and Other Interesting Facts of His Literary Labors and Output." *Atlanta Journal*, 4 July 1908, 1-6.

Index

"A Conscript's Christmas", 158
"A Georgia Fox-Hunt", 165;
A Little Story, 339-341
A Little Union Scout, 249-250
A Mother's List of Books for
  Children, 165
"A Piece of Land", 93-94, 98
"A Rainy Day With Uncle Remus",
  90
"A Shadow Between His Shoulder-
  Blades", 250
ABC-TV, 283
Abernathy, Ralph, 349
Abrahams, Roger D., 67-68, 300
Academy of Arts and Letters, 213,
  214
Academy of Motion Picture Arts
  and Sciences, 281, 286fn
Adair, Forrest, 14, 134, 135-136,
  142
Adams, Henry, 214
Adams, Hut, 10
Addison, Joseph, 7
"Affairs of Georgia", 30
Africanisms in the Gullah Dialect,
  364-365
Afro-American English—See:
  American Black English
Afro-American Folklore—See:
  American Black Folklore
Afro-American Folk Tales, 300
Afro-American Folklore—See:
  American Black Folklore
Afro-American journalists—See:
  Black Journalists)
Agard, John, 313
Allen, Beverly B., xxx
American Black English, xxiii,
  xxvi, xxvii, 41-44 passim, 51,
  56fn, 58fn, 68, 77-80, 96-97,
  147, 148, 150-153, 220, 245,
  271, 272, 296-311 passim,
  361-370
  Creolist theory, 364-368;
  Deficit Theory, 361-368;
  Dialect Geographer Theory,
  360-368; Eradicationist
  Theory, 366-368; Five Cycle
  Theory, 56fn;Gullah, xxvii,
  96, 148, 271, 309, 361-370
  passim;

American Black Folklore, 51-56,
  66-83 passim, 96-97, 152-
  153, 217-222 passim,
  300-309 passim, 310, 359-
  368 passim
African origins, 68, 70-72;
  Trickster Tales, xxvii-xxviii,
  53, 67-68, 73-76, 149, 307
American Folk-Lore Society, 148
American Folklore Society, xxv,
  217
American Library Association, 301
American Mercury, 361
"Ananias", 158
Anderson, Sherwood, 271
Animaniacs, xxviii
Anne Macfarland, 247, 249
Antebellum era, 41-42, 94, 100,
  213, 279-280, 284-285, 290,
  291, 295
Arrowwood, Clinton, 312
"At Teague Poteet's: A Sketch of
  the Hog-Mountain Range",
  92-93, 98, 160
Atlanta, 276
Atlanta Constitution, 33-34, 36-37,
  38fn, 113-116, 118-119, 173,
  184-188, 185 illus., 211 illus.,
  215, 240, 242, 262, 277-278,
  317, 369
Atlanta Daily News, 240
Atlanta Evening Telegram, 44
Atlanta, Ga., 34-36, 346
Atlanta Herald, 36
Atlanta Historical Center, 369
Atlanta Journal, 194
Atlanta Public Library, 303
Atlanta race riot, 239
Atlanta School Board, 346
Atlanta Urban League, 349
Aunt Minervy Ann Perdue, 10,
  169
Aunt Tempy, 96
Avery, Tex, xxviii
"Azalia", 106-107, 155

*Brer Rabbit,
Uncle Remus,
and the 'Cornfield
Journalist'*

386

Baber, Frank, 312
Backus, Emma M., 149
Baer, Florence, 71, 366, 368 fn
Baker, Augusta, 297-298, 310
Baker, Gloria, 348
Baker, Ray Stannard, 183
Bakshi, Ralph, 284
"Balaam", 158
*Balaam and his Master and other
    Sketches and Stories*, 158
Bannerman, Helen, 312
Barwick, J. R., 34
Baskervill, William Malone, xxiv,
    103, 163
Baskett, James, 275, 279, 280, 281
Bass, George Houston, 314
Batten, Barton, Durstine &
    Osborn, 286fn
Beany Baby, 284
Beard, William Holbrook, 94
Bender, James, xxxi
Berry, Loni, 314
Bickley, R. Bruce, vii, xxv, xxxi, 3,
    91, 141, 153, 202, 232, 234
Bierce, Ambrose, 187
Billy May Orchestra, 283
Billy Sanders, 174, 193, 196, 243,
    245-246, 249
Birnbaum, Michele, 368fn
Birth of a Nation, 205
Bits of Louisiana Folk-Lore, 148
Black English and the Mass Media,
    56fn
Black English—See: Amererican
    Black English
Black Folklore—See: American
    Black Folklore
Black Folktales, 310
Black journalists, 149-150
Black music, 270
"Blue Dave", 93, 98
Boccaccio, 51
Bone, Robert, 295-296
Booklist, 243
Borgenicht, David, 313
Boston Daily Advertiser, 163
Boston Globe/Horn Book Award,
    311
Bowles, Samuel, xxxvii
"Br'er Rabbit and Boss Lion", 315
Br'er Rabbit's Big Secret, 304-305

Branham, Henry, 2
Branham, Joel, 2
Brasch, Helen Haskin, ix
Brasch, Milton, ix
Brasch, Rosemary R., ix, xxxi
Brasch, Walter M., vii, viii, 56fn,
    57fn, 266fn, 368 fn
Brer Bar, 284
Brer Bear, 275-276, 284, 309
Brer Fox, 275-276, 284, 309
Brer Frog, 284
Brer Rabbit, 51, 52-56, 68-83 pas-
    sim, 74, 158, 275-276, 284,
    295, 307, 309, 311, 316-317;
    etymology, 53-54
"Brer Rabbit and the Wonderful
    Tar-Baby", 228, 283, 315
Brer Rabbit and His Tricks, 306
Brer Rabbit and Brer Fox, 307
Brer Rabbit in the Americas, 292
Brer Rabbit Motel, 285fn
Brer Rabbit (musical), 314
Brer Rabbit statue, 343
Brer Rabbit Whole, 314
Brer Vulture, 284
Brer Wolf, 309
Breslin, Jimmy, 57fn
Brestensky, Dennis F., 52
Brewer, J. Mason, xxv, 272
Brookes, Stella Brewer, xxvi, 305
Brooklyn College, 366-367
Brooks, Cleanth, 362, 368 fn
Broomheard, Benjamin H., 143fn
"Brother Rabbit's Laughing-Place",
    220, 227-228
Brown, Charles Farrar, 57fn
Brown, Margaret Wise, 298
Brown, Sterling A., 270, 289
Brown University, 314
Bryan, William Jennings, 184
Buchwald, Art, 57fn
Bugs Bunny, xxviii, 305
Burgess, Anthony, 199
Burgess, Thornton, 305
Burlingame, Edward L., 160-161,
    189, 296
Buster John, 170, 173, 220

C

Cable, George Washington, xix, 108, 120, 137-138, 147, 149, 218
Calamus root, 85
Caldwell, Erskine, 165, 271
Calhoun, John C., 1
California Center for the Arts, 314
California State University at San Marcos, 314
California Theatre Center, 313
Camp, Edwin, 242, 253fn
Campbell, Colin, 317
Campbell, James Edwin, 149
Capitol Records, 283
Carnegie, Andrew, xxiv, 242, 247, 252fn, 345
Cavanagh, Maura, 314
Censorship, 15-16, 301-306, 308-309
Century Company, 158
Century Illustrated Monthly Magazine, 90-91, 213, 227
Charles Scribner's Sons, 109fn, 190
Chase, Richard, 58fn, 297, 310
Chatelain, Heli, 70-71
Chaucer, Geoffrey, 51
Chesnutt, Charles Waddell, 149
Chicago Daily News, 133
Chicago Folklore Society, 218
Chicago Tribune, 167, 304-305
Chloe, 169
Chomsky, Noam, 365, 368fn
Christensen, A. M. H., 55, 72-73, 148
"Christmas in the Briar Patch", 317-318
Christopherson, Paul, 368 fn
Church, Frederick S., 65-66, 94, 275
Civil Rights Cycle, xxiii, 290, 302-317 passim
Civil War, 8-18 passim, 81, 162, 174-175, 202-203, 243, 271, 272, 298-299
Clay, G. A., 313, 317
Clemens, Samuel L., 76, 108, 136-138, 214, 290 (Also see: Mark Twain)
Clement, Dr. Rufus, 346
Cloke, Rene, 312, 313

Coca-Cola, 271-272, 285fn
Coile, Mark, xxx
Collier's Weekly, 227, 249
Colonial-Revolutionary era, 41
Come Back to the 5 and Dime, Jimmy Dean, Jimmy Dean, 313
Commentary, 290
Compair Lapin, 147 (Also see: Brer Rabbit)
Confederate States of America, 20fn
Conrad, Joseph, 191
Coolidge, Archibald, 297
Coonskin, 284
Cooper, James Fenimore, 42, 272
Coretta Scott King Award, 310
Cornelison, Gayle, 313
Corrothers, James D., 149
Cosmopolitan, 227
Cousins, Paul M., xxxi, 92-93, 94, 96, 103, 139, 167-168, 291-292
Cousins, Paul M., 318
Crane, Thomas, 70
Creolist Theory—See: American Black English, Creolist Theory
Cresent Monthly, 24
Crossley, Jo, xxx
Crowther, Bosley, 279-280
Crutchfield, Sharon, 349
Cullen Countee, 270

D

D. Appleton, 65, 108, 156. 161-162, 190, 191, 195-196, 228
Daddy Jack, 96, 148, 189, 364
Daddy Jake, 103-104, 243
Daddy Jake the Runaway, and Short Stories Told After Dark, 158
"Daddy Jake", 103
Daily, Don, 313
Dalby, David, 368 fn
Dana, Charles A., 82
Davidson, James Wood, 18fn, 27, 81
Davies, Mark, 312
Davis, Jefferson, xxi, 65, 116-117
Dearmer, Mable, 314

DeCamp, David, 368 fn
Deficit Theory—See: American
    Black English, Deficit Theory
Democratic National Convention,
    62, 115
Derby, James C., xxiv, 65, 82, 92
Deryk, Thomas, 313
Dial, 97, 204, 232
Dialect Geographer Theory—See:
    American Black English,
    Dialect Geographer Theory
Dialect Tales, 149
Dickenson, Susan, 312
Dickey, John M., 142
Disney, Walt, 274-285 passim
    (Also see: *Song of the South*)
Disney World, 284
Disneyland, 283
Disneyy.com, 285
Dixon, Thomas, 205
Dorson, Richard M., 272
Doubleday, Frank N., 190, 197
Doubleday, McClure & Company,
    190
Doubleday, Page & Company, 190,
    191, 193, 194-196 passim,
    228, 231
Downs, Robert B., 74-75, 83
Doyle, Arther Conan, 191
Draper, Dolores, 299-300
Dreiser, Theodore, 271
Drescher, Henrik, 312
Driscoll, Bobby, 275, 279
Drusilla, 170, 173
DuBois, W. E. B., 270, 289
Dumas, Alexandre, 189
Dunbar, Paul Laurence, 149
DuPont Radio Network, 274

E. I. duPont de Nemours &
    Company, 286fn
Eaton, William, 18fn
Eatonton, Ga., 4, 209fn, 274, 288,
    292, 293 illus., 294, 317, 343
Eatonton Literary Festival, 318
Eatonton Male Academy, 3

Eatonton Post Office, 5-6, 317
Eatonton/Putnam County
    Chamber of Commerce, 317
Ebony, 280
Edwards, Harry Stilwell, 139, 147,
    149
Eliot, George, 189
Eliot, T. S., 271
Elliot, David, 282
Ellison, Ralph, 72, 315
Elmer Fudd, xxviii, 305
Emory College, 213,
Emory University, xxx, xxxiifn, 369
English, Thomas H., xxxi, 147,
    149, 262, 263, 303-304
Ennis, Steve, xxx
Eradicationist Theory—See:
    American Black English,
    Eradicationist Theory
Espinosa, Aurelio M., 366
Estill, J. H., 29 illus.
Evans, Betsy, 10, 169
Evelyn, William, 24
Everybody's magazine, 194, 196-197
Everyman Theatre, 314

Fasold, Ralph, 368 fn
Faulkner, William, 271
Faulkner, William J., 299
Fauset, Arthur Huff, 270, 272
Fauset, Jessie Redman, 270
Favorite Uncle Remus, 297
Fay, Donald J., 74, 76-77
Fenly, Leigh, 295
Field, Eugene, 133
Film Daily, 278
Fisk University, 270, 314
Fitzgerald, F. Scott, 271
Fletch Lives, 284-285
Foils, 45, 57fn, 193, 245 (Also see:
    Billy Sanders)
*Forerunners of Revolution:
    Muckrakers in the American
    Social Conscience*, 266fn
Forsyth, John, xxxvii
Fortier, Alcee, 147-148, 320

Forum 104
Foster, Harve, 276
Frankland, David, 312
Free Joe, 101 illus.
*Free Joe and Other Georgian
  Sketches,* 100
"Free Joe", 100-103, 155, 160, 245
Fritz the Cat, 284
Frost, Arthur Burdett, 139, 155-
  156, 161, 169, 228, 275, 309,
  321
Frost, Robert, 271
Fruit, J. P., 361
Fulton County Commission, 303

Gabriel Tolliver, 193, 200-205, 292
Garis, Howard, 305
Garnsey, John Henderson, 134,
  142-143, 181
Garrison, Francis J., 166
Garrison, Wendell P., 247
Georgia Constitutional
  Convention, 204
Georgia Foundation for
  Independent Colleges, 349
Gerber, Adolph, 71
Ghana, 53
Gilbert, Ray, 278
Gilder, Richard Watson, 92, 106,
  107, 155, 186, 224
Gilpin, Charles, 270
Glover, Danny, 315
Golden Book Magazine, 272
Goldsmith, Oliver, 2, 189
Goldthwaite, John, 83, 297, 305
Gompers, Samuel, xxiv
Gone with the Wind, 271, 276
Gonzales, Ambrose, 148, 360
Gorey, Edward, 306
Graczyk, Ed, 313
Grady, Henry W., 29 illus., 33, 36,
  113-115, 118-124, 138, 259,
  264
Grant, Morton, 276
Greeley, Horace, 114
Griffith, D. W., 205

Gullah—See: American Black
  English, Gullah
Gully Minstrels, 8, 10

Hale, Pat, 314
Hall, Robert A., 368 fn
Halsey, Francis W., 228
Hamilton, Virginia, 307
Hancock, Ian, 368 fn
Handt, William M., 261-262
Harlem Renaissance—see: Negro
  Renaissance
Harlow, Alvin F., xxxi
Harper's magazine, 81, 99
Harris, Charles Collier, 225 illus.,
  229 illus., 240
Harris, Esther LaRose, 31, 32 illus.,
  33, 49, 132, 139, 142, 175,
  209fn, 229, 230 illus., 256,
  258, 285fn, 338 illus., 339-
  341, 344 illus.
Harris, Evan Howell, 49, 124, 239
Harris, Evelyn, 31, 32, 132, 133,
  139, 142, 240, 257, 258, 338
  illus., 339-341
Harris, Joe—See: Joel Chandler
  Harris
Harris, Joel Chandler:
Alcoholism, 50, 255; Ancestry, 1;
  Announces end of Uncle
  Remus, 152; Attacks
  Jefferson Davis, 116-117;
  Autobiography, 168-169
  (Also See: *On the Plantation,
  Sister Jane: Her Friends and
  Acquaintances,* and *Gabriel
  Tolliver: A Story of
  Reconstruction*); Begins writ-
  ing dialect tales, 44; Begins
  writing Uncle Remus tales,
  45-46; Birth, xxxviii, 1, 18fn,
  19fn, 20fn; Death of Joseph
  Addison Turner, 124;
  Contradictions, xx-xxii, 181-
  184; Covers Democratic
  convention, 62; Death, 258;

Death of children, 49-50, 124, 239; Defends Mark Twain, 301-302; Discusses American Black English, 77-78; Discusses dialect, 96-97, 151-152; Editorial campaigns, 30, 184-185, 202, 301-302; Editorial views on human rights, 30; Editorial views on segregation, 30; Elected to Academy of Arts and Letters, 213; Employed at *Cresent Monthly*, 24; Employed at *Macon Telegraph*, 23-24 Employed at Monroe Advertiser, 24-26; Employed at Savannah Morning News, 26, 28, 30; Employed at *The Countryman*, 6-18 passim, 117-118; Ethnic jokes, xxxii; Exemption from draft, 13; First job, 6-17 passim; Flees Yellow Fever epidemic, 33; Founds *Uncle Remus's Magazine*, 240-249; Illnesses, 49, 255-256, 258 (Also see: alcoholism); Influences, 42, 56fn, 189; Insecurity, 5; Leave of absence from *Constitution*, 189-190; Looking to leave *Constitution*, 61-63; Love of animals, 13-14, 134-136; Marriage, 31; Meets Esther LaRose, 31; Meets Henry W. Grady, 36; Negotiates new publishing contracts, 190-193; *On the Plantation*, 14; Opinions of academic folklore, 217-221; Philosophy of life, 30, 109, 121-123, 129-130, 202-204, 221, 233-234, 239, 242-243, 245-247, 249, 251-252, 258; Praised by Theodore Roosevelt, xvii, xxiii, 103, 175, 214-216 passim, 264, 318; Praises A.B. Frost, 156-157; Receives honorary doctorate, 213; Reflections upon Georgia journalism, 23;

Relationship with illustrators, 65-66, 155-157, 161-162; Relationship with book publishers, 94, 99-100, 106, 107-108, 190-191, 193-198 passim, 205-208, 223-224, 230-231; Relationship with illustrators (Also see: Frost, Arthur Burdett; Kemble, E. W.; Moser, James Henry; Church, Frederick S.); Religion, 257-258; Resumes folklore writing, 200, 227; Resumes writing Uncle Remus sketches, 46; Retires from *Constitution*, 193-194, 199; Role of a father, 133; Schooling, 3, 5-6, 213; Shyness, 3-4, 89-90, 137-139 passim, 141-143, 213; Speaking tours, 136-138; the *Atlanta Constitution* employs Harris, 36; Views about Henry W. Grady, 113; Views about Reconstruction, 114-124 passim; Views of plantation life, 201; Views on dialect, 150-152, 296-297; Views on slavery, 231-232; Work habits and views upon journalism and writing, 91-92, 98, 107-109 passim, 113, 134, 153, 155, 167-169; Work Habits and Views Upon Journalism and Writing, 176, 181-190, 198-199, 202, 208fn, 248, 250

Friendships with Andrew Carnegie, xxiv, 242, 247; Henry W. Grady, 29, 33, 36, 113-115, 138, 259, 264; Clark Howell, 57fn, 185, 262; Evan P. Howell, 34, 44, 45-46, 57fn, 129, 262, 264; James Whitcomb Riley, 138, 142, 150, 167, 201-202; Georgia Harrison Starke, 26-27; Joseph Addison Turner, 6-7, 16, 23, 25-26, 43, 83, 162, 200, 247; (and defense of)

Mark Twain, 76, 78-79, 91, 108, 136-138, 147, 186, 189, 191, 214, 272, 290, 301-302;
Writings: Articles and Short Stories—
"A Conscript's Christmas," 158; "A Georgia Fox-Hunt", 165; "A Piece of Land", 93-94, 98; "A Shadow Between his Shoulder-Blades", 250; "A Rainy Day With Uncle Remus", 90; "A Story of the War", 118; "Affairs of Georgia", 30; "An Amuscade", 126fn; "Ananias", 158; "At Teague Poteet's: A Sketch of the Hog-Mountain Range", 92-93, 98, 126fn, 160; "A Song of the Mole", 90; "Azalia", 106-107, 155; "Affairs of Georgia", 30; "Balaam", 158; "Blue Dave", 93, 98; "Br'er Rabbit and Boss Lion", 315; "Brer Rabbit and the Tar-Baby", 228, 283; "Brer Rabbit and the Wonderful Tar-Baby", 71-72, 278, 315; "Brother Rabbit's Laughing-Place", 220, 227-228; "Christmas in the Briar Patch", 317-318; "Daddy Jake", 103; "Free Joe", 100-103, 155, 160, 245; "Hog-Killin' Time", 228; "How Brer Rabbit Saved Brer B'ar's Life", 243; "How Mr. Fox Failed to Get His Grapes", 90; "How Mr. Fox Figues as an Inceniary", 90; "How Mr. Rabbit was too Sharp for Mr. Fox", 355-357; "In Plain Black and White", 120; "Jeems Roberson's Last Illness", 44; "Little Compton", 105-107, 155, 160; "Manifest Destiny", 147; "Markham's Ball, 44; "Mingo", 90, 91, 98, 160; "Mr. Fox, Mr. Rabbit, and Mr. Terrapin", 314; "Mr. Rabbit Run Fur—Mr. Rabbit Run Fas'", 228; "Revival Hymn", 44; "Running Away", 283; "Rosalie", 126fn; "Showing How Brer Rabbit Was too Sharp for Brer Fox", 55; "The Cornfield Story", 278; "The Kidnapping of President Lincoln", 174-175, 193; "The Late Mr. Watkins of Georgia", 217; "The Laughing Place", 278, 283; "The Old Bascomb Place", 158-160; "The Wonderful Tar-baby Story", 351-354; "Tracking a Runaway", 165; "Trouble on Lost Mountain", 126fn; "Uncle Remus and the Savannah Darkey", 44; "Where's Duncan?", 158-159; "Why the Alligator's Back is Rough", 96, 84fn, 90.
Writings: Books—
A Little Union Scout, 249-250; Azalia, 126fn; Daddy Jake the Runaway, and Short Stories Told After Dark, 158; Free Joe and Other Georgian Sketches, 100; Gabriel Tolliver, 193, 200-205, 292; Herndon Wood: A Plantation Comedy, 175-176; Little Mr. Thimblefinger and His Queer Country, 173-174; Mingo and Other Sketches in Black and White, 98-99, 108; Mr. Rabbit at Home, 173; Nights with Uncle Remus: Myths and Legends of the Old Plantation, 94-98, 108, 165, 296; On the Plantation, 161, 162-163, 165, 176fn-177fn, 208; On the Wing of Occasions, 174, 191, 192, 194, 196; Qua: A Romance of the Revolution, 175; Sister Jane: Her Friends and Acquaintances, 165-167, 181; Tales of the Home Folks, 217; The Bishop, the

Boogerman, and the Right of Way, 104, 243; The Chronicles of Aunt Minervy Ann, 170; The Romance of Rockville, 50, 176fn; The Tar-Baby and Other Rhymes of Uncle Remus, 228, 231; Told by Uncle Remus:New Stories of the Old Planatation, 227, 232-233, 278; Uncle Remus and His Friends, 151-152, 153, 218; Uncle Remus, His Songs and His Sayings; The Folk-Lore of the Plantation, 65-84, 141, 155, 157, 165, 191, 195, 294; Uncle Remus, Mythology of the Plantation, 65; Wally Wanderoon, 174, 219 illus., 217-221

Harris, Joel Chandler Jr., 226 illus., 275, 338 illus.

Harris, Julia Collier, 2, 26, 153, 188, 199, 240, 241 illus., 247, 255-256, 257, 297

Harris, Julian, 49, 199-200, 215, 239-240, 247, 255, 256, 264-265, 318, 338 illus.

Harris, Lillian, 189, 257, 338 illus.

Harris, Linton, 49, 124, 239

Harris, Lucien, 49, 338 illus.

Harris, Mary (mother) 1-2, 49, 50, 124, 125 illus., 162, 166, 257

Harris, Mary Esther (daughter), 130, 132-133, 239

Harris, Mildred, 237 illus., 253fn, 338 illus.

Harris, Pierre LaRose, 240

Harrison, James P., 24, 33

Harte, Bret, xxvi

Hawthorne, Nathaniel, 272

Hayes, Barbara, 46, 114-115, 312

Hearn, Lafcadio, 24, 147, 149

Heavy Traffic, 284

Hecht, Ben, 271

Hemenway, Robert, 294

Hemingway, Ernest, 271

Henry, O., 191

Herndon, Jerry Allen, 111fn

Herndon Wood: A Plantation Comedy, 175-176

Hersholt, Jean, 281, 286fn

Herskovits, Melville, 364, 365

Hessey, Anne, 312

Heyward, DuBose, 271

"Hidden Name and Complex Fate", 315

Higginson, Thomas Wentworth, xix

"Hog-Killin' Time", 228

Houghton, Miffin & Co., 108, 161, 166, 190, 297

"How Brer Rabbit Saved Brer B'ar's Life", 243

"How Mr. Fox Figues as an Inceniary", 90

"How Mr. Fox Failed to Get His Grapes", 90

"How Mr. Rabbit was too Sharp for Mr. Fox", 355-357

Howell, Clark, 57fn, 185 illus., 262

Howell, Evan P., 34, 44, 45-46, 57fn, 129, 262, 264

Howells, William Dean, 214

Huckleberry Finn, 301

Hughes, Langston, 270

Hurston, Zora Neale, 270, 272

Hutchins, Stilson, 61-62, 63

I

Imhotep, Akbar, 348 illus.

In Ole Virginia, 157

In the Old South with Brer Rabbit and his Neighbors, 307

Inscoe, John C., 162

Invisible Man, 315

Irish, discrimination against, 4

Ives, Sumner, 79-80, 363, 368 fn

J

J. H. Winchester Shipping Company, 274

Jack Daniel's, 349

Jackson, "Stonewall", xxi, 126fn

Jackson, Maynard, 349

Jackson, Wilfred, 276
Jahdu, 307
James, Henry, 189, 214
James, William, 214
Jazz Age, 270
"Jeems Roberson's Last Illness", 44
Jefferson, Thomas, 214
Joel Chandler Harris Elementary
    School, 306
Joel Chandler Harris Association,
    317, 369
John Henry, 311, 312
Johnson, Charles S., 270
Johnson, F. Mark, 307
Johnson, F. Roy, 307
Johnson, Guy B., 362
Johnson, James Weldon, 270, 289
Johnson, Janet P., 313
Johnson Publishing Company, 307
Johnson, Robert Underwood, 91,
    102, 161, 213-214, 227,
Johnston, Richard Malcomb, 139
Jolley, Marc A., xxxi
Jones, Charles Colcock, 141, 148
Jones, Malcolm, 308, 309, 324fn
Jordan, June, 311
Jump!, 307-308
Jump Again! More Adventures of
    Brer Rabbit, 309
Jump on Over!, 309
Jungle Books, 158
Junior League of Atlanta, 279

Kantrowitz, Barbara, 282
Keenan, Hugh P., xxv, xxxi, 57fn-
    58fn, 74, 77, 133
Kelly, Catherine, xxxi
Kemble, E. W., 155, 161, 228, 275
"Kinlaw Tales", 148, 360
Kipling, Rudyard, 82, 158, 189,
    191, 305
Kitt, Eartha, 312
Knight, Bill, xxx-xxxi
Krapp, George Philip, 297, 361-
    363
Kurath, Hans, 361
Labov, William, 368 fn

Lanier, Clifford, 42
Lanier, Henry, 193, 194, 197-198
Lanier, Sidney, 42, 79, 147, 149,
    193
LaRose, Mary Esther (Essie)—See:
    Harris, Esther LaRose
LaRose, Pierre, 31
Larsen, Nella, 270
Ledford, Mark, 317
Lee, James W., 132, 133, 258-259
Lee, Robert E., xxi, 16, 126fn
Lester, Julius, xxv, 75, 307, 310-
    312
Lewis, Sinclair, 271
Life on the Mississippi, 137
Lincoln, Abraham, xxi, 116, 174-
    175, 262
Linguistic Atlas of The United States,
    361
Literary World, 81
Little Black Sambo, 311, 312
"Little Compton", 105-107, 155,
    160
Little Mr. Thimblefinger and His
    Queer Country, 173-174
Livin' de Life, 313
Livraghi, Virginio, 312
Locke, Alain, 270, 289
Locke, David R., 57fn
Lomax, Michael, 303, 304
Long, Richard L., 368 fn
Longstreet, A. B., 139
Lorimar, George, 174-175, 200
Louisiana Folk-Tales in French
    Dialect and English
    Translation, 148
Ludlum, Robert, 316

MacDowell, Katherine Sherwood
    Bonner, 149
Macon Telegraph, 23-24, 149
Mandy Satterlee, 166
"Manifest Destiny", 147
Markham, Edwin, 191
"Markham's Ball", 44
Marquis, Don, 57fn, 136, 215, 242,
    252fn

Marvin the Martian, xxviii
Master John, 52, 118, 275
Mathews, Denise, xxx
Mathews, Tabitha, xxx
Matthews, Linda, xxx
Maverick, Bret and Bart, xxviii
Maxwell, Joe, 162-163
May, Lyn, 349
McBee, Silas, 214
McClure, Phillips & Company,
    190, 197, 205-108, 232. 249
McClure, Samuel S., 161, 190,
    197, 208
McClure, T. C., 207
McClure's Magazine, 197, 206
McDaniel, Hattie, 275, 279
McDavid, Raven I., 367
McKay, Claude, 270
Mercer, Johnny, 283
Merchants Association (Boston),
    124
Metaxas, Eric, 312, 315
Metropolitan, 227
Miller, Arthur, 274
Milne, A. A., 305
"Mingo", 91, 98, 160
*Mingo and Other Sketches in Black
    and White*, 98-99, 108
Minstrel, 10, 19fn, 290
Miss Sally, 52, 94, 118, 234, 275
Mitchell, Margaret, 271
Mixon, Wayne,, vi, xxxi, 73, 77,
    223
Modern Language Association, 367
Monroe Advertiser, 24
Moorhead, Agnes, 274
More of Brer Rabbit's Tricks, 306
Morrow, James B., 173
Moser, James Henry, 65-66
Moser, Mary, 309
"Mr. Fox, Mr. Rabbit, and Mr.
    Terrapin", 314
Mr. Rabbit at Home, 173
"Mr. Rabbit Run Fur—Mr. Rabbit
    Run Fas'", 228
Muckraking era, 183, 190, 264-265
Muldoon, 222 illus., 225 illus.
Mumford, Carole, xxx, xxxi, 349
Muse, Clarence, 279
Muse, George, 143fn

Nash, Evelyn, 294-295
Nash, J. V., 72
National Association for the
    Advancement of Colored
    People, 270, 280, 289, 366-
    367
National Council of Teachers of
    English, 367
National Endowment for the Arts,
    308
National Institute of Arts and
    Letters, 213
National Public Radio, 349
National Urban League, 270, 280,
    349
Negro Legion of Decency, 280
*Negro Myths from the Georgia Coast
    Told in the Vernacular*, 148
Negro Renaissance Cycle, 269-272,
    289
Neumer, Jennifer, xxxi
Neumeyer, Peter, 309
New England Society, 119
New Herald Tribune, 320
New Orleans Daily Picuyne, 81, 170
New York Daily Tribune, 99, 114,
    167
New York Evening Post, 56, 65, 155
New York Herald-Tribune, 278, 320
New York Independent, 148
New York Journal, 187, 193
New York Public Library, 297
New York Times Saturday Review,
    228
New York Times, 97, 157-158, 167,
    170, 204, 232, 245, 250, 309,
    311
Newsweek, 278
Niger-Congo Language Family,
    364, 368fn
Nigeria, 53
*Nights with Uncle Remus: Myths and
    Legends of the Old Plantation*,
    94-98, 108, 165, 296
Nixon, Raymond B., 114
Norris, Thaddeus, 54
North Carolina Symphony, 307-
    308

O'Hern, Edna, 368 fn
O'Neil, Eugene, 271
O'Shea, Brian P., xxxi
Odum, Howard W., 116
Ohl, J.K., 185 illus.
Old Creole Days, 137
Olympics, Atlanta, 316-317
On the Plantation, 161, 162-163, 165, 176fn-177fn, 208
On the Wing of Occasions, 174, 191, 192, 194, 196
Opportunity, 270
Osgood, James R., 91, 98, 108
Outlook, 22204
Ovid, 136
Owens, William, 51, 55

Page, Thomas Nelson, xix, 83, 138, 147, 150, 157, 204
Page, Walter Hines, xxv, 79, 89-90, 166, 183, 191, 194, 195-198 passim
Page, William Eugene, xxx
Parks, VanDyke, 307-310
Parsons, Elsie Clews, 272
Patten, Luana, 279
Paul, Korky, 313
Pederson, Lee, 80-81, 368 fn
Peed, William, 276
Pennsylvania Dutch, 14, 105, 162
People, 282-283
Philadelphia Freedom Theater, 314
Philadelphia Inquirer, 262
Phillips, John S., 198, 205-206
Phoenix, Arizona, 276
Pinkney, Jerry, 311-312
Plantation economy, 17
Poe, Edgar Allan, 42, 272
Pogue, Mike, 315
Pond, James B., 138
Popular Science Monthly, 70
Porgy, 271
Potter, Beatrix, xix
Powell, J. W., 70
Powers, David, xxxi
Presidential Election of 1877, 115

Publishers Weekly, 312
Puppet Theatre Barge, 314
Putnam County Elementary School, 318
Putnam County, Ga., 8, 18fn, 153, 303
Putnam County Middle School, 318
Putnam, Israel, 18fn
Putnam, George M., 368 fn

Qua: A Romance of the Revolution, 175

Rabbit Ears Productions 314-315
Race riots, 239, 269
Racial stereotypes, 33-34, 41-42, 150, 153, 155, 271-272, 278-282, 289, 292, 294, 298, 302-306, 309, 312, 323fn, 340-341 (Also see: *Song of the South*)
Raglin, Tim, 315
Ralph David Abernathy Boulevard, 143fn
Ramage, Lynda, xxx
Ranger Summer Theater, 314,325fn
Rapf, Maurice, 276
Reasoner, Charles, 313
Reconstruction era, 23-37 passim, 41-42, 114-124 passim, 169, 200-205, 243, 269, 272, 285fn, 290-291,321
Reed, Wallace P., 185 illus
Rees, Ennis, 306
Reid, Andrew, 2
Reid, William A., 23
Renn, Rick, xxx
Repplier, Agnes, 170
Republican party, 115, 169, 203
"Revival Hymn", 44

Reymond, Dalton, 276
Reynolds, Paul R., 249
Ricker, Michael, 284
Riley, James Whitcomb, xix, 138,
140 illus., 142, 150, 167, 201-
202
Riley Rabbit, 74 (Also see: Brer
Rabbit)
Roadrunner and Coyote, 305
Roberts, Frank Sloval, 29 illus.
Robinson, Roby, 240
Roby, William, 18fn
Rocky and Bullwinkle, xxviii, 306
Roger Rabbit, xxviii
Rogers, Joseph M., 262
Rolf, Eric, 275
Rome Commercial, 36
Rome Daily, 36
Roosevelt, Theodore, xvii, xxiii,
103, 175, 214-216, 264, 318,
345
Rorabaugh, W. J., 18fn
Rose, Billy, 279
Rose, Michael, xxx
Rosewood Bed and Breakfast, 317-
318
Rowell, Jr., Edmon L., xxxi
Royko, Mike, 57fn
Rubin, Louis D., xxvi
"Running Away", 283
Russell, Irwin, 42-43, 147, 149

S. S. Joel Chandler Harris, 274
Sabine Farm, 144fn
Saint Anthony's Catholic Church,
257
Saint Joseph's Academy, 257
Sam and the Tigers, 312
San Diego Union, 282, 295
San Francisco Chronicle, 167
Saturday Evening Post, 174-175,
193, 200, 249
Saturday Review of Literature, 163,
270, 272, 297
Savanna-Chatham County School
District, 304-305
Savannah, Ga., 26-28, 34-36

Savannah Morning News, 26-28, 39
illus.
Savannah Theatre Company, 304-
305
Scarborough, W. S., 51
Schneider, Gilbert, 365, 368fn
Schnell, Frank, 343
Scribner's Monthly, 42, 81, 82, 90-
91, 109fn, 169
Sea Islands, 189-190
Segregation, 120-121, 122 (Also
see: Racial Stereotypes and
Slavery)
"Sense and Non-Since about
American Dialects", 367
Seward, William H., 19fn
Shachter, Jacqueline, 292
Shadow and Act, 315
Shady Dale, 201, 209fn
Shannon, Margaret, xxxi
Shaw, Jane, 307
Sherman, William T., 13, 16, 119
Shiner, Alex, xxx
Shoemaker, Kathy, xxx
"Showing How Brer Rabbit Was
too Sharp for Brer Fox", 55
Shuy, Roger, 368 fn
Sierra Leone, 53
"Silhouettes", 148, 360
Simms, William Gilmore, 41
Sister Jane: Her Friends and
Acquaintances, 165-167, 181
Slave narratives, 41
Slavery, 1, 7-8, 17, 41-42, 53-54,
70, 73, 81, 100-104 passim,
162, 221, 231-232, 295 (Also
see: Racial Stereotypes)
Slocum, Henry, 13-14
Small, Sam W., 44, 45, 46, 48, 204
Smith, C. Alphonso, xxvi, 48
Smith, Michele, xxx
Smithies, Richard, 314
Snap-Bean Farm, 133, 134 (Also
see: Wren's Nest)
Song of the South, 274-285 passim,
290, 291, 298, 299-300, 304,
311, 320, 325fn (Also see:
Disney, Walt)
Sottnick, Mark, 315
Sources and Analogs of the Uncle
Remus Tales, 71, 366

Spectator, 73
Splash Mountain, 283-284
Spriggs, Ruth, 312
Springfield Republican, 55, 56, 148
St. Helena Island, 362
Stagolee, 310
Stallings, George, 276
Stanislavsky, Konstantin, 184
Stanton, Frank L., 185 ill.
Starke, Georgia Harrison, 26-27
Steele, Richard, 7
Steinbeck, John, 271
Stewart, William, 368 fn
Stowe, Harriet Beecher, 42
Strickland, William Bradley, xxxi,
    295
Styles, Carey W., 34
Sunny South, 242
Sweetest Susan, 170, 173, 220
Swinson, Karl, 274

Tales of the Home Folks, 217
Tales of Uncle Remus for Children,
    283
Tang, Yen, xxx
Tar Baby, 316
Tar-Baby's pancakes, 285fn
Tarkington, Booth, 190
Tasmanian Devil, xxviii
Taylor, Wyndel, 343
Tempy, 275
Terrell, George, 10, 11, 47
"The "Great Migration", 269
The Bishop, the Boogerman, and the
    Right of Way, 104, 243
The Book Buyer, 165
The Bourne Ultimatum, 316
The Chataquan, 165
The Chronicles of Aunt Minervy
    Ann, 170
The Clansman, 205
The Colonel's Dream, 149-150
The Color Purple, 292
The Conjure Woman, 149
"The Cornfield Story", 278
The Countryman, 6-18, passim,
    117-118

The Crisis, 270, 289, 366-367
The Critic, 90, 160, 165, 167, 204
The Days when Animals Talked, 299
The English Language in America,
    362
"The Goophered Grapevine", 149
The Home Magazine, 245, 255
The Horn Book, 309
The Independent, 170
"The Kidnapping of President
    Lincoln", 174-175, 193
The Knee-High Man and Other
    Tales, 310
"The Late Mr. Watkins of
    Georgia", 217
"The Laughing Place", 278, 283
The Little Boy, 10, 49, 52, 72, 118,
    152, 169, 171 illus., 233, 275
"The Lost Generation", 270
The Myth of the Negro Past, 364
The Nation, 97, 99, 160, 204 243-
    245, 247, 270
The Natural History of Make-
    Believe, 305
The New Era, 201
The New Republic, 270
"The Old Bascomb Place", 158-
    160
The Optimist, 243
The People Could Fly, 307
The Plantation, 8
The Return of Brer Rabbit, 317, 319
    ilus.
The Romance of Rockville, 50, 176fn
The Sign of the Wren's Nest (See:
    Wren's Nest)
The Spectator, 7
The State, 148
The Sting, xxviii
The Tales of Uncle Remus, 310
The Tar-Baby, 54-56, 58fn, 141,
    147, 153, 174, 228, 230, 308,
    315-316 (Also see: Brer
    Rabbit)
The Tar-Baby and Other Rhymes of
    Uncle Remus, 228, 231
The Tattler, 7
The Three Caballeros, 286fn
The Vicar of Wakefield, 2
"The Wonderful Tar-Baby Story",
    71-72, 278, 351-354

"The Wonderful World of Disney",
283
The World's Wit and Humor, 231-
232
Thomas, Jr., Kenneth H., xxx, 18fn
Thompson, Harold W., xxv
Thomson, William Tappan, 28, 36-
37, 139
Thurber, James, 271
Ticknor, Benjamin H., 98
Ticknor, Francis O., 139
Tilden, Samuel, 115
Time, 279
Toggle, William Orrie, 51
Tokyo Disneyland, 284
*Told by Uncle Remus: New Stories of
the Old Planatation*, 227, 232-
233, 278
Tom and Jerry, 305
Toomer, Jean, 270
Tourgee, Albion, 104-105
Townsend, Robert, 315
"Tracking a Runaway", 165
Transformational Grammar Theory,
365, 368fn,,
Tri-State Actors' Theater, 325fn
Trickster tales—See: American
Black Folklore, trickster tales
Turks and Caicos Islands, 282
illus., 283,
Turner, Billy, 6
Turner, Darwin, 17, 292
Turner, Joe Syd, 10-11
Turner, Joseph Addison, 6-7, 16,
23, 25-26, 43, 83, 121, 124,
162, 200, 247, 343
Turner, Lorenzo Dow, 364-365
Turner Park, 343
Turnwold, 6, 9, 19fn, 51, 105, 162,
169
Twain, Mark, xxiv, xix, xxvii, 78-
79, 91, 137, 138, 147, 186,
189, 191, 234fn, 272, 301-
302, 323fn (Also see: Samuel
L. Clemens)

U. S. Post Office, 274, 318
Uncle Julius, 149
Uncle Remus, xxiv, xxvi-xxvii, 10,
24, 44-49, 51, 55, 64 illus.,
79, 118, 148, 149, 151-152,
158, 169, 171 illus., 184, 204,
220, 232-233, 271, 274-283
passim, 290, 291, 295, 304-
305, 307, 308, 311, 316, 322
Description, 45, 46, 48, 52, 66
Uncle Remus, advertising, 271
"Uncle Remus and the Savannah
Darkey", 44
Uncle Remus and His Friends, 151-
152, 153, 218
Uncle Remus Day, 274
Uncle Remus Golf Course, 285fn
*Uncle Remus, His Songs and His
Sayings; The Folk-Lore of the
Plantation*, 64 illus, 65-84,
141, 155, 157, 165, 191, 195,
294,
Uncle Remus Library System, 303
Uncle Remus Memorial
Association, 279, 344 illus.,
345, 346,
Uncle Remus Museum, xxx, 332
illus, 343, 369
*Uncle Remus, Mythology of the
Plantation*, 65
Uncle Remus Realty Company,
285fn
Uncle Remus Restaurant, 285fn,
294, 323fn
Uncle Remus Sausage Company,
285fn
Uncle Remus's Home Magazine, 254
illus.
Uncle Remus's Magazine, 215, 240-
249, 255, 302
Uncle Tom's Cabin, 42
University of Missouri, 234fn
University of Pennsylvania, 213
University of Virginia, 369

*Brer Rabbit,
Uncle Remus,
and the 'Cornfield
Journalist'*

Van Santvoord, George, 297
Van Vechten, Carl, 270
Variety, 281
Violence in literature, 305-306

Walker, Alice, 292, 294
Walker, J. Randolph, 227
Walker, Stanley, 321
Wallace, Lew, 82
Waller, Laura Ramey, 349
Wally Wanderoon, 174, 219 illus.,
    217-221
Walt Disney Collectors' Society,
    284
Walt Disney Studios, 274-285 pas-
    sim, 325fn (Also see: Disney,
    Walt and *Song of the South*)
Wanamaker, John, 196-197
Warner Brothers, 308
Warner, Charles Dudley, xxiv
Warwick, Ruth, 275
Washington, Booker T., 123, 224
Washington Post, 61-64 passim
Watterson, Henry, 18fn, 97
Watterson, Norma, xxx
Weiss, Jacqueline Shachter, 312
Wells-Barnett, Ida B., 270
Werner, Craig, 296
Wes-Kos, 365
West African Pidgin English, 365
West End, 129, 134
Westview Cemetery, 263-264, 321
Whatizit, 317
"Where's Duncan?", 158-159
Whitman, Walt, 272
"Why the Alligator's Back is
    Rough", 96, 84fn, 90
Wiggins, Robert L., xxxi
William Wornum, 165-166
Williams, Clyde, 346
Winsell, Keith A., xxx, 273 illus.
Wise, Ron, 281
Wolfe, Bernard, 75-76, 290, 311
Wolfram, Walt, 368 fn
World War I, 269
World's Work, 193, 196

Wornum, William, 165-166
Wren's Nest, 129-132, 135 illus.,
    142, 143fn, 145 illus., 237
    illus., 303, 317, 320-321,
    343-349, 347 illus.
Wright, Mildred Harris Camp, 346
Wright, Ralph, 276
Wrubel, Allie, 278

Yosemite Sam, xxviii
Young, Andrew, 316

"Zip-a-Dee-Doo-Dah", 278, 285
Zola, Emile, 82

About the Author

Walter M. Brasch

Walter M. Brasch, Ph.D., an award-winning former newspaper reporter and editor in California, Iowa, Indiana, and Ohio, is a university professor of journalism and mass communications, author of a biweekly syndicated newspaper column, and multi-media wirter-producer.

He is also the author of ten other books, most of them focusing upon the fusion of historical and contemporary social issues, including *Black English and the Mass Media* (1981); *Forerunners of Revolution: Muckrakers and the American Social Conscience* (1991); *With Just Cause: The Unionization of the American Journalist* (1991); and two books largely of humor and satire about the media, *Enquiring Minds and Space Aliens: Wandering Through the Mass Media and Popular Culture* (1995) and *Sex and the Single Beer Can: Probing the Media and American Culture* (1997). He is also co-author of *The Press and the State* (1986), awarded Outstanding Academic Book distinction by *Choice* magazine, published by the American Library Association.

Among his recent writing awards are those from the National Society of Newspaper Columnists, Society of Professional Journalists, National Federation of Press Women, Pennsylvania Press Club, Pennsylvania Women's Press Association, Pennwriters, International Association of Business Communicators, Pacific Coast Press Club, and Press Club of Southern California. He is also a co-recipient of the Civil Liberties Award of the American Civil Liberties Union, 1996; and was honored by San Diego State University as a Points of Excellence winner in 1997. At Bloomsburg University, he earned the Creative Arts Award, the Creative Teaching Award, and was named an Outstanding Student Advisor. For the Pennsylvania Humanities Council, he was a Commonwealth Speaker.

He was president of the Keystone State professional chapter and deputy regional director of the Society of Professional Journalists, from which he received the Director's Award and the National Freedom of Information Award. He is founding coordinator of Pennsylvania Journalism Educators, and is a member of the National Society of Newspaper Columnists, the Authors' Guild, National Writers Union (UAW/AFL-CIO), and The Newspaper Guild (CWA/AFL-CIO). He is listed in *Who's Who in the East*, *Contemporary Authors*, and *Who's Who in the Media*.

Dr. Brasch earned an A.B. in sociology from San Diego State College, an M.A. in journalism from Ball State University, and a Ph.D. in mass communication/journalism, with a cognate area in language and culture studies, from Ohio University.